NUREG-0133

I0448238

Preparation of Radiological Effluent Technical Specifications for Nuclear Power Plants

A Guidance Manual for Users of Standard Technical Specifications

U.S. Nuclear Regulatory Commission

Office of Nuclear Reactor Regulation

J. S. Boegli, R. R. Bellamy,
W. L. Britz, R. L. Waterfield

Reprinted October 1987

NUREG-0133

PREPARATION OF
RADIOLOGICAL EFFLUENT TECHNICAL SPECIFICATIONS
FOR NUCLEAR POWER PLANTS

A Guidance Manual for Users of Standard Technical Specifications

Editors

J. S. Boegli
R. R. Bellamy
W. L. Britz
R. L. Waterfield

Principal Investigators

W. C. Burke
F. J. Congel

Other Participating Staff

J. E. Fairobent	K. F. Eckerman
P. G. Stoddart	J. H. Osloond
L. G. Bell	F. M. Akstolewicz
F. P. Cardile	D. L. Ondish
J. T. Collins	W. E. Kreger

Manuscript Completed: October 1978
Date Published: October 1978

Division of Site Safety and Environmental Analysis
Office of Nuclear Reactor Regulation
U.S. Nuclear Regulatory Commission

TABLE OF CONTENTS

Chapter	Page
1 INTRODUCTION	1
1.1 Purpose	1
1.2 Background	1
2 DEFINITIONS AND STAFF POSITIONS	5
2.1 Definitions	5
2.2 Staff Positions Augmenting Standard Definitions	5
3 SPECIAL CONSIDERATIONS	7
3.1 Multi-Unit Sites with Shared Radioactive Waste Management Systems	7
3.2 Population Exposure	7
3.3 Meteorological Data	8
3.4 National Interim Primary Drinking Water Regulations	8
3.5 Solid Waste Management System - Process Control Program	9
3.6 Offsite Dose Calculation Manual (ODCM)	9
3.7 Identification of Radionuclides in Effluents	9
3.8 Environmental Radiation Protection Standards for Nuclear Power Operations	10
4 LIQUID EFFLUENTS	12
4.1 Instrumentation	12
4.2 Requirement for Implementing 10 CFR Part 20	13
4.3 Requirement for Implementing 10 CFR Part 50	14
4.4 Specification on Radioactivity Contents in Liquid-Containing Tanks	17
4.5 Specification on the Use of Liquid Radioactive Waste Management System	18
5 GASEOUS EFFLUENTS	20
5.1 Instrumentation	20
5.2 Dose Limit for Implementing 10 CFR Part 20	21
5.3 Dose Limit for Implementing 10 CFR Part 50	27
5.4 Specification on the Use of Gaseous Radioactive Waste Management System	36
5.5 Specification on Explosive Gas Mixture Limitation	37
5.6 Specification Unique to LWR Design Features	38
REFERENCES	42
APPENDIX A	A-1
APPENDIX B	B-1
APPENDIX C	C-1
APPENDIX D	D-1
ADDENDUM	AA-1

CHAPTER 1

INTRODUCTION

1.1 PURPOSE

The purpose of this manual is to describe methods found acceptable to the staff of the U.S. Nuclear Regulatory Commission (NRC) for the calculation of certain key values required in the preparation of proposed radiological effluent Technical Specifications using the Standard Technical Specifications for light-water-cooled nuclear power plants. This manual also provides guidance to applicants for operating licenses for nuclear power plants in the preparation of proposed radiological effluent Technical Specifications or in preparing requests for changes to existing radiological effluent Technical Specifications for operating licenses. The manual additionally describes current staff positions on the methodology for estimating radiation exposure due to the release of radioactive materials in effluents and on the administrative control of radioactive waste treatment systems.

1.2 BACKGROUND

Section 50.36, "Technical Specifications," of 10 CFR Part 50, "Licensing of Production and Utilization Facilities" (Ref. 1), requires that each nuclear power reactor operating license issued by the NRC contain Technical Specifications that set forth limits, operating conditions, and other regulatory requirements imposed on the facility operation for the protection of the health and safety of the public. Conditions and limitations corresponding to certain key values which are system-dependent and site-related are to be incorporated in these Technical Specifications for compliance with 10 CFR 50.36a, "Technical Specifications on Effluents from Nuclear Power Reactors." Under the provisions of Section 50.36, each applicant for an operating license is required to submit proposed Technical Specifications for his facility, including the supporting bases. These are reviewed by the NRC staff to assure that the proposed Technical Specifications contain such conditions and limitations as deemed appropriate and necessary; approved Technical Specifications are then included as Appendix A of the operating license.

Standard Technical Specifications have been developed by the staff for each appropriate nuclear steam supply system (NSSS) vendor to provide guidance to applicants for the preparation of proposed Technical Specifications. These are as follows:

NUREG-0212 - "Standard Technical Specifications for Combustion Engineering Pressurized Water Reactors"

NUREG-0103 - "Standard Technical Specifications for Babcock and Wilcox Pressurized Water Reactors"

NUREG-0452 - "Standard Technical Specifications for Westinghouse Pressurized Water Reactors"

NUREG-0123 - "Standard Technical Specifications for General Electric Boiling Water Reactors"

Current Standard Technical Specifications are available from the National Technical Information Service (NTIS), Springfield, Virginia, 22161. These Standard Technical Specifications will contain the radiological effluent Technical Specifications to be used by the applicant for an operating license. In the interim, model radioactive effluent Technical Specifications have been provided in NUREG-0472 (Ref. 2) for pressurized water reactors, and NUREG-0473 (Ref. 3) for boiling water reactors. Table 1.1 provides a summary of those applicable sections in the Standard Technical Specifications which contain conditions and limitations relative to the radiological effluent Technical Specifications to be discussed in this manual.

The Standard Technical Specifications contain the limiting conditions for operation necessary for complying with the Commission's regulations and are in a format that is acceptable to the NRC staff. The reporting requirements reflect the guidelines provided in Regulatory Guide 1.16, "Reporting of Operating Information - Appendix A Technical Specifications," Revision 4, August 1975 (Ref. 4) and Regulatory Guide 10.1, "Compilation of Reporting Requirements for Persons Subject to NRC Regulations," Revision 3, May 1977 (Ref. 5).

The methodology discussed in this manual and used to implement the requirements of 10 CFR Part 50, Appendix I, "Numerical Guides for Design Objectives and Limiting Conditions for Operation to Meet the Criterion 'As Low As Practicable' for Radioactive Material in Light-Water-Cooled Nuclear Power Reactor Effluents" (Ref. 1), is consistent with the Regulatory Guides used in the staff's safety evaluations pursuant to 10 CFR 50.34a(c). These guides are as follows:

Regulatory Guide 1.109 - "Calculation of Annual Doses to Man from Routine Releases of Reactor Effluents for the Purpose of Evaluating Compliance with 10 CFR Part 50, Appendix I" (Revision 1), October 1977. (Ref. 6)

Regulatory Guide 1.110 - "Cost-Benefit Analysis for Radwaste Systems for Light-Water-Cooled Nuclear Power Reactors," March 1976. (Ref. 7)

Regulatory Guide 1.111 - "Methods for Estimating Atmospheric Transport and Dispersion of Gaseous Effluents in Routine Releases from Light-Water-Cooled Reactors" (Revision 1), July 1977. (Ref. 8)

Regulatory Guide 1.112 - "Calculation of Releases of Radioactive Materials in Gaseous and Liquid Effluents from Light-Water-Cooled Power Reactors," April 1976. (Ref. 9)

TABLE 1.1

SUMMARY OF APPLICABLE SECTIONS IN THE STANDARD TECHNICAL SPECIFICATIONS
CONSIDERED IN THIS MANUAL

| PLANT TYPE | Standard Technical Specification or Model Technical Specification in NUREG-0472 (Ref. 2) or NUREG-0473 (Ref. 3) | | | | SECTION REFERENCE IN THIS MANUAL |
	SECTION	TABLES	BASES	TITLE	
PWR BWR	1.0	Yes	No	Definitions	2.0
PWR BWR	3/4.3.3.8	Yes	Yes	Radioactive Liquid Effluent Instrumentation	4.1
PWR BWR	3/4.3.3.9	Yes	Yes	Radioactive Gaseous Effluent Instrumentation	5.1
PWR BWR	3/4.11.1.1	Yes	Yes	Liquid Effluents, Concentration	4.2
PWR BWR	3/4.11.1.2	No	Yes	Liquid Effluents, Dose	4.3
PWR BWR	3/4.11.1.3	No	Yes	Liquid Effluents, Liquid Waste Treatment	4.5
PWR BWR	3/4.11.1.4	No	Yes	Liquid Effluents, Liquid Holdup Tanks	4.4
PWR BWR	3/4.11.2.1	Yes	Yes	Gaseous Effluents, Dose Rate	5.2
PWR BWR	3/4.11.2.2	No	Yes	Dose, Noble Gases	5.3
PWR BWR	3/4.11.2.3	No	Yes	Dose Radioiodines, Radioactive Material in Particulate Form and Radionuclides Other than Noble Gases	5.3
PWR BWR	3/4.11.2.4	No	Yes	Gaseous Effluents, Gaseous Waste Treatment	5.4
PWR BWR	3/4.11.2.5	No	Yes	Gaseous Effluents, Dose	3.8
PWR BWR	3/4.11.2.6A	No	Yes	Explosive Gas Mixtures (Systems designed to withstand a hydrogen explosion)	5.5
PWR BWR	3/4.11.2.6B	No	Yes	Explosive Gas Mixtures (Systems not designed to withstand a hydrogen explosion)	5.5
PWR	3/4.11.2.7	No	Yes	Gaseous Effluents, Gas Storage Tanks	5.6
BWR	3/4.11.2.7	No	Yes	Gaseous Effluents, Main Condenser	5.6
BWR	3/4.11.3.8	No	Yes	Gaseous Effluents, Mark I or II Containment (Optional)	3.0
PWR BWR	3/4.11.3.1	No	Yes	Solid Radioactive Waste	3.0
PWR BWR	3/4.12.1	Yes	Yes	Monitoring Program	4.3, 5.3
PWR BWR	3/4.12.2	No	Yes	Land Use Census	4.3, 5.3
PWR BWR	Fig. 3.11-1	No	No	Unrestricted Area Boundary for Liquid Effluents	2.0
PWR BWR	Fig. 5.1-1	No	No	Unrestricted Area Boundary for Gaseous Effluents	2.0
PWR BWR	6.9	No	No	Reporting Requirements	General

Regulatory Guide 1.113 - "Estimating Aquatic Dispersion of Effluents from Accidental and
Routine Reactor Releases for the Purpose of Implementing Appendix I"
(Revision 1), April 1977. (Ref. 10)

Computer codes used to determine certain values and parameters used with the Regulatory
Guides listed above are described in the following documents:

NUREG-0017 - "Calculation of Releases of Radioactive Materials in Gaseous and Liquid
Effluents from Pressurized Water Reactors (PWR-GALE Code)," April 1976
(Ref. 11)

NUREG-0016 - "Calculation of Releases of Radioactive Materials in Gaseous and Liquid
Effluents from Boiling Water Reactors (BWR-GALE Code) " April 1976 (Ref. 12)

NUREG-0324 - "XOQDOQ, Program for the Meteorological Evaluation of Routine Effluent
Releases at Nuclear Power Stations," September 1977 (Ref. 13)

These guides and computer codes provide acceptable methods of complying with the Commission's regulations; however, conformance with the staff's guidelines on Standard Technical
Specifications, Regulatory Guides, and dose calculation methodology is not required. If the
proposed Technical Specifications include mathematical models and parameters that differ
from the methodology used by the staff to calculate set points and release rates or estimate
doses due to releases of radioactive materials in effluents, the parameters and calculations
used shall be substantiated in the Offsite Dose Calculation Manual.

Based on the findings of the Environmental and Safety Hearings, the Commission may
impose certain additional or alternative limiting conditions for operation based on values
that are more restrictive than those determined using this manual or provided in the Standard
Technical Specifications. In such cases, the limiting conditions will be based on the decisions
of the Atomic Safety and Licensing Board rather than the limiting values determined by this
manual or included in the Standard Technical Specifications.

CHAPTER 2

DEFINITIONS AND STAFF POSITIONS

2.1 DEFINITIONS

Section 1.0, DEFINITIONS, of the Standard Technical Specifications provides standard definitions of terms and phrases which appear capitalized throughout the specifications. Standard definitions are provided to assure licensing consistency. When a term or phrase is used in a limited subject area of the Standard Technical Specifications, it is defined in the limited subject area and referenced by Specification number, table, figure or footnote.

2.2 STAFF POSITIONS AUGMENTING STANDARD DEFINITIONS

In certain circumstances, terms used in the Standard Technical Specifications are defined or specified in applicable regulations, such as 10 CFR Part 50 (Ref. 1). Staff positions clarifying certain of these definitions are as discussed below.

LIMITING CONDITIONS FOR OPERATION (LCO) is defined in 10 CFR 50.36(c)(2) as "the lowest functional capability or performance levels of equipment required for safe operation of the facility." This definition is applicable to the components of the radioactive waste management systems during normal reactor operations, including anticipated operational occurrences. When an LCO for a nuclear power reactor is not met, the licensee shall either shut down the reactor or follow any remedial action permitted by the Technical Specifications until the LCO can be met. Remedial action by the licensee may include processing by normal or alternate modes of operation for the control of radioactive effluents using such existing equipment as may be installed in the radioactive waste management systems.

MAINTENANCE AND USE of the equipment installed in the radioactive waste management systems is required in 10 CFR 50.34a(c) and in 10 CFR 50.36a(a)(1). The term, MAINTENANCE AND USE, is applicable to the installed components of the liquid, gaseous, and solid radioactive waste management systems and to instrumentation installed for the monitoring and control of potentially radioactive effluents. MAINTENANCE AND USE does not require the installation of fully redundant systems; however, prudent management procedures, such as scheduled standby and maintenance periods should be employed. The Standard Technical Specifications specify levels or values above which equipment installed in the radioactive waste management systems shall be used to enable the licensee to show that he is exerting his best efforts to maintain levels of radioactive effluents "as low as is reasonably achievable," in accordance with 10 CFR 50.36a.

UNRESTRICTED AREA is defined in 10 CFR 20.3(a)(17) (Ref. 14), as "any area access to which is not controlled by the licensee for purposes of protection of individuals from exposure to radiation and radioactive materials, and any area used for residential quarters."

For purposes of implementation, the definition of UNRESTRICTED AREA has been expanded as follows: "any area at or beyond the site boundary access to which is not controlled by the licensee for purposes of protection of individuals from exposure to radiation and radioactive materials, and any area within the site boundary used for residential quarters or industrial, commercial, institutional and recreational facilities". The UNRESTRICTED AREA boundary may coincide with the exclusion (fenced) area boundary, as defined in 10 CFR 100.3(a) (Ref. 15), may include land areas owned by the licensee, provided that occupancy is controlled by the licensee for the purposes of meeting the requirements of 10 CFR Part 20, but does not include areas over water bodies.

To assure that the UNRESTRICTED AREA boundary is defined in each license, the Standard Technical Specifications require two maps, one for liquid effluents (Figure 3.11-1)[*] and one for gaseous effluents (Figure 5.1-1)[*] locating all points surrounding the facility at which the licensee shall comply with the expanded definition, given above. These boundaries shall be consistent with those established in the Safety Analysis Report, or the Final Hazard Summary for the facility. The UNRESTRICTED AREAS, established at or beyond these boundaries, are also considered in the LIMITING CONDITIONS FOR OPERATION to keep levels of radioactive materials in effluents as low as is reasonably achievable, pursuant to 10 CFR 50.36a.

RELEASE RATE used in this manual is defined as, "the discharge of radioactive materials in liquid or gaseous effluents per unit time." The "second" is used as the practical reporting time unit for establishing release rates to show compliance with the requirements of 10 CFR Part 20 and for establishing instantaneous limitations based on potentially radioactive releases. The "hour" is used as the practical reporting time unit in establishing average release rates to show conformance with the requirements of 10 CFR Part 50 for noble gas releases, for gaseous radioactive effluents other than noble gases (radioiodines and particulates) and for radioactive materials released in liquid effluents. Liquid releases are further subdivided into batch and continuous releases. Gaseous releases are subdivided into short- and long-term releases. These gaseous release subdivisions classify cumulative releases as being either less than or greater than 500 hrs/year, respectively, for gaseous effluents. Further discussion is provided in Sections 3.3, 4.2 and 5.2 of this manual.

RADIOACTIVE WASTE MANAGEMENT SYSTEMS are defined as all process and control equipment provided to reduce the amount or concentration of radioactive materials (in any form) released from the facility. The overall systems may be divided into subsystems to handle the radioactive materials contained in liquid and gaseous streams and in solid waste. The Standard Technical Specifications have adopted nomenclature for systems and components which are in common use in the industry. In preparing proposed Technical Specifications, the system and component names may be changed to correspond to the terminology used in the Final Safety Analysis Report (FSAR) or the Final Hazard Summary, if applicable. Engineered Safety Feature (ESF) atmospheric cleanup systems are not considered to be radioactive waste management system components and, therefore, are not within the scope of this manual.

---

[*] This Figure is to be included in proposed Technical Specifications.

CHAPTER 3

SPECIAL CONSIDERATIONS

3.1 MULTI-UNIT SITES WITH SHARED RADIOACTIVE WASTE MANAGEMENT SYSTEMS

The Standard Technical Specifications are written on a "per unit" basis, since this is the format in which operating licenses are issued. When shared radioactive waste management systems are used by more than one reactor unit on a site, the wastes from all units are mixed for shared treatment; by such mixing, the effluent releases cannot accurately be ascribed to a specific reactor unit. The licensee should estimate the contributions from each unit based on input conditions, e.g., flow rates and radioactivity concentrations, or, if not practicable, the treated effluent releases may be allocated equally to each of the radioactive waste producing reactors sharing the treatment system. For determining conformance to LCOs, these allocations from shared treatment systems are to be added to the releases specifically attributed to each unit to obtain the total releases per unit.

It is preferred that discharge lines leading to common release points be separately controlled and monitored, and the licensee should consider instrumentation which will provide volumetric recording and radiological effluent monitoring, sampling and analyses on a unit basis. This has been accomplished for some units by continuous representative sampling and analysis of the streams prior to mixing and continuously monitored and controlled at the common release point. Multi-unit sites with common release points, but without shared radioactive waste management systems, are also required to determine the alarm/trip setpoints in Sections 4.1 and 5.1 of this manual to assure compliance with the requirements of 10 CFR Part 20 (Ref. 14) at each release point.

In preparing Technical Specifications for units at adjacent sites (multi-unit stations with a common boundary), the sites should be considered as a multi-unit site.

3.2 POPULATION EXPOSURE

The Standard Technical Specifications 3.11.1.3 and 3.11.2.4 require the use of equipment installed in the radioactive waste management system to meet the requirements of 10 CFR 50.36a (Ref. 1).

To assure that the Technical Specifications consider the population radiation doses, the use of the installed radioactive waste management system is required when the projected cumulative doses exceed an appropriate fraction of the individual dose limitations. This method of establishing use of the radwaste equipment assures that the staff's Appendix I cost-benefit analysis in the safety evaluation is not invalidated. Sections 4.5 and 5.4 of this manual provide these values for the Standard Technical Specifications. Guidance on reporting population exposures is provided in Regulatory Guide 1.21 (Ref. 17).

3.3 METEOROLOGICAL DATA

The Standard Technical Specifications consider the historical annual average atmospheric dispersion condition rather than real time dispersion conditions in determining the LCO for radioactive materials in gaseous effluents.

Releases are characterized as "long" or "short" term, depending on the frequency and duration of the releases. This characterization permits the matching of the releases to more appropriate atmospheric diffusion, dispersion and decay conditions.

"Long-term" refers to releases that are generally continuous and stable in release rate with some anticipated variation (i.e., <50%, based on a running monthly average) in release rate, such as is experienced in normal ventilation system effluents at nuclear power plants. Determination of doses due to long-term releases should use the historical annual average relative concentration (χ/Q) based on meteorological data summarized, as recommended in Regulatory Guide 1.111 (Ref. 8).

"Short-term" refers to releases that are intermittent in radionuclide concentrations or flow, such as releases from PWR gas storage tanks, PWR containment ventings and purges, BWR drywell purges (See Standard Technical Specification 3.11.3.8), BWR mechanical vacuum pump exhausts, and systems or components with infrequent use. Short-term releases may be due to operational variations which result in radioactive releases greater than 50% of the releases normally considered as long-term. Short-term releases from these sources during normal operation, including anticipated operational occurrences, are defined as those which occur for a total of 500 hours or less in a calendar year but not more than 150 hours in any quarter. Determination of doses due to short-term releases can use the annual average relative concentration (long-term) if it can be demonstrated that past short-term releases were sufficiently random in both time of day and duration (e.g., the short-term release periods were not dependent solely on atmospheric conditions or time of day) to be represented by the annual average dispersion conditions. Otherwise, the short-term relative concentration value should be calculated in accordance with the guidelines provided in NUREG-0324 (Ref. 13) for short-term release.

Even though "annual average" atmospheric dispersion conditions are used as basis for the Standard Technical Specifications, "real time" meteorological data should be summarized hour-by-hour and coupled with the corresponding releases, and the summary should be included in the SEMIANNUAL RADIOACTIVE EFFLUENT RELEASE REPORT.

3.4 NATIONAL INTERIM PRIMARY DRINKING WATER REGULATIONS

Operators of nuclear power plants located on fresh water bodies which are used as sources of water for drinking water supply systems, are required to make a special report concerning the impact on the water supply system due to liquid effluent releases into the water bodies which are above the value(s) permitted in Specification 3.11.1.2 of the Standard Technical Specifications. The NRC has no legal responsibility to implement 40 CFR Part 141, "National Interim Primary Drinking Water Regulations" (Ref. 16), or to assure routine conformance to the Act since this is the responsibility of the Environmental Protection Agency and the water plant operator. This special report is intended for public information and as a tool to assure awareness by the licensee of the impact of radioactive liquid releases on the community's water supply system. The impact within the water supply system is dependent on treatment given to the water taken into the system. The water plant operator is responsible for providing appropriate treatment to assure that 40 CFR Part 141 requirements are met. While the operator of the nuclear power plant is not responsible for meeting the requirements of 40 CFR Part 141 in the water supply system, his success in meeting the requirements of Specification 3.11.1.2 will assure an environmentally acceptable impact on the water supply system. The non-radiological impact is separately considered in the Appendix B Technical Specifications.

3.5 SOLID WASTE MANAGEMENT SYSTEM - PROCESS CONTROL PROGRAM

Standard Technical Specification 3.11.3.1 requires the operator of each nuclear power plant to establish a PROCESS CONTROL PROGRAM for the solid radioactive waste management system. The purpose of the PROCESS CONTROL PROGRAM is to provide reasonable assurance of the complete SOLIDIFICATION of processed wastes and of the absence of free water in the processed waste. At the time the applicant submits proposed Technical Specifications, he should submit the PROCESS CONTROL PROGRAM for NRC review and approval prior to implementation. The PROCESS CONTROL PROGRAM should consist of the processing steps and a set of established process parameters, which include but are not limited to pH, oil content, ratio of solidification agent to influent waste, water content, and ratio of solidification agent to chemical additive for each type of anticipated waste (filter sludges, spent resins, evaporator bottoms, boric acid solutions, sodium sulfate solutions and filter media). The surveillance requirements in the Standard Technical Specifications provide the steps to be taken to assure that operation is within the parameters established by the PROCESS CONTROL PROGRAM. Packaging procedures should demonstrate conformance with Specification 3.11.3.1. The PROCESS CONTROL PROGRAM required by the Standard Technical Specifications is to be documented in the operating procedures for each reactor and available for review by the NRC inspector. A summary of changes to the PROCESS CONTROL PROGRAM shall be provided in the SEMIANNUAL RADIOACTIVE EFFLUENT RELEASE REPORT.

3.6 OFFSITE DOSE CALCULATION MANUAL (ODCM)

Standard Technical Specifications 3.3.3.8 and 3.3.3.9 require the operator of each nuclear power plant to establish alarm and trip action setpoints for each radioactive liquid and gaseous effluent release point in maintained, auditable records, determined in accordance with the OFFSITE DOSE CALCULATION MANUAL (ODCM). The ODCM shall contain the methodology and parameters to be used in the calculation of offsite doses due to radioactive liquid and gaseous effluents pursuant to Specifications 3.11.1.2, 3.11.2.2 and 3.11.2.3, and the established limits of Specifications 3.11.1.1 and 3.11.2.1. The ODCM shall be submitted to the NRC with the proposed Technical Specifications for review and approval by the NRC. Changes to the ODCM shall be provided in the SEMIANNUAL RADIOACTIVE EFFLUENT RELEASE REPORT.

3.7 IDENTIFICATION OF RADIONUCLIDES IN EFFLUENTS

In order to determine the radiological impact associated with the release of radioactive materials in liquid and gaseous effluents, the principal radionuclides contributing to the dose must be identified. Tables 4.11-1 and 4.11-2** of the Standard Technical Specifications contain the sampling and analysis programs required for identifying principal radionuclides in effluents. These tables were compiled using the guidelines of Regulatory Guide 1.21 (Ref. 17) and reflect current radiochemical analytical methods. Other methods may be necessary to enhance identification and analysis, as provided by the footnotes to Tables 4.11-1 and 4.11-2. In lieu of sample-analysis, if the applicant does not consider that the collection, radio-chemical separation, and analytical methods are technically feasible or practical at the speci-fied LLD, then the dose limitations in Specifications 3.11.1.2, 3.11.2.2, and 3.11.2.3 should be proportionally reduced by assuming the continued presence and release concentrations of those radionuclides as determined by the source term (GALE Code, Ref. 11 or 12). For example, the dose LCO may be reduced based on predicted radioactive materials in gaseous effuents from PWR turbine buildings if sampling is not provided. For BWRs and PWRs it may be reduced if carbon-14 analysis is not provided.

3.8 ENVIRONMENTAL RADIATION PROTECTION STANDARDS FOR NUCLEAR POWER OPERATIONS

Standard Technical Specification 3.11.2.5 specifies in the Action that when the cal-culated doses associated with the effluent releases exceed twice* the limits of any one of the Specifications 3.11.1.2, 3.11.2.2 or 3.11.2.3, the licensee shall prepare and submit a Special Report to the Commission and limit subsequent releases such that the dose or dose commitment to a real individual from all uranium fuel cycle sources is limited to $\leq$ 25 mrem to the total body or any organ (except the thyroid, which is limited to $\leq$ 75 mrem) over 12 consecutive months. This Special Report shall include an analysis which demonstrates that radiation exposures to all real individuals from all uranium fuel cycle sources (including all liquid and gaseous effluent pathways and direct radiation) are less than the standards in 40 CFR Part 190, Environmental Radiation Protection Standards for Nuclear Power Operations (Ref. 18). If analysis indicates that releases resulting in doses that exceed the 40 CFR 190 Standard could occur, obtain a variance from the Commission to permit such releases. The Standard Technical Specifications 3.11.1.2, 3.11.2.2 and 3.11.2.3 consider doses to a real individual and apply to each reactor but do not include any other portion of the uranium fuel cycle or direct shine from the reactor.

The "Uranium fuel cycle" is defined in 40 CFR Part 190.02(b) as:

"Uranium fuel cycle means the operations of milling of uranium ore, chemical conversion of uranium, isotopic enrichment of uranium, fabrication of uranium fuel, generation of electricity by a light-water-cooled nuclear power plant using uranium fuel, and repro-cessing of spent uranium fuel, to the extent that these directly support the production of electrical power for public use utilizing nuclear energy, but excludes mining opera-tions, operations at waste disposal sites, transportation of any radioactive material in support of these operations, and the reuse of recovered non-uranium special nuclear and by-product materials from the cycle."

The following general guidelines are presented for preparation of the Special Report:

1) determine which uranium fuel cycle facilities or operations, in addition to the nuclear power reactor units at the site, contribute to the annual dose to the maximum exposed member of the public. The maximum exposed member of the public for

_____

*This value may be reduced for multi-unit sites depending on staff analysis.

**These Tables are to be included in proposed Technical Specifications.

this evaluation may or may not correspond to the individual considered in the Technical Specification;

2) determine the total annual dose to this person from all existing pathways and sources of radioactivity and radiation using the methodologies described in this NUREG document and applicable references. Where additional information on pathways and nuclides is needed, the best available information should be used and documented;

3) include direct radiation from the site in the dose determination. An acceptable method for calculating radiation from the N-16 component of direct radiation is: SKYSHINE, A Computer Procedure for Evaluating Effects of Structure Design on N-16 Gamma-Ray Dose Rates, Radiation Research Associates, Inc. Report RRA-T7209, November 1972 (Ref. 19).

In addition to N-16, all direct radiation from the plant and storage facilities should be considered in the dose determination. The direct dose component (including N-16) may be determined by calculation or actual measurement (e.g., high pressure ionization chamber). The calculation or actual measurement must be documented in this Special Report.

The 25 mrem and 75 mrem dose standards are effective December 1, 1979, except for doses arising from operations associated with the milling of uranium ore which is effective December 1, 1980.

Further information on the method of implementation of 40 CFR Part 190 is being developed by the NRC staff.

CHAPTER 4

LIQUID EFFLUENTS

4.1 INSTRUMENTATION

Standard Technical Specification 3.3.3.8 requires that:

"The radioactive liquid effluent monitoring instrumentation channels shown in Table 3.3-11* shall be OPERABLE with their alarm/trip setpoints set to ensure that the limits of Specification 3.11.1.1 are not exceeded. The setpoints shall be determined in accordance with procedures as described in the ODCM, and shall be recorded in the station log."

Table 3.3-11* provides a list of radioactive liquid effluent monitoring instrumentation needed to comply with the requirements of General Design Criteria (GDC) 60, 63, and 64 of Appendix A to 10 CFR Part 50 (Ref. 1). The list includes instrumentation such as radioactivity monitoring and sampling devices, automatic control devices, and essential flow and level devices which are components of the monitoring channels. The list uses common nomenclature for the effluent streams; however, the names may be revised, as necessary, to conform with a particular plant's nomenclature. Deletion of any item listed should be justified. Clarification of proposed Technical Specifications should be provided by a simple drawing or sketch showing stream intersections, instrumentation, and control features. Duplicate instrumentation (i.e., instruments that measure different sensor parameters or ranges) should be listed separately. The channel logic should assure that the alarmed trip action is not negated by switching.

The plant procedures should contain a quality assurance program for instruments as recommended in Regulatory Guide 4.15 (Ref. 20).

4.1.1 Setpoint Determination to be Provided in the ODCM

The alarm and trip setpoint(s) for each instrument channel listed in Table 3.3-11* should be provided and should correspond to a value(s) which represents a safe margin of assurance that the instantaneous liquid release limit of 10 CFR Part 20 is not exceeded. If the alarm and the automatic control trip are separate devices, the alarm/trip setpoint in the ODCM should list the separate trip setpoints. The alarm/trip setpoint in the ODCM should list the alarm setpoint where any trip actions are by manual initiation. The method for calculating fixed and adjustable setpoints shall be provided in the ODCM and auditable records shall be maintained indicating the actual setpoints used at all times. For setpoint calculations, see the Addendum to this manual.

---

*This Table is to be included in proposed Technical Specifications.

The alarm/trip setpoint for a liquid effluent radiation monitor should be determined based on the instantaneous concentration limits of 10 CFR Part 20, Appendix B, Table II, Column 2, and are to be applied at the point of discharge for that stream, pipe or conduit into the unrestricted area, as defined by Figure 3.1-1.[*] The alarm/trip setpoint should not consider dilution, dispersion or decay in the unrestricted area beyond the release point. An isolation control valve or system shall be provided on the discharge line prior to the release point to permit termination of radioactive releases prior to exceeding the instantaneous concentration limits of 10 CFR Part 20. The isolation and radiation monitoring points are to be located upstream of the release point far enough to assure that the time lag between the established alarm and isolation of the release will not permit a release exceeding these limits. If the stream is diluted by non-radioactive effluents, and the stream dilution and effluent isolation control system is in the exclusion area, the monitor's alarm/trip setpoint may be determined by considering the known in-plant dilution. In-plant dilution is the ratio of the total release rate at the release point into the unrestricted area to the release rate of the undiluted stream, and should be based on continuous measurement of these liquid flows. In such cases, alarm/trip setpoints should also be provided on the flow or level instrumentation with indication in the main control room. The minimum or actual instantaneous in-plant dilution ratio on which the liquid effluent radiation monitor alarm/trip setpoint has been based, should be continuously measured to aid prompt corrective action to satisfy Specification 3.11.1.1.

Conservative assumptions may be included in establishing setpoints to account for such system variables as the control and measurement system efficiency and detection capabilities during normal and anticipated operating conditions, the effects of multiple release points with common or shared in-plant dilution, variability of dilution flow and principal radio-nuclide composition, and the time lag between alarm/trip action and final isolation of the radioactive effluent. A record of analyses showing current spectra of radionuclides used to calibrate radiation monitors should be maintained in the plant records.

The instruments listed in Table 3.3-11[**] should also be included in Table 4.3-11[**] to provide the instrument surveillance requirements, such as calibration, source checking, functional testing and channel checking.

4.2 REQUIREMENT FOR IMPLEMENTING 10 CFR PART 20

In preparing proposed Technical Specifications, Figure 3.11-1[*] should consist of a map of the site area, showing the unrestricted area boundary for liquid effluents, as defined in 10 CFR 20.3(a)(17). Guidelines for preparing the figure are contained in Section 2.1.1 of Regulatory Guide 1.70 (Ref. 21).

Standard Technical Specification 3.11.1.1 specifies that:

---

[*] This Figure is to be included in proposed Technical Specifications.
[**] See footnote on page 12.

13

"The concentration of radioactive material released from the site to unrestricted areas (see Figure 3.11-1)* shall be limited to the concentrations specified in 10 CFR Part 20, Appendix B, Table II, Column 2 for radionuclides other than noble gases and 2×10^{-4} µCi/ml total activity concentration for all dissolved or entrained noble gases."

The concentration limits provided in 10 CFR Part 20, Appendix B, Table II, Column 2, do not include an MPC for noble gases dissolved or entrained in liquid effluents. An MPC of 2×10^{-4} µCi/ml has been established, based on the assumption that xenon-135 is the controlling radionuclide; the Xe-135 MPC in air (submersion) was converted to an equivalent concentration in water using the method described in International Commission on Radiological Protection (ICRP) Publication 2 (Ref. 22). The value of 2×10^{-4} µCi/ml shall be used for a mixture of dissolved or entrained noble gases, not otherwise identified in liquid releases.

To demonstrate that the Specifications are being met, the surveillance requirements specify that a sampling and analysis program be implemented according to Table 4.11-1.[**] There are two general types of releases: batch and continuous. A batch release is the discharge of liquid waste of a discrete volume. A continuous release is the discharge of liquid wastes of a nondiscrete volume; e.g., from a volume or system that has an input flow during the continuous release. For example, releases from sample monitor tanks are batch, and releases from steam generator blowdown are continuous. The sampling and analysis frequency and the type of analysis required by the Standard Technical Specifications is given in Table 4.11-1 for each type of release. The lower limit of detection is also specified in Table 4.11-1 for typical in-plant radiochemical analysis equipment. This program meets the requirements of 10 CFR Part 50, GDC 64, and conforms to the guidelines given in Regulatory Guides 1.21 (Ref. 17) and 4.15 (Ref. 20).

4.3 REQUIREMENT FOR IMPLEMENTING 10 CFR PART 50

The Standard Technical Specification 3.11.1.2 requires that the cumulative dose contributions be determined in accordance with the ODCM at least once per 31 days. The cumulative dose contributions should consider the dose contributions from the maximum exposed individual's consumption of fish, invertebrates and potable water, as appropriate. Normally, the adult is the maximum exposed individual. All of these pathways should be considered in the calculation unless demonstrated not to be present. For many plant sites, the dose calculations may be performed assuming conservative dilution factors and receptor locations to show compliance with the Technical Specification rather than a more rigorous determination. The relationships presented below are acceptable for inclusion in the ODCM. If other methods are selected to implement this Specification, it is expected that the alternate method will include the same general features considered below.

---

[*] See footnote on page 13.

[**] See footnote on page 12.

The dose contributions for the total time period $\sum_{\ell=1}^{m} \Delta t_\ell$ should be determined by calculation at least once per 31 days and a cumulative summation of these total body and any organ doses should be maintained for each calendar quarter. These dose contributions should be calculated for all radionuclides identified in liquid effluents released to unrestricted areas using the following expression:

$$D_\tau = \sum_i [A_{i\tau} \sum_{\ell=1}^{m} \Delta t_\ell \; C_{i\ell} \; F_\ell]$$

where:

D_τ = the cumulative dose commitment to the total body or any organ, τ, from the liquid effluents for the total time period $\sum_{\ell=1}^{m} \Delta t_\ell$, in mrem.

Δt_ℓ = the length of the ℓth time period over which $C_{i\ell}$ and F_ℓ are averaged for all liquid releases, in hours.

$C_{i\ell}$ = the average concentration of radionuclide, i, in undiluted liquid effluent during time period Δt_ℓ from any liquid release, in μCi/ml.

$A_{i\tau}$ = the site related ingestion dose commitment factor to the total body or any organ τ for each identified principal gamma and beta emitter listed in Table 4.11-1,* in mrem-ml per hr-μCi.

F_ℓ = the near field average dilution factor for $C_{i\ell}$ during any liquid effluent release. Defined as the ratio of the maximum undiluted liquid waste flow during release to the product of the average flow from the site discharge structure to unrestricted receiving waters times ___. (___ is the site specific applicable factor for the mixing effect of the discharge structure.)

The term $C_{i\ell}$ is the composite undiluted concentration of radioactive material in liquid waste at the common release point determined from the Radioactive Liquid Waste Sampling and Analysis Program, Table 4.11-1* in the Standard Technical Specifications. All dilution factors beyond the sample point(s) are to be included in the F_ℓ and $A_{i\tau}$ terms.

The term F_ℓ is a near field average dilution factor, considering the combined liquid releases from each unit even if there is more than one release point to the unrestricted area per unit within one-quarter mile of each other. As described in Section 3.1 of this manual, multi-unit sites with shared radioactive waste management systems should calculate the total continuous and batch liquid release concentrations for each reactor. The value of the term F_ℓ should be determined as:

---

* See footnote on page 12.

$$F_\ell = \frac{\text{liquid radioactive waste flow per unit}}{\text{discharge structure exit flow per unit} \times \text{applicable factor}}$$

The liquid radioactive waste flow is the maximum flow from all continuous and batch radioactive effluent releases specified in Table 4.11-1, from all liquid radioactive waste management systems, per unit. The discharge structure exit flow is the average flow during disposal from the discharge structure release point into the receiving water body (in an unrestricted area) per unit. The definition of F_ℓ also requires a value to be included in Specification 3.11.1.2 for the dilution as a result of mixing effects in the near field of the discharge structure. For plants with once through cooling, the applicable factor is set equal to one, i.e., no additional dilution is considered. For plants with cooling towers, onsite ponds, or lagoons, the factor shall be a number such that the product of the average blowdown flow to the receiving water body, in cfs and the applicable factor, is 1000 cfs or less. The 1000 cfs figure was selected to correspond to a typical flow for a unit with once-through cooling water and agrees with the staff method for determining compliance with Appendix I (Ref. 1) at the OL stage. The value of this applicable factor is to be included in the blank provided for the term F_ℓ. The actual dilution factor value is dependent upon the dilution available in the near field of the receiving water body; however, the applicable factor is limited, as stated above.

4.3.1 Dose Factor Related to Liquid Effluents

The above equation for calculating the dose contributions requires the use of a dose factor $A_{i\tau}$ for each nuclide, i, which embodies the dose factors, pathway transfer factors (e.g., bioaccumulation factors), pathway usage factors, and dilution factors for the points of pathway origin. The adult total body dose factor and the maximum adult organ dose factor for each radionuclide will be used from Table E-11 of Regulatory Guide 1.109 (Ref. 6); thus the list should contain critical organ dose factors for various organs. The dose factor may be written:

$$A_{i\tau} = k_o(U_W/D_W + U_F BF_i + U_I BI_i)DF_i$$

where

$A_{i\tau}$ = composite dose parameter for the total body or critical organ of an adult for nuclide, i, for all appropriate pathways, mrem/hr per μCi/ml.

k_o = units conversion factor, $1.14 \times 10^5 = 10^6$ pCi/μCi $\times 10^3$ml/kg $\div$ 8760 hr/yr.

U_W = 730 kg/yr, adult water consumption (fresh water site only).

U_F = 21 kg/yr, adult fish consumption (all sites).

U_I = 5 kg/yr, adult invertebrate consumption (salt water site only).

BF_i = Bioaccumulation factor for nuclide, i, in fish (fresh or salt water site, as applicable), pCi/kg per pCi/l, from Table A-1 of Regulatory Guide 1.109 (Ref. 4).

BI_i = Bioaccumulation factor for nuclide, i, in invertebrates (salt water only), pCi/kg per pCi/l, from Table A-1 of Regulatory Guide 1.109 (Ref. 4).

DF_i = Dose conversion factor for nuclide, i, for adults in pre-selected organ, τ, in mrem/pCi, from Table E-11 of Regulatory Guide 1.109 (Ref. 4).

D_W = Dilution factor from the near field area within one-quarter mile of the release point(s) to the potable water intake for the adult water consumption (fresh water site only).

Inserting the usage factors of Regulatory Guide 1.109 (Ref. 6) as appropriate into the equation gives the following expressions:

For Fresh Water sites: $A_{i\tau} = 1.14 \times 10^5 (730/D_W + 21BF_i)DF_i$

For Salt Water sites: $A_{i\tau} = 1.14 \times 10^5 (21BF_i + 5BI_i)DF_i$

As noted, all the factors required to calculate the values of $A_{i\tau}$ should be contained in the ODCM. The staff's method of calculating dilution factors for aquatic dispersion is provided in Regulatory Guide 1.113 (Ref. 10). The ODCM should include a detailed presentation of the calculation model and a tabulation of all values assigned to the parameters in expressions used to implement the Specification 3.11.1.2.

4.3.2 Special Reports

The Standard Technical Specifications 3.11.1.2, 3.11.1.3, 3.11.2.2, 3.11.2.3, 3.11.2.4 and 3.11.3.1 require that action be taken when the Specification cannot be met. The action is in the form of special reports, in lieu of licensee event reports, indicating the corrective action to be taken to reduce the dose impact due to the release of radioactive materials in liquid effluents.

These special reports should be prepared using the methodology provided in this manual to determine the dose impact. Such information in the special reports will be used by the staff in determining if the corrective action proposed by the licensee is adequate to bring the releases within the design objectives of Appendix I to 10 CFR Part 50. These special reports may also require submitting additional information as described in Section 3.4 of this manual.

4.4 SPECIFICATION ON RADIOACTIVITY CONTENTS IN LIQUID-CONTAINING TANKS

Standard Technical Specification 3.11.1.4 and Tables 3.3-11* and 4.3-11* list liquid-containing tanks outside containment that are to be analyzed periodically to verify that the radioactivity content (in curies, excluding tritium and dissolved or entrained noble gases) is below the specified value. Tanks included in this Specification are those that are not surrounded by liners, dikes or walls capable of holding the tank contents and do not have tank overflow and drains connected to the liquid radioactive waste management system. Indoor tanks are not included unless an analysis based on design basis fission product leakage from the fuel results in radionuclide concentrations in excess of the limits of 10 CFR Part 20, Appendix B, Table II, Column 2, where leaked fluid is capable of affecting the nearest existing or known future water supply** in an unrestricted area.

---

*See footnote on page 12.

**"Supply" means a well or surface water intake that is used as a water source for direct human consumption or indirectly through animals, crops or food processing. "Known future" water supply means potential wells or surface water intakes which are identified, or may be reasonably deduced from available information.

For those tanks that are determined to be included in Specification 3.11.1.4 and Tables 3.3-11 and 4.3-11, a curie limit should be determined based on the methodology presented in Appendices A or B of this manual, using the PWR-RATAFR Computer Code for pressurized water reactor plants, or the BWR-RATAFR Computer Code for boiling water reactor plants, respectively. The methodology is based on the calculated radionuclide inventory in the tank at 80% capacity using a design basis fission product source term of (1) 1% of the operating fission product inventory in the core being released to the primary coolant for a PWR, or (2) a fission product release consistent with a noble gas release rate of 100 μCi/MWt-sec at 30 minutes decay for a BWR. These Computer Codes determine the radionuclide inventory in a tank that would result in concentrations equal to the limits of 10 CFR Part 20, Appendix B, Table II, Column 2, at (1) the nearest potable water supply and (2) the nearest surface water supply in an unrestricted area.

By excluding tritium and dissolved or entrained noble gases from the surveillance analyses, since these can be estimated for any licensee event report, Specification 3.11.1.4 should include the lowest curie quantity of activation and mixed fission products determined for any tank listed in Specification 3.11.1.4 as the curie limit for all tanks included in that Specification.

Most operating reactors have required the use of temporary process and storage tanks during maintenance and service periods, or when temporary solidification equipment is used at the facility; therefore, the Specification 3.11.1.4 should indicate a "temporary tank." The curie limit for a temporary tank may be calculated by the above method, but should be limited to $\leq$ 10 curies, excluding tritium and dissolved or entrained gases. If the temporary tank is mobile and not used for more than a calendar quarter, it need not be included in Tables 3.3-11* and 4.3-11.*

4.5 SPECIFICATION ON THE USE OF LIQUID RADIOACTIVE WASTE MANAGEMENT SYSTEM

Standard Technical Specification 3.11.1.3 specifies that:

"The liquid radwaste treatment system shall be OPERABLE. The appropriate subsystems shall be used to reduce the radioactive materials in liquid wastes prior to their discharge when the projected doses due to the liquid effluent releases to unrestricted areas (see Figure 3.11-1)* when averaged over 31 days, exceeds 0.06 mrem to the total body or 0.2 mrem to any organ."

The operability of the liquid radioactive waste management system ensures that this system will be available for use whenever liquid effluents require treatment prior to release to the environment. The term "liquid radwaste treatment system" involves all of the installed and available liquid radioactive waste management system equipment, as well as their controls, power instrumentation, and services that make the system functional. Equipment that is considered standby or redundant is also included, since their function is to assure operability. The specification also permits alternate treatment paths using alternate subsystems and equipment to be used in the event that the normal treatment is inoperable.

---

*See footnote on page 13.

This Specification requires maintenance and use of the liquid radioactive waste management system for conformance to 10 CFR Part 50.36a. Maintenance and use of the radioactive waste management system components are discussed in Section 2.2 of this manual.

To determine if use of the installed equipment is necessary, the licensee must project the cumulative liquid effluent releases over the ensuing 31 days. These releases should include all plant effluents from all liquid radioactive waste management and liquid waste disposal system components that are planned to be operated at the projected capacity and performance of each component used during the specified time. These releases should include a margin, based on operating data, for anticipated and unplanned operational occurrences and should use the methodology discussed in Section 4.3 of this manual. The impact from this projected cumulative release is to be compared to 0.06 mrem for the total body or 0.2 mrem for any organ. If the projection indicates these values will be exceeded, then the installed liquid radioactive waste management system components that will reduce those radioactive materials in liquid effluents and the projected impact, must be used.

The values for the projected impact, given above, correspond to approximately one forty-eighth of the design objective values of Appendix I, Section II.A of 10 CFR Part 50 in a month, and if continued at this rate for a year, they would correspond to less than one-fourth the values limited by Specification 3.11.1.2.b. The calculations of projected cumulative dose impact that could result from the proposed operation should use the methodology provided in Section 4.3 of this manual.

CHAPTER 5

GASEOUS EFFLUENTS

5.1 INSTRUMENTATION

Standard Technical Specification 3.3.3.9 requires that:

"The radioactive gaseous process and effluent monitoring instrumentation channels shown in Table 3.3-12* shall be OPERABLE with their alarm/trip setpoints set to ensure that the limits of Specification 3.11.2.1 are not exceeded. The setpoints shall be determined in accordance with procedures as described in the ODCM, and shall be recorded in the station log."

Table 3.3-12* provides a list of the radioactive gaseous effluent monitoring instrumentation needed to comply with the requirements of General Design Criteria (GDC) 60, 63, and 64 of Appendix A to 10 CFR Part 50. The list includes instrumentation such as radioactivity monitoring and sampling devices, automatic control devices and essential flow and level devices that are components of the monitoring systems. The list uses common nomenclature for the effluent streams; however, the names may be revised as necessary, to conform with a particular plant's nomenclature. The list may include effluent streams which are not applicable to a given plant, or which may be duplicated and, therefore, should be tailored for the proposed Technical Specifications. Clarification of proposed Technical Specifications should be provided by a simple drawing or sketch, showing stream intersections, instrumentation and control features. Duplicate instrumentation (i.e., instruments that measure different sensor parameters or ranges) should be listed separately in Tables 3.3-12* and 4.3-12.* The channel logic should assure that the alarmed trip action is not negated by switching.

The plant procedures should contain a quality assurance program for instruments as recommended in Regulatory Guide 4.15 (Ref. 20).

5.1.1 Setpoint Determination to be Provided in the ODCM

The alarm/trip setpoint or automatic control trip setpoint for each instrument channel listed in Table 3.3-12* should be provided and should correspond to a value(s) which represents a safe margin of assurance that the instantaneous gaseous release limit of Specification 3.11.2.1(a) will not be exceeded. For channels with separate alarm and automatic control trips, the setpoint for the automatic control trip should be the established value referenced above; the corresponding setpoint for alarm/trip should be established such that an alarm trip will occur either in advance of the automatic control trip or simultaneously with the automatic control trip. For channels with alarm trips only, the setpoint for the alarm/trip should be the established value referenced above, provided that the manual or procedural response to the alarm represents a safe margin of assurance that the instantaneous gaseous release limit of 10 CFR Part 20 will not be exceeded. The alarm/trip setpoint in the ODCM should list the alarm setpoint for those channels where any trip actions are by

---

*This Table is to be included in the proposed Technical Specifications.

manual initiation. The method for calculating fixed or adjustable setpoints shall be provided in the ODCM and auditable records shall be maintained indicating the actual setpoints used at all times.

The alarm/trip setpoint for any gaseous effluent radiation monitor should be determined based on the instantaneous (see RELEASE RATE fundamental time units in Section 2.2 of this manual) concentration limits of 10 CFR Part 20, Appendix B, Table II, Column 1, and are to be applied at the point at which the discharge leaves the restricted area boundary into an unrestricted area, as defined by Figure 5.1-1.** The bases for each setpoint should consider the type of release at the monitor's location, e.g., long-term releases using the long-term atmospheric dispersion conditions or, if applicable (see Section 3.3 of this manual), short-term releases using the short-term atmospheric dispersion conditions. An isolation control valve or system shall be provided on the discharge line upstream of the release point to permit isolation prior to exceeding the specified release limits.

If the alarm/trip setpoints are based on predetermined factors accounting for atmospheric conditions, the elevation of the release point should be considered. The symbols used in the equations in this manual use a subscript (s) for a free-standing stack for elevated releases (or vents that take the plume out of the building wake) and a subscript (v) for vent for releases that are not completely elevated. Guidance on the staff's method for estimating atmospheric transport and dispersion of gaseous effluents in routine releases is provided in Regulatory Guide 1.111 (Ref. 8). The radiation monitor alarm/trip setpoints for each release point should be based on the radioactive noble gases in gaseous effluents. It is not considered to be practicable to apply instantaneous alarm/trip setpoints to integrating radiation monitors sensitive to radioiodines, radioactive materials in particulate form and radionuclides other than noble gases. Alarm/trip setpoints should also be provided in the main control room for flow measurement devices which are part of continuous monitoring or sampling systems and should alarm on loss-of-flow or departure from an established flow range. In all cases, conservative assumptions may be necessary in establishing these setpoints to account for system variables, such as the control and measurement system efficiency and detection capabilities during normal, anticipated, and unusual operating conditions, the variability in release flow and principal radionuclides, and the time lag between alarm/trip action and the final isolation of the radioactive effluent. The current spectrum of radionuclides used to calibrate radiation monitors should be maintained in the plant records. The instruments listed in Table 3.3-12* should also be included in Table 4.3-12,* to provide the instrument surveillance requirements, such as calibration, source checking, functional testing, and channel checking.

5.2 DOSE LIMIT FOR IMPLEMENTING 10 CFR PART 20

In preparing proposed Technical Specifications, Figure 5.1-1** should consist of a map of the site area showing the exclusion boundary, as defined in 10 CFR 100.3(a) (Ref. 15) and the unrestricted area boundary, as defined in 10 CFR 20.3(a)(17) (Ref. 14). Guidelines for this figure are contained in Section 2.1.1 of Regulatory Guide 1.70 (Ref. 21). Details on the release point locations and significant elevations should be given in Figure 5.1-1.**

---

*See footnote on page 20.
**This Figure is to be included in proposed Technical Specifications.

5.2.1 Implementation of 10 CFR Part 20 - Airborne Releases

The Standard Technical Specification 3.11.2.1 implements 10 CFR Part 20 as follows:

"The instantaneous dose rate in unrestricted areas (see Figure 5.1-1)** due to radioactive materials released in gaseous effluents from the site shall be limited to the following values:

a.   The dose rate limit for noble gases shall be < 500 mrem/yr to the total body and < 3000 mrem/yr to the skin, and

b.   The dose rate limit for all radioiodines and for all radioactive materials in particulate form and radionuclides other than noble gases with half lives greater than 8 days shall be < 1500 mrem/yr to any organ."

The ODCM should provide the mathematical relationships used to implement the above specification. The relationships presented below are acceptable for inclusion in the ODCM. If other methods are selected to implement the specification, it is expected that the alternative method will include the same general features considered below.

a.   Release rate limit for noble gases:

$$\sum_i [V_i \dot{Q}_{is} + K_i ((\overline{x/Q})_v \dot{Q}_{iv})] < 500 \text{ mrem/yr, and}$$

$$\sum_i [(L_i (\overline{x/Q})_s + 1.1 B_i) \dot{Q}_{is} + (L_i + 1.1 M_i)((\overline{x/Q})_v \dot{Q}_{iv})] < 3000 \text{ mrem/yr}$$

where the terms are defined below.

b.   Release rate limit for all radionuclides and radioactive materials in particulate form and radionuclides other than noble gases:

$$\sum_i P_i [W_s \dot{Q}_{is} + W_v \dot{Q}_{iv}] < 1500 \text{ mrem/yr}$$

where:

K_i =   The total body dose factor due to gamma emissions for each identified noble gas radionuclide, in mrem/yr per $\mu Ci/m^3$.

L_i =   The skin dose factor due to beta emissions for each identified noble gas radionuclide, in mrem/yr per $\mu Ci/m^3$.

M_i =   The air dose factor due to gamma emissions for each identified noble gas radionuclide, in mrad/yr per $\mu Ci/m^3$ (unit conversion constant of 1.1 mrem/mrad converts air dose to skin dose).

P_i =   The dose parameter for radionuclides other than noble gases for the inhalation pathway, in mrem/yr per $\mu Ci/m^3$ and for food and ground plane pathways, in m^2(mrem/yr per $\mu Ci/sec$). The dose factors are based on the critical individual organ and most restrictive age group (infant).

V_i =   The constant for each identified noble gas radionuclide accounting for the gamma radiation from the elevated finite plume, derived in accordance with the dose methodology in Regulatory Guide 1.109, Appendix B, Section 1, in mrem/yr per $\mu Ci/sec$.

B_i =   The constant for long-term releases (greater than 500 hrs/yr) for each identified noble gas radionuclide accounting for the gamma radiation from the elevated finite plume, derived in accordance with the dose methodology in Regulatory Guide 1.109, Appendix B, Section 1, in mrad/yr per $\mu Ci/sec$.

**See footnote on page 21.

$\dot{Q}_{is}$ = The release rate of radionuclides, i, in gaseous effluents from free-standing stack, in μCi/sec (per unit, unless otherwise specified.)

$\dot{Q}_{iv}$ = The release rate of radionuclides, i, in gaseous effluent from all vent releases, in μCi/sec (per unit, unless otherwise specified).

$(\overline{\chi/Q})_s$ = _____ sec/m³. For free-standing stack releases. The highest calculated annual average relative concentration for any area at or beyond the unrestricted area boundary.

$(\overline{\chi/Q})_v$ = _____ sec/m³. For all vent releases. The highest calculated annual average relative concentration for any area at or beyond the unrestricted area boundary.

W_v = The highest calculated annual average dispersion parameter for estimating the dose to an individual at the controlling location due to all vent releases:

W_v = _____ sec/m³, for the inhalation pathway. The location is the unrestricted area boundary in the ___ sector.

W_v = _____ meters^{-2}, for the food and ground plane pathways. The location is the unrestricted area boundary in the ___ sector.

W_s = The highest calculated annual average dispersion parameter for estimating the dose to an individual at the controlling location due to free-standing stack releases:

W_s = _____ sec/m³, for the inhalation pathway. The location is the unrestricted area boundary in the ___ sector.

W_s = _____ meters^{-2}, for the food and ground plane pathways. The location is the unrestricted area boundary in the ___ sector."

SPECIAL NOTES: (1) If there are no free-standing stacks, the factors denoted by the subscript, s, need not be considered. (2) In all cases, the tritium releases use the first W parameter, based on relative concentration (sec/m³). (3) All radioiodines are assumed to be released in elemental form. If analysis includes the capability of determining elemental and nonelemental forms in all releases, the food pathway parameters may be adjusted accordingly.

The Specification is applicable to the location (unrestricted area boundary or beyond), characterized by the values of the parameters V_i, B_i or $(\overline{\chi/Q})$ which result in the maximum total body or skin dose commitment. In the event that the analyses indicates a different location for the total body and skin dose limitations, the location selected for consideration shall be that which minimizes the allowable release values.

The factors K_i, L_i, and M_i relate the radionuclide airborne concentrations to various dose rates assuming a semi-infinite cloud. These factors may be taken directly from Table B-1 of the Regulatory Guide 1.109 (Ref. 6), if the values therein are multiplied by 10^6 to convert picocuries^{-1} to microcuries^{-1} as used in the above equations. A tabulation of these factors should be included in the ODCM.

The B_i and V_i factors for the radionuclides are based on the finite plume model of Regulatory Guide 1.109 (Ref. 6). From Equation 6 of Section 6.2 of this Regulatory Guide, B_i can be expressed as:

$$B_i = \frac{K}{r_d} \sum_{jk\ell} \frac{f_{jk} A_{\ell i} \mu_a E_\ell I}{u_j} \left(\frac{mrad/yr}{\mu Ci/sec}\right)$$

Where:

I = the results of numerical integration over the plume spatial distribution of the airborne activity as defined by the meteorological condition of wind speed (u_j) and atmospheric stability class k for a particular wind direction.

K = a numerical constant representing unit conversions, presented below.

r_d = the distance from the release point to the receptor location, in meters.

u_j = the mean wind speed assigned to the jth wind speed class, in meters/sec.

f_{jk} = the joint frequency of occurrence of the jth wind speed class and kth stability class (dimensionless).

$A_{\ell i}$ = the number of photons of energy corresponding to the ℓth energy group emitted per transformation of the ith radionuclide, in number/transformation.

E_ℓ = the energy assigned to the ℓth energy group, in Mev.

μ_a = the energy absorption coefficient in air for photon energy E_ℓ, in meters^{-1}.

The constant K follows from Equation 6 of Section C.2.a of Regulatory Guide 1.109 (Ref. 6), as:

$$K = \frac{260 \text{ mrad(radians)}(m^3)(\text{transformation})}{\text{sec(Mev)(Ci)}} \left(\frac{16 \text{ sectors}}{2\Pi \text{ radians}}\right)\left(10^{-6} \frac{Ci}{\mu Ci}\right)\left(3.15\times10^7 \frac{sec}{yr}\right)$$

$$= 2.1\times10^4 \text{ mrad } (m^3)(\text{transformation})/yr(Mev)(\mu Ci).$$

The V_i factor is computed with conversion from air dose to tissue depth dose, thus:

$$V_i = 1.1 \frac{K}{r_d} \sum_{jk\ell} \frac{f_{jk} A_{\ell i} \mu_a E_\ell I}{u_j} [e^{-\mu_T T_d}] \left(\frac{mrem/yr}{\mu Ci/sec}\right)$$

where:

μ_T = the tissue energy absorption coefficient for photons of energy E_ℓ, in cm^2/gm.

T_d = the tissue density thickness taken to represent the total body dose (5gm/cm^2).

1.1 = the ratio of the tissue to air absorption coefficients over the energy range of photons of interest. This ratio converts dose (mrad) to dose equivalent (mrem).

The parameter, P_i, contained in the radioiodine and particulates Specification 3.11.2.1.b includes pathway transport parameters of the ith radionuclide, the receptor's usage of the pathway media and the dosimetry of the exposure. Pathway usage rates and the internal dosimetry are functions of the receptor's age; however, the youngest age group, the infant, will always receive the maximum dose under the exposure conditions for Specification 3.11.2.1. For the infant exposure, separate values of P_i may be calculated using the PARTS computer program given in Appendix D of this manual for the inhalation pathway which uses a W parameter based on $(\overline{\chi/Q})$, and the food (milk) and ground pathway which uses a W parameter normally based on $\overline{(D/Q)}$, except for tritium, for application in the ODCM. The following sections provide detail on calculating these P_i values for inclusion in the ODCM.

The values of P_i are independent of vent and stack release elevation. In the case of tritium, $\overline{(\chi/Q)}$ is the W parameter for the food (milk) pathway as well as the inhalation pathway. As tritium is a weak beta emitter, the ground plane contribution is zero for tritium. (NOTE: The value for the P_i (food) for tritium is 2.4×10^3 mrem/yr per µCi/m³.) If the controlling locations for vent and stack releases are different, the controlling location for vent releases should be used in Specification 3.11.2.1.

Omitting the subscripts for vent and stack releases, the dose rate from the ith radionuclide (except tritium) is:

$$P_i \text{ (inhalation)} (\overline{\chi/Q})\ Q + [P_i \text{(food)} + P_i \text{(ground plane)}]\ \overline{(D/Q)} Q \text{ (mrem/yr)}$$

and for tritium, is:

$$P_i \text{ (inhalation)} (\overline{\lambda/Q}) Q + P_i \text{(food)} \overline{(\chi/Q)} Q = 3.0 \times 10^3 \overline{(\chi/Q)} Q \text{ (mrem/yr)}$$

5.2.1.1   Calculation of P_i (Inhalation)

$$P_i = K'(BR)\ DFA_i \text{ (mrem/yr per µCi/m}^3)$$

where:

K' = a constant of unit conversion, 10^6 pCi/µCi.

BR = the breathing rate of the infant age group, in m³/yr.

DFA_i = the maximum organ inhalation dose factor for the infant age group for the ith radionuclide, in mrem/pCi. The total body is considered as an organ in the selection of DFA_i.

The age group considered is the infant group. The infant's breathing rate is taken as 1400 m³/yr from Table E-5 of Regulatory Guide 1.109 (Ref. 6). The inhalation dose factors for the infant, DFA_i are presented in Table E-10 of Regulatory Guide 1.109, in units of mrem/pCi.

Resolution of the units yields:

$$P_i \text{ (inhalation)} = 1.4 \times 10^9\ DFA_i$$

5.2.1.2   Calculation of P_i (Ground Plane)

$$P_i = K'K''DFG_i \ (1-e^{-\lambda_i t})/\lambda_i \quad (m^2 \cdot mrem/yr \text{ per } \mu Ci/sec)$$

Where:

K' = a constant of unit conversion, 10^6 pCi/μCi.

K'' = a constant of unit conversion, 8760 hr/year.

λ_i = the decay constant for the ith radionuclide, sec^{-1}.

t = the exposure period, 3.15×10^7 sec (1 year).

DFG_i = the ground plane dose conversion factor for the ith radionuclide (mrem/hr per pCi/m^2).

The deposition rate onto the ground plane results in a ground plane concentration that is assumed to persist over a year with radiological decay the only operating removal mechanism for each radionuclide. The ground plane dose conversion factors for the ith radionuclide, DFG_i, are presented in Table E-6 of Regulatory Guide 1.109 (Ref. 6), in units of mrem/hr per pCi/m^2.

Resolution of the units yields:

$$P_i \text{ (Ground)} = 8.76 \times 10^9 \ DFG_i \ (1-e^{-\lambda_i t})/\lambda_i .$$

5.2.1.3   Calculation of P_i (Food)

$$P_i = K'r \frac{Q_F(U_{ap})}{Y_p(\lambda_i + \lambda_w)} F_m DFL_i [e^{-\lambda_i t_f}] \quad (m^2 \cdot mrem/yr \text{ per } \mu Ci/sec)$$

where:

K' = a constant of unit conversion, 10^6 pCi/μCi.

Q_F = the cow's consumption rate, in kg/day (wet weight).

U_{ap} = the infant's milk consumption rate, in liters/yr.

Y_p = the agricultural productivity by unit area, in kg/m^2

F_m = the stable element transfer coefficients, in days/liter.

r = fraction of deposited activity retained on cow's feed grass.

DFL_i = the maximum organ ingestion dose factor for the ith radionuclide, in mrem/pCi.

λ_i = the decay constant for the ith radionuclide, in sec^{-1}.

λ_w = the decay constant for removal of activity on leaf and plant surfaces by weathering, 5.73×10^{-7} sec^{-1} (corresponding to a 14 day half-time).

t_f = the transport time from pasture to cow, to milk, to infant, in sec.

A fraction of the airborne deposition is captured by the ground plant vegetation cover. The captured material is removed from the vegetation (grass) by both radiological decay and weathering processes.

The values of Q_F, U_{ap}, and Y_p are provided in Regulatory Guide 1.109 (Ref. 6), Tables E-3, E-5, and E-15, as 50 kg/day, 330 liters/day and 0.7 kg/m^2, respectively. The value t_f is provided in Regulatory Guide 1.109 (Ref. 6), Table E-15, as 2 days (1.73x10^5 seconds). The fraction, r, has a value of 1.0 for radioiodines and 0.2 for particulates, as presented in Regulatory Guide 1.109 (Ref. 6), Table E-15.

Table E-1 of Regulatory Guide 1.109 (Ref. 4) provides the stable element transfer coefficients, F_m, and Table E-14 provides the ingestion dose factors, DFL_i, for the infant's organs. The organ with the maximum value of DFL_i is to be used.

Resolution of the units yields:

$$P_i \text{ (food)} = 2.4 \times 10^{10} \frac{rF_m}{\lambda_i + \lambda_w} DFL_i \left[e^{-\lambda_i t_f}\right] \text{ (m}^2 \cdot \text{mrem/yr per } \mu\text{Ci/sec)}$$

for all radionuclides, except tritium.

The concentration of tritium in milk is based on its airborne concentration rather than the deposition rate.

$$P_i = K'K'''F_m Q_F U_{ap} DFL_i \left[0.75(0.5/H)\right] \text{ (mrem/yr per } \mu\text{Ci/m}^3)$$

where:

K''' = a constant of unit conversion, 10^3 gm/kg.

H = absolute humidity of the atmosphere, in gm/m^3.

0.75 = the fraction of total feed that is water.

0.5 = the ratio of the specific activity of the feed grass water to the atmospheric water.

From Table E-1 and E-14 of Regulatory Guide 1.109 (Ref. 6), the values of F_m and DFL_i for tritium are 1.0x10^{-2} day/liter and 3.08x10^{-7} mrem per pCi, respectively. Assuming an average absolute humidity of 8 grams/meter^3, the resolution of units yields:

$$P_i \text{ (food)} = 2.4 \times 10^3 \text{ mrem/yr per } \mu\text{Ci/m}^3$$

for tritium, only.

5.3 DOSE LIMIT FOR IMPLEMENTING 10 CFR PART 50

In preparing proposed Technical Specifications, Figure 5.1-1* should consist of a map of the site area showing the unrestricted area boundary for gaseous effluents as defined in Section 5.2 of this manual. Guidelines for this figure are contained in Regulatory Guide 1.70, Section 2.1.1 (Ref. 21).

---

*See footnote on page 21.

5.3.1 REQUIREMENTS FOR IMPLEMENTING 10 CFR PART 50

The Standard Technical Specifications 3.11.2.2 and 3.11.2.3 implement 10 CFR Part 50, Appendix I, as follows:

"The air dose in unrestricted areas (see Figure 5.1-1)* due to noble gases released in gaseous effluents shall be limited to the following:

a.   During any calendar quarter, to $\leq$ 5 mrad for gamma radiation and $\leq$ 10 mrad for beta radiation;

b.   During any calendar year, to $\leq$ 10 mrad for gamma radiation and $\leq$ 20 mrad for beta radiation;

   (The dose design objectives may be reduced based on expected public occupancy of areas, e.g., beaches and visitor centers within the unrestricted area boundary. (For PWRs only) the dose design objectives may be reduced based on predicted noble gas releases from the turbine building, if effluent sampling is not provided.)"

"The dose to an individual from radioiodines, radioactive materials in particulate form, and radionuclides other than noble gases with half-lives greater than 8 days in gaseous effluents released to unrestricted areas (see Figure 5.1-1)* shall be limited to the following:

a.   During any calendar quarter to $\leq$ 7.5 mrem; and

b.   During any calendar year to $\leq$ 15 mrem."

The ODCM should provide the mathematical relationships used to implement the Specifications. The relationships presented below are acceptable for inclusion in the ODCM. If other methods are selected to implement these Specifications, it is expected that the alternative method will include the same general features considered below.

The air dose in unrestricted area (see Figure 5.1-1)* due to noble gases released in gaseous effluents should be determined by the following expressions:

a.   During any calendar quarter, for gamma radiation:

$$3.17 \times 10^{-8} \sum_i \left[M_i \left[(\overline{\chi/Q})_v \tilde{Q}_{iv} + (\overline{\chi/q})_v \tilde{q}_{iv} \right] + \left[B_i \tilde{Q}_{is} + b_i \tilde{q}_{is} \right] \right] \leq 5 \text{ mrad, and}$$

During any calendar quarter, for beta radiation:

$$3.17 \times 10^{-8} \sum_i N_i \left[(\overline{\chi/Q})_v \tilde{Q}_{iv} + (\overline{\chi/q})_v \tilde{q}_{iv} + (\overline{\chi/Q})_s \tilde{Q}_{is} + (\overline{\chi/Q})_s \tilde{q}_{is} \right] \leq 10 \text{ mrad, and}$$

b.   During any calendar year, for gamma radiation:

$$3.17 \times 10^{-8} \sum_i \left[M_i \left[(\overline{\chi/Q})_v \tilde{Q}_{iv} + (\overline{\chi/q})_v \tilde{q}_{iv} \right] + \left[B_i \tilde{Q}_{is} + b_i \tilde{q}_{is} \right] \right] \leq 10 \text{ mrad, and}$$

During any calendar year, for beta radiation:

$$3.17 \times 10^{-8} \sum_i N_i \left[(\overline{\chi/Q})_v \tilde{Q}_{iv} + (\overline{\chi/q})_v \tilde{q}_{iv} + (\overline{\chi/Q})_s \tilde{Q}_{is} + (\overline{\chi/q})_s \tilde{q}_{is} \right] \leq 20 \text{ mrad}$$

   where:

   M_i = The air dose factor due to gamma emmissions for each identified noble gas radionculide, in mrad/yr per $\mu Ci/m^3$.

---

*See footnote on page 21.

N_i = The air dose factor due to beta emissions for each identified noble gas radionuclide, in mrad/yr per $\mu Ci/m^3$.

$(\overline{\chi/Q})_v$ = _____ sec/m^3. For vent releases. The highest calculated annual average relative concentration for area at or beyond the unrestricted area boundary for long term releases (greater than 500 hrs/year).

$(\overline{\chi/q})_v$ = _____ sec/m^3. For vent releases. The relative concentration for areas at or beyond the unrestricted area boundary for short term releases (equal to or less than 500 hrs/year).

$(\overline{\chi/Q})_s$ = _____ sec/m^3. For free-standing stack releases. The highest calculated annual average relative concentration for areas at or beyond the unrestricted area boundary for long term releases (greater than 500 hrs/year).

$(\overline{\chi/q})_s$ = _____ sec/m^3. For free-standing stack releases. The relative concentration for areas at or beyond the unrestricted area boundary for short term releases (equal to or less than 500 hrs/year).

$\tilde{q}_{is}$ = The average release of noble gas radionuclides in gaseous effluents, i, for short term releases (equal to or less than 500 hrs/year) from the free-standing stack, in μCi. Releases shall be cumulative over the calendar quarter or year as appropriate.

$\tilde{q}_{iv}$ = The average release of noble gas radionuclides in gaseous effluents, i, for short term releases (equal to or less than 500 hrs/year) from all vents, in μCi. Releases shall be cumulative over the calendar quarter or year as appropriate.

$\tilde{Q}_{is}$ = The average release of noble gas radionuclides in gaseous releases, i, for long term releases (greater than 500 hrs/year) from the free-standing stack, in μCi. Release shall be cumulative over the calendar quarter or year as appropriate.

$\tilde{Q}_{iv}$ = The average release of noble gas radionuclides in gaseous effluents, i, for long term releases (greater than 500 hrs/yr) from all vents, in μCi. Releases shall be cumulative over the calendar quarter or year as appropriate.

B_i = The constant for long term releases (greater than 500 hrs/yr) for each identified noble gas radionuclide accounting for the gamma radiation from the elevated finite plume, derived in accordance with the dose methodology in Regulatory Guide 1.109, Appendix B, Section 1, in mrad/yr per $\mu Ci/sec$.

b_i = The constant for short term releases (equal to or less than 500 hrs/yr) for each identified noble gas radionuclide accounting for the gamma radiation from the elevated finite plume, derived in accordance with the dose methodology in Regulatory Guide 1.109, Appendix B, Section 1, in mrad/yr per $\mu Ci/sec$.

3.17×10^{-8} = The inverse of the number of seconds in a year.

The dose to an individual from radioiodines, radioactive materials in particulate form, and radionuclides other than noble gases with half-lives greater than 8 days in gaseous effluents released to unrestricted areas (see Figure 5.1-1)* should be determined by the following expressions:

a. During any calendar quarter:

$$3.17 \times 10^{-8} \sum_i R_i [W_s\tilde{Q}_{is} + w_s\tilde{q}_{is} + W_v\tilde{Q}_{iv} + w_v\tilde{q}_{iv}] \le 7.5 \text{ mrem, and}$$

---

*See footnote on page 21.

29

b. During any calendar year:

$$3.17 \times 10^{-8} \sum_i R_i \left[W_s \tilde{Q}_{is} + w_s \tilde{q}_{is} + W_v \tilde{Q}_{iv} + w_v \tilde{q}_{iv} \right] \leq 15 \text{ mrem}$$

where:

$\tilde{Q}_i$ = The releases of radionuclides, radioactive materials in particulate form, and radionuclides other than noble gases in gaseous effluents, i, for long term releases greater than 500 hrs/yr, in μCi. Releases shall be cumulative over the calendar quarter or year as appropriate.

$\tilde{q}_i$ = The releases of radionuclides, radioactive materials in particulate form and radionuclides other than noble gases in gaseous effluents, i, for short term releases equal to or less than 500 hrs/yr, in μCi. Releases shall be cumulative over the calendar quarter or year as appropriate.

W = The dispersion parameter for estimating the dose to an individual at the controlling location for long term releases (greater than 500 hrs/yr):

W = $(\overline{\chi/Q})$ for the inhalation pathway, in sec/m^3.

W = $(\overline{D/Q})$ for the food and ground plane pathways in meters^{-2}.

w = The dispersion parameter for estimating the dose to an individual at the controlling location for short term releases (equal to or less than 500 hrs/yr):

w = $(\overline{\chi/q})$ for the inhalation pathway in sec/m^3.

w = $(\overline{D/q})$ for the food and ground plane pathway in meters^{-2}.

3.17×10^{-8} = The inverse of the number of seconds in a year.

R_i = The dose factor for each identified radionuclide, i, in m^2(mrem/yr) per μCi/sec or mrem/yr per μCi/m^3.

For the direction sectors with existing pathways within 5 miles from the unit, use the values of R_i for these pathways. If no real pathway exists within 5 miles from the center of the building complex, use the cow-milk R_i assuming that this pathway exists at the 4.5 to 5.0 mile distance in the worst sector. If the R_i for an existing pathway within 5 miles is less than a cow-milk R_i at 4.5 to 5.0 miles, then use the value of the cow-milk R_i at 4.5 to 5.0 miles. The pathway values used for calculating dose contributions shall be consistent with the results of the land use census performed pursuant to Specification 3.12.2. The controlling value of R_i for each radionuclide shall be determined and provided in tabular form in the ODCM. The parameters W and w shall correspond to the applicable pathway location.

SPECIAL NOTES: (1) If there is no free-standing stack, the factors denoted by the subscript, s, need not be considered. (2) In all cases, the tritium releases use the first W or w parameter, based on relative concentration (sec/m^3). (3) All radioiodines are assumed to be released in elemental form. If analysis includes the capability of determining the elemental and non-elemental forms in all releases, the food pathway parameters may be adjusted accordingly.

The following information is provided to further clarify the application of these Specifications and provide more information regarding the individual factors. The ODCM should include a detailed presentation of the calculational model and a complete tabulation of all values assigned to each parameter.

The noble gas Specification 3.11.2.2 is to be evaluated at the location in the unrestricted area where analyses of annual average air doses were found to be maximum. In the event that the analyses indicate different locations for the beta and gamma limitations, the location selected for consideration shall be that which minimizes the allowable release values due to gamma radiation.

The radioiodine and particulate Specification 3.11.2.3 is applicable to the location in the unrestricted area where the combination of existing pathways and receptor age groups indicates the maximum potential exposures. The inhalation and ground plane exposure pathways shall be considered to exist at all locations. The grass-cow-milk, grass-cow-meat, and vegetation pathways are considered based on their existence at the various locations. Of the various age groups, the infant or child receives the largest dose; thus, only these two age groups will be discussed. It is the intent, however, that a licensee undertake annual surveys of the age groups and the land use at the various locations about the site, reports these results according to Specification 3.12.2 and determines the applicable parameters of R_i for tabulation in the ODCM. The new parameters shall be submitted to the NRC for review and approval prior to implementation.

The M_i and N_i factors of the noble gas relationship relate the airborne concentration of the noble gas to the air dose rates assuming a semi-infinite cloud. These factors may be taken directly from Table B-1 of the Regulatory Guide 1.109 (Ref. 6), and the values therein have been multiplied by 10^6 to convert picocuries^{-1} to microcuries^{-1}.

The factor, B_i, is defined in Section 5.2.1 of this manual. The corresponding short-term factor, b_i is computed following the same procedure replacing the meteorological variables, j, k, and ℓ, for long-term releases with variables for short-term releases using the methodology provided in Regulatory Guide 1.111 (Ref. 8), NUREG-0324 (Ref. 13), and NUREG-75/087 (Ref. 23). Such information should be provided in tabular form in the ODCM.

In developing the R_i values, separate expressions are written for each of the potential pathways. These expressions are similar to those developed in Section 5.2.1 of this manual for P_i, and are denoted by $R_i^G[D/Q]$, $R_i^I[\chi/Q]$, $R_i^C[D/Q]$, $R_i^M[D/Q]$ and $R_i^V[D/Q]$, where the superscripts G, I, C, M, and V refer to ground plane, inhalation, cow's milk, meat and vegetation, respectively. The 'argument' notation, [ ], indicates the appropriate dispersion parameter, W, to be applied with the R_i factor. Note that the argument is not included in the following expressions. In the case of tritium, the dispersion parameter, W, is always taken as $(\overline{\chi/Q})$. The R_i parameter is independent of long-term or short-term releases and should be provided in tabular form in the ODCM.

5.3.1.1 Inhalation Pathway Factor, $R_i^I[\chi/Q]$

$$R_i^I[\chi/Q] = K'(BR)_a (DFA_i)_a \text{ (mrem/yr per } \mu Ci/m^3)$$

where:

K' = a constant of unit conversion, $10^6 pCi/\mu Ci$.

31

$(BR)_a$ = the breathing rate of the receptor of age group (a), in m^3/yr.

$(DFA_i)_a$ = the maximum organ inhalation dose factor for the receptor of age group (a) for the ith radionuclide, in mrem/pCi. The total body is considered as an organ in the selection of $(DFA_i)_a$.

The breathing rates $(BR)_a$ for the various age groups are tabulated below, as given in Table E-5 of the Regulatory Guide 1.109 (Ref. 6).

Age Group (a)	Breathing Rate (m^3/yr)
Infant	1400
Child	3700
Teen	8000
Adult	8000

Inhalation dose factors $(DFA_i)_a$ for the various age groups are given in Tables E-7 through E-10 of Regulatory Guide 1.109 (Ref. 6).

5.3.1.2 Ground Plane Pathway Factor, R_i^G [D/Q]

$$R_i^G[D/Q] = K'K''(SF)DFG_i[(1-e^{-\lambda_i t})/\lambda_i] \ (m^2 \cdot mrem/yr \ per \ \mu Ci/sec)$$

where:

K' = a constant of unit conversion, 10^6 pCi/μCi.

K'' = a constant of unit conversion, 8760 hr/year.

λ_i = the decay constant for the ith radionuclide, sec^{-1}.

t = the exposure time, 4.73×10^8 sec (15 years).

DFG_i = the ground plane dose conversion factor for the ith radionuclide (mrem/hr per pCi/m^2).

SF = the shielding factor (dimensionless).

A shielding factor of 0.7 is suggested in Table E-15 of Regulatory Guide 1.109 (Ref. 6). A tabulation of DFG_i values is presented in Table E-6 of Regulatory Guide 1.109 (Ref. 6).

5.3.1.3 Grass-Cow-Milk Pathway Factor, R_i^C [D/Q]

$$R_i^C[D/Q] = K' \ \frac{Q_F(U_{ap})}{\lambda_i + \lambda_w} \ F_m(r)(DFL_i)_a \left[\frac{f_p f_s}{Y_p} + \frac{(1-f_p f_s)e^{-\lambda_i t_h}}{Y_s} \right] e^{-\lambda_i t_f}$$

$$(m^2 \cdot mrem/yr \ per \ \mu Ci/sec)$$

where:

K' = a constant of unit conversion, 10^6 pCi/µCi.

Q_F = the cow's consumption rate, in kg/day (wet weight).

U_{ap} = the receptor's milk consumption rate for age (a), in liters/yr.

Y_p = the agricultural productivity by unit area of pasture feed grass, in kg/m^2.

Y_s = the agricultural productivity by unit area of stored feed, in kg/m^2.

F_m = the stable element transfer coefficients, in days/liter.

r = fraction of deposited activity retained on cow's feed grass.

$(DFL_i)_a$ = the maximum organ ingestion dose factor for the ith radionuclide for the receptor in age group (a), in mrem/pCi.

λ_i = the decay constant for the ith radionuclide, in sec^{-1}.

λ_w = the decay constant for removal of activity on leaf and plant surfaces by weathering, 5.73×10^{-7} sec^{-1} (corresponding to a 14 day half-life).

t_f = the transport time from pasture to cow, to milk, to receptor, in sec.

t_h = the transport time from pasture, to harvest, to cow, to milk, to receptor, in sec.

f_p = fraction of the year that the cow is on pasture (dimensionless).

f_s = fraction of the cow feed that is pasture grass while the cow is on pasture (dimensionless).

SPECIAL NOTE: The above equation is applicable in the case that the milk animal is a goat.

Milk cattle are considered to be fed from two potential sources, pasture grass and stored feeds. Following the development in Regulatory Guide 1.109 (Ref. 6), the values of f_p and f_s will be considered unity, in lieu of site specific information provided in the annual land census report by the licensee.

Tabulated below are the appropriate parameter values and their reference to Regulatory Guide 1.109 (Ref. 6). In the case that the milk animal is a goat, rather than a cow, refer to Regulatory Guide 1.109 for the appropriate parameter values.

Parameter	Value	Table (Ref. 6)
r (dimensionless)	1.0 for radioiodine	E-15
	0.2 for particulates	E-15
F_m (days/liter)	Each stable element	E-1
U_{ap} (liters/yr) - Infant	330	E-5
- Child	330	E-5
- Teen	400	E-5
- Adult	310	E-5
$(DFL_i)_a$ (mrem/pCi)	Each radionuclide	E-11 to E-14
Y_p (kg/m^2)	0.7	E-15
Y_s (kg/m^2)	2.0	E-15
t_f (seconds)	1.73×10^5 (2 days)	E-15
t_h (seconds)	7.78×10^6 (90 days)	E-15
Q_F (kg/day)	50	E-3

The concentration of tritium in milk is based on the airborne concentration rather than the deposition. Therefore, the R_i^C is based on $[\chi/Q]$:

$$R_i^C[\chi/Q] = K'K'''F_mQ_FU_{ap}(DFL_i)_a [0.75(0.5/H)] \text{ (mrem/yr per } \mu Ci/m^3)$$

where:

$K''' = $ a constant of unit conversion, 10^3 gm/kg.

$H = $ absolute humidity of the atmosphere, in gm/m^3.

$0.75 = $ the fraction of total feed that is water.

$0.5 = $ the ratio of the specific activity of the feed grass water to the atmospheric water.

and other parameters and values are given above. The value of H may be considered as 8 grams/meter^3, in lieu of site specific information (Ref. 6).

5.3.1.4 Grass-Cow-Meat Pathway Factor, $R_i^M[D/Q]$

The integrated concentration in meat follows in a similar manner to the development for the milk pathway, therefore:

$$R_i^M[D/Q] = K' \frac{Q_F(U_{ap})}{\lambda_i + \lambda_w} F_f(r)(DFL_i)_a \left[\frac{f_pf_s}{Y_p} + \frac{(1-f_pf_s)e^{-\lambda_i t_h}}{Y_s} \right] e^{-\lambda_i t_f}$$

$(m^2 \cdot mrem/yr \text{ per } \mu Ci/sec)$

where:

$F_f = $ the stable element transfer coefficients, in days/kg.

$U_{ap} = $ the receptor's meat consumption rate for age (a), in kg/yr.

$t_f = $ the transport time from pasture to receptor, in sec.

$t_h = $ the transport time from crop field to receptor, in sec.

Tabulated below are the appropriate parameter values and their reference to Regulatory Guide 1.109 (Ref. 6).

Parameter	Value	Table (Ref. 6)
r (dimensionless)	1.0 for radioiodine	E-15
	0.2 for particulates	E-15
F_f (days/kg)	Each stable element	E-1
U_{ap} (kg/yr) - Infant	0	E-5
- Child	41	E-5
- Teen	65	E-5
- Adult	110	E-5
$(DFL_i)_a$ (mrem/pCi)	Each radionuclide	E-11 to E-14
Y_p (kg/m^2)	0.7	E-15

Parameter	Value	Table (Ref. 6)
Y_s (kg/m^2)	2.0	E-15
t_f (seconds)	1.73 X 10^6 (20 days)	E-15
t_h (seconds)	7.78 X 10^6 (90 days)	E-15
Q_F (kg/day)	50	E-3

The concentration of tritium in meat is based on its airborne concentration rather than the deposition. Therefore, the R_i^M is based on $[\chi/Q]$:

$$R_i^M[\chi/Q] = K'K'''F_f Q_F U_{ap}(DFL_i)_a [0.75(0.5/H)] \quad (mrem/yr \text{ per } \mu Ci/m^3)$$

where all terms are defined above and Section 5.3.1.3 of this manual.

5.3.1.5 Vegetation Pathway Factor, $R_i^V[D/Q]$

The integrated concentration in vegetation consumed by man follows the expression developed in the derivation of the milk factor. Man is considered to consume two types of vegetation (fresh and stored) that differ only in the time period between harvest and consumption, therefore:

$$R_i^V[D/Q] = K' \left[\frac{(r)}{Y_v(\lambda_i + \lambda_w)} \right] (DFL_i)_a \left[U_a^L f_L e^{-\lambda_i t_L} + U_a^S f_g e^{-\lambda_i t_h} \right]$$

$$(m^2 \cdot mrem/yr \text{ per } \mu Ci/sec)$$

where:

K' = a constant of unit conversion, 10^6 pCi/μCi.

U_a^L = the consumption rate of fresh leafy vegetation by the receptor in age group (a), in kg/yr.

U_a^S = the consumption rate of stored vegetation by the receptor in age group (a), in kg/yr.

f_L = the fraction of the annual intake of fresh leafy vegetation grown locally.

f_g = the fraction of the annual intake of stored vegetation grown locally.

t_L = the average time between harvest of leafy vegetation and its consumption, in seconds.

t_h = the average time between harvest of stored vegetation and its consumption, in seconds.

Y_v = the vegetation areal density, in kg/m^2.

and all other factors are defined in Section 5.3.1.3 of this manual.

Tabulated below are the appropriate parameter values and their reference to Regulatory Guide 1.109 (Ref. 6).

35

Parameter	Value	Table (Ref. 6)
r (dimensionless)	1.0 for radioiodines	E-1
	0.2 for particulates	E-1
$(DFL_i)_a$ (mrem/pCi)	Each radionuclide	E-11 to E-14
U_a^L (kg/yr) - Infant	0	E-5
- Child	26	E-5
- Teen	42	E-5
- Adult	64	E-5
U_a^S (kg/yr) - Infant	0	E-5
- Child	520	E-5
- Teen	630	E-5
- Adult	520	E-5
f_L (dimensionless)	site specific (default = 1.0)	
f_g (dimensionless)	site specific (default = 0.76) (see Ref. 6, page 28)	
t_L (seconds)	8.6×10^4 (1 day)	E-15
t_h (seconds)	5.18×10^6 (60 days)	E-15
Y_v (kg/m^2)	2.0	E-15

The concentration of tritium in vegetation is based on the airborne concentration rather than the deposition. Therefore, the R_i^V is based on [x/Q]:

$$R_i^V[x/Q] = K'K''' \quad U_a^L f_L + U_a^S f_g \quad (DFL_i)_a \quad [0.75(0.5/H)] \quad (\text{mrem/yr per } \mu Ci/m^3).$$

where all terms have been defined above and in Section 5.3.1.3 of this manual.

The staff has developed a computer code PARTS for calculating the R_i parameters, which is described in Appendix D of this manual.

5.4 SPECIFICATION ON THE USE OF GASEOUS RADIOACTIVE WASTE MANAGEMENT SYSTEM

Standard Technical Specification 3.11.2.4 specifies that:

"The gaseous radwaste treatment system shall be OPERABLE. The appropriate subsystems shall be used to reduce radioactive materials in gaseous waste prior to their discharge when the projected gaseous effluent releases from all release points to unrestricted areas (see Figure 5.1-1)* would result in a dose in any period of 31 days that exceeds 0.2 mrad for gamma radiation, 0.4 mrad for beta radiation, or 0.3 mrem to any organ for that same 31 day period."

The operability of the gaseous radioactive waste management system ensures that this system will be available for use whenever gaseous effluents require treatment prior to release to the environment. The term "gaseous radwaste treatment system" includes all of the installed and available gaseous radioactive waste management system equipment, as well as their controls, power, instrumentation and services that make the system functional. Equipment that is considered standby or redundant is also included, since the function is to assure operability. The action also permits alternate treatment paths using alternate subsystems and equipment to be used in the event that the normal treatment is inoperable.

---

*See footnote on page 21.

This Specification provides impetus to maintain and use the gaseous radioactive waste management system as required in 10 CFR 50.36a. Maintenance and use of the gaseous radioactive waste management system components are discussed in Section 2.2 of this manual. Since features; such as, free-standing stacks or elevated vents are not considered to be treatment systems, the NRC staff considers that BWR offgas systems must be used without bypassing normal treatment during reactor operation.

To determine if use of the installed equipment, other than in BWR offgas systems, is necessary, the licensee should calculate the expected dose to an individual in the unrestricted area by projecting the plant's cumulative gaseous effluent release over a 31-day period. These releases should include all potentially radioactive plant gaseous effluents from all gaseous radioactive waste management systems and ventilation exhaust treatment systems. Calculations should include a margin, based on operating data, for anticipated operational occurrences and should use the dose calculation models discussed in Section 5.3 of this manual. The dose impact from the projected 31-day release should be compared to 0.2 mrad for gamma radiation, 0.4 mrad for beta radiation, or 0.3 mrem to any organ. If the projection indicates these values will be exceeded, then installed radwaste treatment system components, which are capable of reducing the quantities or concentrations of radioactive materials in gaseous effluents and which are capable of reducing the projected impact to less than the values specified above, must be used. The values for the projected impact, given above, corresponds to approximately one forty-eighth of the annual design dose objective values of Appendix I, Section II.B and II.C of 10 CFR Part 50 in a month, and if continued for a year, these values would correspond to less than one-fourth the values limited by Specifications 3.11.2.2.b and 3.11.2.3.b. The calculation of projected cumulative dose impact that could result from the proposed operation may use the methodology provided in Section 5.3 of this manual.

5.5 SPECIFICATION ON EXPLOSIVE GAS MIXTURE LIMITATION

The Standard Technical Specifications for BWRs and PWRs contain Specification 3.11.2.6A and alternate Specification 3.11.2.6B for the limiting conditions for operation for systems designed to treat and store radioactive gases which also contain quantities of uncombined hydrogen and oxygen. Specification 3.11.2.6A applies to a system designed to withstand a hydrogen explosion. If all components of the system, from containment to the release point, are designed and tested to 20 times the normal operating pressure, the system is considered to be designed to withstand a hydrogen explosion. Alternate Specification 3.11.2.6B applies to a system not considered to be designed to withstand a hydrogen explosion.

The functional name, "waste gas holdup system," has been used in this manual to include the various system designs found in BWRs and PWRs which serve the same basic purpose, i.e., to remove radioactive waste gases from the reactor coolant, to treat and hold gases for radioactive decay, and to monitor and control the radioactive materials in the gaseous waste prior to final release.

The potentially explosive components of the waste gas holdup system may be effectively inerted by nitrogen or steam, treated and re-used in the plant or stored and released after delay. The treatment may involve hydrogen-oxygen recombiners, filters, holdup tanks, decay pipes, charcoal adsorbers, and cryogenic stills. The Specification is provided to ensure that the concentrations of potentially explosive gases contained in the system are maintained outside the explosive envelope for hydrogen and oxygen (i.e., less than 4% H_2 by volume or less than 4% O_2 by volume). The alternate Specification 3.11.2.6B provides an additional setpoint limitation to ensure that the automatic dilution, inerting or recombiner control is functioning to maintain the relative concentration of components of potentially explosive gas mixtures outside one-half the above flammability limits (i.e., 2% H_2 and/or O_2). Based on the design, the licensee should specify the gas to be measured: hydrogen, oxygen or both hydrogen and oxygen.

5.6 SPECIFICATIONS UNIQUE TO LWR DESIGN FEATURES

The Standard Technical Specifications contain several Specifications unique to certain design features of PWRs and BWRs; in general, these Specifications contain limiting conditions for operation. The following Sections describe these limitations and the method for determining the limiting values.

5.6.1 PWR Gas Storage Tank Specification 3.11.2.7

Specification 3.11.2.7 requires that the quantity of radioactive gas in each gas storage tank at a PWR be limited to a predetermined curie content. It is not applicable to PWRs that use adsorption units for gas holdup, but is applicable for compressed gas storage and for cryogenic storage systems. The purpose of this Specification is to assure that, in the event of an uncontrolled release of the tank contents, the resulting total body exposure to an individual at the nearest exclusion area boundary will not exceed 0.5 rem.

Determination of the curie limit should consider the following expression;

$$\sum Q_{iT} \leq \frac{500 \text{ mrem } (3.15 \times 10^7 \text{ sec/year})}{10^6 \text{ } \mu Ci/Ci \sum_i K_i (\overline{x/Q})_{DBA} \text{ (mrem} \cdot \text{sec/}\mu Ci \cdot \text{yr)}}$$

where:

- $\sum Q_{iT}$ = The sum quantity of all noble gas nuclides (i) in a gas storage tank based on a gas mixture resulting from gaseous wastes, in curies.

- K_i = The total body dose factor due to gamma emissions for each identified noble gas radionuclide, in mrem/yr per $\mu Ci/m^3$. (See Section 5.2.1 of this manual.)

- $(\overline{x/Q})_{DBA}$ = The relative concentration at the exclusion area boundary used for evaluation of design basis accidents for ground release conditions, in sec/m^3. Guidelines are provided in Standard Review Plan 2.3.4 (Ref. 23).

Normally the major radioactive nuclide constituent in PWR waste gas storage tanks is Xe-133. Radiation monitoring and sampling of these tanks should consider the Xe-133 (equivalent) concentration. Plant procedures shall not permit operation with communication between tanks.

Alternate Specification 3.11.2.7, "PWR Waste Gas Processing System," should be used for plants that use adsorption units for gas holdup prior to release. This Specification requires that the gross radioactivity in noble gases removed from the waste gas system by means of steam jet air ejectors (or other devices) and as measured prior to entering the adsorption systems at PWR plants shall be limited by a release rate alarm setpoint with indication in the main control room. The purpose of this pretreatment continuous radiation monitor setpoint is to provide reasonable assurance that the potential accident total body dose to an individual at the exclusion area boundary will not exceed a small fraction of the limits specified in 10 CFR Part 100 in the event this effluent is inadvertently discharged directly to the environment without treatment. Guidelines for determining the release rate limit are provided in Standard Review Plan 15.7.1 (Ref. 24), and guidance on the radiation monitoring instrumentation is given in Regulatory Guide 1.97 (Ref. 25).

5.6.2 BWR Main Condenser Evacuation System Specification 3.11.2.7

This Specification requires that the gross radioactivity in noble gases removed from the main condenser by means of steam jet air ejectors (or other devices) and as measured prior to entering the treatment, adsorption and delay systems at BWR plants shall be limited by a release rate alarm setpoint with indication in the main control room. The purpose of this pretreatment continuous radiation monitor setpoint is to provide reasonable assurance that the potential total body accident dose to an individual at the exclusion area boundary will not exceed a small fraction of the limits specified in 10 CFR Part 100 in the event this effluent including the radioactivity accumulated in the treatment system is inadvertently discharged directly to the environment without treatment.

The method for determining the specified rate limit, in µCi/sec, should use the following assumptions:

1. The release of radioactive material from the fuel is postulated to have an isotopic composition of noble gases determined from noble gas source term distribution for a 3500 MWt reactor. These values should be scaled linearly for reactors of higher and lower powers.

2. The assumptions related to the release of radioactive material from the system following the accident are:

    a. For systems which are not fully detonation-resistant or for those systems which are equipped with rupture discs that have not been isolated or loop seals which do not vent back to the main condenser, release occurs from a break just downstream of the main condenser evacuation system. Release from the main condenser evacuation system is assumed to be at ground level and a delay of five minutes is assumed to account for radioactive decay during transit from the release point to the exclusion area boundary.

39

NOBLE GAS SOURCE TERM

Isotope	Approx. Half-Life	Source Term, μCi/sec, at the main condenser evacuation system (SJAE) O Decay
Xe-140	13.7 s	1.1×10^6
Kr-90	33 s	9.8×10^5
Xe-139	41.0 s	9.8×10^5
Kr-89	3.2 m	4.6×10^5
Xe-137	3.8 m	5.3×10^5
Xe-138	14.0 m	3.1×10^5
Xe-135m	15.6 m	9.1×10^4
Kr-87	76 m	7.0×10^4
Kr-83m	1.86 hr	1.2×10^4
Kr-88	2.8 hr	7.0×10^4
Kr-85m	4.4 hr	1.1×10^4
Xe-135	9.2 hr	7.7×10^4
Xe-133m	2.3 d	1.0×10^3
Xe-133	5.27 d	2.9×10^4
Xe-131m	11.9 d	5.2×10^1
Kr-85	10.76 y	7.0×10^1
	Total	$\sim\!4.7 \times 10^6$

b.   For systems which are detonation-resistant (i.e., rupture discs have been isolated and loop seals are vented back to the main condenser), release from the main condenser evacuation system exits via the normal release point.

c.   Activity release into the system continues for one hour following the accident at the Technical Specification limit unless positive means (such as automatic isolation) are provided to limit the releases from this source.

d.   Radioiodines and activation gases may be ignored.

e.   No deposition during downwind transport occurs.

f.   The total radioactive inventory (neglecting radioiodines and activation gases) in any delay lines and from the process equipment is released within a two-hour period with no decay.

g.   The total noble gas content of all charcoal delay beds is released over a period of two hours. A fractional release of the particulate inventory on the charcoal beds should be assumed. The rate of release is equal to the rate of absorption using the information contained in NUREG-0016 (Ref. 12).

h.   The main condenser air inleakage is 6 scfm for three shell main condensers.

3. The relative concentration, $(\overline{\chi/Q})_{DBA}$, to be used is described in Section 5.6.1 of this manual.

Based on these assumptions, the applicant should backcalculate from a whole body dose of 2.5 rem to an individual at the exclusion area boundary to obtain the main condenser evacuation system rate limit, in µCi/sec, having a noble gas isotopic distribution proportional to the noble gas source term, given above. For licensed BWR facilities that have a Technical Specification limit, in µCi/sec, based on a 5 rem consequence criteria, a reevaluation of the specified limit is not required. Guidance on the radiation monitoring instrumentation is given in Regulatory Guide 1.97 (Ref. 25).

5.6.3 PWR Monitoring of Steam Generator Blowdown Flask Tank Vent

Standard Technical Specification 3.3.3.9, including Tables 3.3-12* and 4.3-12,* requires that PWRs continuously monitor the steam generator blowdown tank vent for gross noble gas radioactivity and continuously sample for radioactive iodines and particulates. Many PWRs with U-tube steam generators direct their blowdown to a blowdown treatment system without venting, so that item f in Tables 3.3-12 and 4.3-12 is not applicable. Others vent their flash tank to the main condenser, where the airborne radionuclides are either removed by condensing steam or drawn into the main condenser evacuation system, where they are then monitored prior to release to the atmosphere; therefore, this design provision makes item f not applicable. However, there are several operating PWR's that direct their blowdown to a flash tank which is vented directly to the atmosphere. Monitoring these releases presents serious difficulties, due to the presence of steam in the exhaust. In lieu of a flash tank vent radiation monitor, a determination of the release of radioiodine-131 via the flash tank vent can be made by calculating from a measured concentration in the secondary water by the following equation:

$$\dot{Q}_y = \overline{C}_y [R_{SGB}] f_{FT} (1 - SQ_{FTv})$$

where:

$\dot{Q}_y$ = The release rate of radioiodine-131, y, from the steam generator flash tank vent, in µCi/sec.

$\overline{C}_y$ = The concentration of radioiodine-131, y, in the secondary coolant water averaged over not more than one week, in µCi/ml.

R_{SGB} = The steam generator blowdown rate to the flash tank, in ml/sec.

f_{FT} = The fraction of blowdown flashed in the falsh tank determined from a heat balance taken around the flash tank at the applicable reactor power level.

SQ_{FTv} = The measured steam quality in the flash tank vent; or an assumed value of 0.85, based on NUREG-0017 (Ref. 11).

If this option is chosen, the applicant shall perform this calcuation every time measurements of secondary water radioiodine concentrations are required by Technical Specifications, and the calculated release shall be assumed at this calculated level until the next secondary water analysis is completed. These calculations shall be provided by the applicant in his semiannual effluent release report.

*See footnote on page 20.

REFERENCES

1. Title 10, "Energy," Chapter I, Code of Federal Regulations; Part 50, pages 250 to 327, U.S. Government Printing Office, Washington, D.C. 20402, January 1, 1977.

2. U.S. Nuclear Regulatory Commission, "Draft Radiological Effluent Technical Specifications for PWR's," USNRC NUREG-0472, Revision 1, Washington, D.C. 20555, October 1978.

3. U.S. Nuclear Regulatory Commission, "Draft Radiological Effluent Technical Specifications for PWR's," USNRC NUREG-0473, Revision 1, Washington, D.C. 20555, October 1978.

4. Regulatory Guide 1.16, "Reporting of Operating Information - Appendix A Technical Specifications," Revision 4, U.S. Nuclear Regulatory Commission, Washington, D.C. 20555, August 1975.

5. Regulatory Guide 10.1, "Compilation of Reporting Requirements for Persons Subject to NRC Regulations," Revision 3, U.S. Nuclear Regulatory Commission, Washington, D.C. 20555, May 1977.

6. Regulatory Guide 1.109, "Calculation of Annual Doses to Man from Routine Releases of Reactor Effluents for the Purpose of Evaluating Compliance with 10 CFR Part 50, Appendix I," Revision 1, U.S. Nuclear Regulatory Commission, Washington, D.C. 20555, October 1977.

7. Regulatory Guide 1.110, "Cost-Benefit Analysis for Radwaste Systems for Light-Water-Cooled Nuclear Power Reactors," U.S. Nuclear Regulatory Commission, Washington, D.C. 20555, March 1976.

8. Regulatory Guide 1.111, "Methods for Estimating Atmospheric Transport and Dispersion of Gaseous Effluents in Routine Releases from Light-Water-Cooled Reactors," Revision 1, U.S. Nuclear Regulatory Commission, Washington, D.C. 20555, July 1977.

9. Regulatory Guide 1.112, "Calculation of Releases of Radioactive Materials in Gaseous and Liquid Effluents from Light-Water-Cooled Power Reactors," U.S. Nuclear Regulatory Commission, Washington, D.C. 20555, April 1976.

10. Regulatory Guide 1.113, "Estimating Aquatic Dispersion of Effluents from Accidental and Routine Reactor Releases for the Purpose of Implementing Appendix I," Revision 1, U.S. Nuclear Regulatory Commission, Washington, D.C. 20555, April 1977.

11. U.S. Nuclear Regulatory Commission, "Calculation of Releases of Radioactive Materials in Gaseous and Liquid Effluents from Pressurized Water Reactors (PWR-GALE Code)," USNRC Report NUREG-0017, Washington, D.C. 20555, April 1976.

12. U.S. Nuclear Regulatory Commission, "Calculation of Releases of Radioactive Materials in Gaseous and Liquid Effluents from Boiling Water Reactors (BWR-GALE Code)," USNRC Report NUREG-0016, Washington, D.C. 20555, April 1976.

13. U.S. Nuclear Regulatory Commission, "XOQDOQ, Program for the Meteorological Evaluation of Routine Effluent Releases at Nuclear Power Stations," USNRC Report NUREG-0324, Washington, D.C. 20555, September 1977.

14. Title 10, "Energy," Chaper I, Code of Federal Regulations; Part 20, pages 144 to 172, U.S. Government Printing Office, Washington, D.C. 20402, January 1, 1977.

15. Title 10, "Energy," Chapter I, Code of Federal Regulations; Part 100, pages 409 to 421, U.S. Government Printing Office, Washington, D.C. 20402, January 1, 1977.

16. Title 40, "Protection of Environment," Chapter I, Code of Federal Regulations, Part 141, pages 169 to 182, U.S. Government Printing Office, Washington, D.C. 20402, January 1, 1977.

17. Regulatory Guide 1.21, "Measuring, Evaluating, and Reporting Radioactivity in Solid Wastes and Releases of Radioactive Materials in Liquid and Gaseous Effluents from Light-Water-Cooled Nuclear Power Plants," Revision 1, U.S. Nuclear Regulatory Commission, Washington, D.C. 20555, June 1974.

18. Title 40, "Protection of Environment," Chapter I, Code of Federal Regulations, Part 190, Federal Register, Vol. 42, No. 9, pages 2858 to 2861, Washington, D.C. 20402, January 13, 1977.

19. "SKYSHINE, A Computer Program for Evaluating Effects of Structure Design on N-16 Gamma-Ray Dose Rates," Radiation Research Associates, Inc., Report RRA-T7209, Fort Worth, Texas, 76107, November 1972.

20. Regulatory Guide 4.15, "Quality Assurance for Radiological Monitoring Programs (Normal Operation) - Effluent Streams and the Environment," U.S. Nuclear Regulatory Commission, Washington, D.C. 20555, December 1977.

21. Regulatory Guide 1.70, "Standard Format and Content of Safety Analysis Reports for Nuclear Power Plants, LWR Edition," Revision 2, USNRC Report NUREG-75/094, Washington, D.C. 20555, September 1975.

22. International Commission on Radiological Protection, Report of ICRP Committee II on Permissible Dose for Internal Radiation, ICRP Publication 2, Pergamon Press, New York 10022, 1959.

23. U.S. Nuclear Regulatory Commission, "Short Term Diffusion Estimates," Section 2.3.4, Standard Review Plan for the Review of Safety Analysis Reports for Nuclear Power Plants - LWR Edition, USNRC Report NUREG-75/087, Washington, D.C. 20555, November 1975.

24. U.S. Nuclear Regulatory Commission, "Waste Gas System Failure," Section 15.7.1 (Draft Revision) Standard Review Plan for the Review of Safety Analysis Reports for Nuclear Power Plants - LWR Edition, USNRC Report NUREG-75/087, Washington, D.C. 20555, 1978.

25. Regulatory Guide 1.97, "Instrumentation for Light-Water-Cooled Nuclear Power Plants to Assess Plant Conditions During and Following an Accident," Revision 1, U.S. Nuclear Regulatory Commission, Washington, D.C. 20555, August 1977.

APPENDIX A

RATAFR CODE FOR PRESSURIZED WATER REACTORS
Input Cards and Sample Calculation

1. ## Parameters Required for the PWR-RATAFR Code
   Complete the cards from information given in the Applicant's Safety Analysis and
   Environmental Reports and in Section 2 of this Appendix.

   a. ### CARD 1: Name of Reactor
      Enter in spaces (33-60) the name of the reactor.

   b. ### CARD 2: Thermal Power Level
      Enter in spaces (73-80) the maximum thermal power level (MWt) evaluated for safety
      considerations in the Safety Analysis Report.

   c. ### CARD 3: Mass of Coolant in Primary System
      Enter in spaces (73-80) the mass of coolant (10^3 lbs) in the primary system at
      operating temperature and pressure.

   d. ### CARD 4: Primary System Letdown Rate
      Enter in spaces (73-80) the average letdown rate (gpm) from the primary system to
      the purification demineralizers.

   e. ### CARD 5: Letdown Cation Demineralizer Flow Rate
      Enter in spaces (73-80) the annual average flow rate (gpm) through the cation
      demineralizers for the control of cesium in the primary coolant. The average flow
      rate is determined by multiplying the average letdown rate (value entered on Card 4)
      by the fraction of time cation demineralizers are in service to obtain the average
      cation demineralizer flow rate.

   f. ### CARD 6: Hydrological Travel Time
      Enter in spaces (73-80) the travel time (days) it takes for the liquid waste of a
      failed tank to reach the nearest potable water supply or nearest surface water in
      an unrestricted area.

   g. ### CARD 7: Hydrological Dilution Factor
      Enter in spaces (73-80) the dimensionless value of:
      The annual volume of water flowing past the potable water supply divided by the
      total volume of liquid waste in the failed tank (80% of design capacity).

   h. ### CARDS 8-16: Liquid Tank Parameters
      Tanks in two separate processing systems are considered in the PWR-RATAFR Code:
      (1) Shim Bleed Processing System, Cards 8-12;
      (2) Waste Drain Processing System, Cards 13-16.

In each of the processing systems considered, the Code can calculate the tank concentrations in either the collector tank or the evaporator bottoms tank. However, separate computer runs must be made for these two tank classifications. If it is desired, the Code can calculate concentrations in one tank of each of the processing systems in one computer run by making the appropriate entries in CARDS 8-16. If a tank in only one of the processing systems is to be considered, then the appropriate entries need only be made in CARDS 8-12 or 13-16, depending on which system contains the tank of interest.

Five input data cards define the major parameters for the failed tank in the shim bleed processing system. The first two cards (CARDS 8 and 9) describe the inputs to the tank. The shim bleed wastes are entered on CARD 8. For reactor designs which combine the shim bleed with other reactor grade wastes prior to processing, the other wastes are entered as equipment drain wastes on CARD 9.

Four input data cards define the major parameters for the failed tank in the waste drain processing system. The first card (CARD 13) describes the inputs to the tank. Essentially the same information is required on CARDS 8, 9 and 13, on CARDS 10 and 14, on CARDS 11 and 15, and on CARDS 12 and 16.

The following information explains the use of the parameters in this Appendix and information given in the SAR/ER to complete the input data cards.

For CARD 8, enter in spaces (42-49) the flow rate (gpd) of the inlet stream. The value of the shim bleed rate must always be entered, even if the tank being evaluated is not in this system, since it is used in determining the primary coolant concentrations. Do not enter inlet waste activity for the shim bleed since the activity for this waste stream is calculated by the Code.

The following information is required on CARDS 9 and 13 for both of the processing systems considered in the Code.

(1) Enter in spaces (17-40) the name of the waste stream (e.g., clean wastes).
(2) Enter in spaces (42-49) the flow rate (gpd) of the inlet stream.
(3) Enter in spaces (57-61) the activity of the inlet stream expressed as a fraction of primary coolant activity (PCA).

For CARDS 10 and 14, the following information is required:

(1) Enter in spaces (27-50) the name of the tank to be failed (e.g., shim bleed collector).

(2) Enter in spaces (65-73) the volume (gallons) of the tank to be failed. If a tank in either of the two processing streams is not being considered, leave spaces (65-73) blank for that tank.

For CARDS 11 and 15, enter a 1 in space (80) if the tank to be failed is an evaporator bottoms tank. Otherwise leave space (80) blank.

CARDS 12 and 16 for both waste streams contain the overall system "tank" factors. The "tank" factors indicate the type of processing the waste has undergone prior to its entry into the tank. The tank factors should be entered as follows:

(1) For a collector tank in either waste stream, without demineralizers upstream of the tank, values of TF=1.0 should be entered in the appropriate spaces.

(2) For a collector tank in either waste stream with demineralizers upstream of the tank, or for an evaporator bottoms tank in either waste stream, TF's based on the description given in Section 2.a(3) should be entered in the appropriate spaces.

The appropriate spaces for the TFs are:

(1) Enter in spaces (21-28) the TF for iodine.
(2) Enter in spaces (34-41) the TF for cesium and rubidium.
(3) Enter in spaces (47-54) the TF for other nuclides.

The following section explains the use of the parameters in this note and information given in the SAR/ER to complete data input CARDS 8-16.

2. Explanation of Parameters used in Filling out CARDS 8-16
  a. Liquid Waste Flow Rates and Activities

  (1) Shim Bleed Wastes and Equipment Drain Wastes
  The flow rates of the shim bleed waste stream and equipment drain wastes processed with the shim bleed and the activity of the equipment drain wastes are based on information given in the SAR/ER. The activity of the shim bleed wastes is based on the primary coolant letdown system effluent activity and is calculated in the Code.

  The activity of the combined inlet stream is calculated by the Code based on the weighted average of the composite stream entering the tanks.

  (2) Waste Drain Tank Wastes
  Flow rates and activities are calculated using the waste volumes and activities given in NUREG-0017, Table 1-2, "PWR Liquid Wastes" (Ref. 11).

  These input flow rates are supplemented by the use of expected flows and activities more specific to the plant design as given in the SAR/ER. The individual streams are combined based on the radwaste treatment system described in the SAR/ER. Input activities are based on the weighted average activity of the composite stream entering the waste collection tanks. The input flow rates and activities are entered in units of gpd and fractions of PCA.

(3) Tank Factors

The tank factors indicate the type of processing the waste has undergone prior to its entry into the tank. The tank factors provide the capability to consider radionuclide removal by demineralizers or other treatment equipment prior to the tank. For evaporator bottoms tanks, the tank factors provide the capability to consider the effects of radionuclide concentration in the evaporator. Therefore, in determining the radionuclide concentration in the tank, the type of processing upstream of the tank must be considered and entered as tank factors on CARDS 12 and 16.

The following factors are considered in calculating overall tank factors for the systems.

(a) TFs are categorized by radionuclides.
Halogens
Cs, Rb
Other Nuclides
Note: TF of 1 is assumed for tritium.

(b) The system TF is the product of the individual equipment TF in each of the systems, e.g., the effect of the demineralizer removal, if any, is multiplied by the effect of the evaporator concentration, if any.

(c) Tank Factors for Demineralizers
The tank factors for demineralizers are entered in the same manner as decontamination factors (DFs) are entered in the PWR-GALE Code. Therefore, the values used for TFs for demineralizers are the same as those given in NUREG-0017, Table 1-3, "Decontamination Factors for PWR Liquid Waste Treatment Systems" (Ref. 11).

(d) Tank Failures for Evaporators
The tank factors for evaporators express the increase in concentration of radionuclides in the evaporator bottoms resulting from evaporator operation. The values entered on the CARDs are the ratio of the evaporator bottom stream flow to the evaporator inlet stream flow. Therefore, the TFs for evaporators are as follows:

Evaporator	All Nuclides
Waste Drain Stream	0.02
Shim Bleed Stream	0.02

U.S. NUCLEAR REGULATORY COMMISSION

ADP TRANSCRIPTION SHEET

INPUT DATA PWR-RATAFR CODE

Card	Code	Description
CARD 1	REACTR	NAME OF REACTOR [ ] TYPE=[ ] PWR
CARD 2	POW1	THERMAL POWER LEVEL (MEGAWATTS) [ ]
CARD 3	PCVOL	MASS OF PRIMARY COOLANT (THOUSAND LBS) [ ]
CARD 4	LETDWN	PRIMARY SYSTEM LETDOWN RATE (GPM) [ ]
CARD 5	CBFLR	LETDOWN DEMINERALIZER FLOW (GPM) [ ]
CARD 6	HYTRTM	HYDROLOGICAL TRAVEL TIME (DAYS) [ ]
CARD 7	HYDF	HYDROLOGICAL DILUTION FACTOR [ ]
CARD 8	SBLDR	SHIMBLEED RATE [ ]GPD [ ]GPD AT [ ]PCA
CARD 9	EDFLR	EQUIPMENT DRAINS INPUT [ ]GPD AT [ ]
CARD 10	SBTANK	TANK NAME [ ] IN SYSTEM A BOTTOMS TANK [ ] TANK VOLUME [ ]GAL
CARD 11	KEVBTS	IS TANK IN SYSTEM A BOTTOMS TANK? 0 IF NO, 1 IF YES IN (8.0) TFI=[ ] TFO=[ ]
CARD 12		TFI=[ ] TFO=[ ]
CARD 13	DWFLR	CLEAN WASTE INPUT [ ]GPD
CARD 14	DWTANK	TANK NAME [ ] IN SYSTEM A BOTTOMS TANK [ ] TANK VOLUME [ ]GAL
CARD 15	KEVBTD	IS TANK IN SYSTEM A BOTTOMS TANK? 0 IF NO, 1 IF YES IN (8.0) TFI=[ ] TFO=[ ]
CARD 16		TFI=[ ] TFO=[ ]
CARD 17		
CARD 18		
CARD 19		
CARD 20		
CARD 21		
CARD 22		
CARD 23		

```
                                        NAME OF REACTOR    SAMPLE CASE PWR  4/78          TYPE = PWR
CARD  1     NAME    NAME OF REACTOR    SAMPLE CASE PWR  4/78                              3391.
CARD  2     POWTH   THERMAL POWER LEVEL (MEGAWATTS)                                        561.
CARD  3     PCVOL   MASS OF PRIMARY COOLANT (THOUSANDS LBS)                                75.
CARD  4     LETDWN  PRIMARY SYSTEM LETDOWN RATE (GPM)                                      7.5
CARD  5     CBFLR   LETDOWN CATION DEMINERALIZER FLOW (GPM)                                1.
CARD  6     HYTRTM  HYDROLOGICAL TRAVEL TIME (DAYS)                                        1000.
CARD  7     HYDF    HYDROLOGICAL DILUTION FACTOR
CARD  8     SHIMBLEEC RATE              16200.        GPD
CARD  9     EQUIPMENT DRAINS INPUT        810.        GPD AT 1.0
CARD 10     TANK NAME CONDENSATE HOLDUP                TANK VOLUME 250000.
CARD 11     IS TANK IN SYSTEM A BOTTOMS TANK 0 IF NO  1 IF YES
CARD 12     DFI=  1.0E03DFCS=  1.0E05DFO=  1.0E05
CARD 13     DIRTY WASTES        INPUT    1375.        GPD AT .075 PCA
CARD 14     TANK NAME WASTE HOLDUP                     TANK VOLUME 250000.
CARD 15     IS TANK IN SYSTEM A BOTTOMS TANK 0. IF NO  1 IF YES
CARD 16     DFI=  1.0E03DFCS=  1.0E04DFO=  1.0E04
```

A-6

```
                    SAMPLE CASE PWR   4/78

                                               PWR
THERMAL POWER LEVEL (MEGAWATTS)             3391.0000
PLANT CAPACITY FACTOR                          0.80
MASS OF PRIMARY COOLANT (THOUSANDS LBS)      561.0000
PERCENT FUEL WITH CLADDING DEFECTS             1.0000
PRIMARY SYSTEM LETDOWN RATE (GPM)             75.0000
LETDOWN CATION DEMINERALIZER FLOW (GPM)        7.5000
HYDROLOGICAL TRAVEL TIME (DAYS)                1.00
HYDROLOGICAL DILUTION FACTOR                1000.
SHIMBLEED RATE           GPD                1.62E+04
EQUIPMENT DRAINS INPUT   GPD                8.10E+02
DIRTY WASTES    INPUT    GPD                1.38E+03

FAILED TANK PARAMETERS

                                                   TANK FACTORS
                        VOLUME      I          CS        OTHERS
FAILED TANK
CONDENSATE HOLDUP       250000.  1.00E+03  1.00E+05  1.00E+05
WASTE HOLDUP            250000.  1.00E+03  1.00E+04  1.00E+04
```

A-7

SAMPLE CASE PWR 4/78   LIQUID TANK FAILURE
NAME OF TANK FAILED: CONDENSATE HOLDUP
VOLUME OF TANK FAILED: 200000. GAL. (80% OF TANK CAPACITY)
HYDROLOGICAL TRAVEL TIME (DAYS):   1.00
HYDROLOGICAL DILUTION FACTOR: 1000.

NUCLIDE	HALF-LIFE (DAYS)	PRIMARY COOLANT CONC. (UCI/ML)	10CFR20 LIMITS (UCI/ML)	FAILED TANK CONC. (UCI/ML)	CRITICAL RECEPTOR CONC. (UCI/ML)	FRACTION 10CFR20
CORROSION AND ACTIVATION PRODUCTS						
H 3	4.49E+03	1.00E+00	3.00E-03	1.00E+00	1.00E-03	0.3300
FISSION PRODUCTS						
I131	8.05E+00	2.18E+00	3.00E-07	2.00E-04	1.80E-07	0.6000
I133	8.75E-01	3.08E+00	1.00E-06	4.70E-05	2.10E-08	0.0210
ALL OTHERS		6.38E+00		2.40E-05	3.10E-09	0.0003
TOTAL EXCEPT TRITIUM		1.16E+01		2.70E-04	2.00E-07	0.6200

THE MAXIMUM QUANTITY OF TRITIUM IN THE TANK IS 2.3E+03 CURIES.

THE MAXIMUM QUANTITY OF CORROSION AND FISSION PRODUCTS (EXCLUDING TRITIUM) IN THE TANK IS 3.3E-01 CURIES.

SAMPLE CASE PWR 4/78   LIQUID TANK FAILURE
NAME OF TANK FAILED: WASTE HOLDUP
VOLUME OF TANK FAILED: 200000. GAL. (80% OF TANK CAPACITY)
HYDROLOGICAL TRAVEL TIME (DAYS):   1000.
HYDROLOGICAL DILUTION FACTOR: 1.00

NUCLIDE	HALF-LIFE (DAYS)	PRIMARY COOLANT CONC. (UCI/ML)	10CFR20 LIMITS (UCI/ML)	FAILED TANK CONC. (UCI/ML)	CRITICAL RECEPTOR CONC. (UCI/ML)	FRACTION 10CFR20
CORROSION AND ACTIVATION PRODUCTS						
H 3	4.49E+03	1.00E+00	3.00E-03	7.40E-02	7.40E-05	0.0250
FISSION PRODUCTS						
I131	8.05E+00	2.18E+00	3.00E-07	1.30E-05	1.20E-08	0.0400
ALL OTHERS		9.46E+00		6.70E-06	3.60E-09	0.0011
TOTAL EXCEPT TRITIUM		1.16E+01		2.00E-05	1.60E-08	0.0410

THE MAXIMUM QUANTITY OF TRITIUM IN THE TANK IS 2.3E+03 CURIES.

THE MAXIMUM QUANTITY OF CORROSION AND FISSION PRODUCTS (EXCLUDING TRITIUM) IN THE TANK IS 3.6E-01 CURIES.

APPENDIX B

RATAFR CODE FOR BOILING WATER REACTORS
Input Cards and Sample Calculation

1. ## Parameters Required for the BWR-RATAFR Code

   Complete the cards from information given in the Applicant's Safety Analysis and Environmental Reports and in Section 2 of this Appendix.

   a. ### CARD 1: Name or Reactor (SAR/ER)
      Enter in spaces (33-60) the name of the reactor.

   b. ### CARD 2: Thermal Power Level (SAR/ER)
      Enter in spaces (73-80) the maximum thermal power level (MWt) evaluated for safety considerations in the Safety Analysis Report.

   c. ### CARD 3: Total Steam Flow Rate (SAR/ER)
      Enter in spaces (73-80) the total steam flow rate from the reactor (10^6 lbs/hr).

   d. ### CARD 4: Mass of Coolant in Reactor Vessel (SAR/ER)
      Enter in spaces (73-80) the mass of water in the reactor vessel (10^6 lbs).

   e. ### CARD 5: Cleanup Demineralizer Flow (SAR/ER)
      Enter in spaces (73-80) the primary coolant flow rate (10^6 lbs/hr) through the reactor coolant cleanup system demineralizers.

   f. ### CARD 6: Condensate Demineralizer Regeneration Time
      For deep bed condensate demineralizers, use 3.5 day regeneration frequency per demineralizer. If ultrasonic resin cleaning is used, assume 7-day regeneration frequency per demineralizer. Multiply the frequency by the number of demineralizers, and enter the calculated number of days in spaces (73-80). For filter/demineralizers (Powdex), enter zero in spaces (73-80).

   g. ### CARD 7: Fraction of Feed Water Through Condensate Demineralizer (SAR/ER)
      Enter in spaces (73-80) the fraction of feedwater processed through the condensate demineralizers.

   h. ### CARD 8: Hydrological Travel Time
      Enter in spaces (73-80) the travel time (days) it takes for the liquid waste of a failed tank to reach the nearest potable water supply or nearest surface water in an unrestricted area.

   i. ### CARD 9: Hydrological Dilution Factor
      Enter in spaces (73-80) the dimensionless value of:
      The annual volume of water flowing past the potable water supply divided by the **total** volume of liquid waste in the failed tank (80% of design capacity).

j. **CARD 10-17: Liquid Tank Parameters**

Tanks in two separate processing systems are considered in the BWR-RATAFR Code:

(1) Waste Drain Processing System, CARDS 10-13.
(2) Regenerant Solutions Processing System, CARDS 14-17.

In each of the processing systems considered, the Code can calculate the tank concentrations in either the collector tank or the evaporator bottoms tank. However, separate computer runs must be made for these two tank classifications. If it is desired, the Code can calculate concentrations in one tank of each of the processing systems in one computer run by making the appropriate entries in CARDS 10-17. If a tank in only one of the processing systems is to be considered, then the appropriate entries need only be made in CARDS 10-13 or 14-17 depending on which system the tank of interest is in.

Four input data cards are used to define the major parameters for the failed tank in each of the processing systems. Essentially, the same information is required on the four input data cards used for each of the processing systems. The instructions given in this section are applicable to both processing streams, with the following exception. The inlet waste activity is not entered on CARD 14 for the regenerant solutions wastes for systems using regenerable condensate demineralizers, since the activity is calculated by the Code.

The following information explains the use of the parameters in this Appendix and information given in the SAR/ER to complete the input data cards.

The following information is required on CARDS 10 and 14 for both of the streams considered in the Code.

(1) Enter in spaces (18-40) the name of the waste stream (e.g., high-purity wastes).
(2) Enter in spaces (42-49) the flow rate (gpd) of the inlet stream.
(3) Enter in spaces (57-61) the activity of the inlet stream, expressed as a fraction of the primary coolant activity (PCA).

On CARD 14, do not enter the activity of the regenerant solutions waste inlet stream in spaces (57-61).

For CARDS 11 and 15, the following information is required:

(1) Enter in spaces (27-50) the name of the tank to be failed (e.g., High Purity Collector).

(2) Enter in spaces (65-73) the volume (gallons) of the tank to be failed. If a tank in either of the two processing streams is not being considered, leave spaces (65-73) blank for that tank.

For CARDS 12 and 16, enter a 1 in space (80) if the tank to be failed is an evaporator bottoms tank. Otherwise leave space (80) blank.

CARDS 13 and 17 for both waste streams contain the overall system "tank" factors. The "tank" factors indicate the type of processing the waste has undergone prior to its entry into the tank. The tank factors should be entered as follows:

(1) For a collector tank in either waste stream, without demineralizers upstream of the tank, values of TF = 1.0 should be entered in the appropriate spaces.

(2) For a collector tank in either waste stream with demineralizers upstream of the tank, or for an evaporator bottoms tank in either waste stream, TFs based on the description given in Section 2.b should be entered in the appropriate spaces.

The appropriate spaces for the TFs are:

(1) Enter in spaces (21-28) the TF for iodine.
(2) Enter in spaces (34-41) the TF for cesium and rubidium.
(3) Enter in spaces (47-54) the TF for other nuclides.

The following section explains the use of the parameters in this note and information given in the SAR/ER to complete data input CARDS 10-17.

2. Explanation of Parameters used in Filling out Cards 10-17

a. Liquid Waste Flow Rates and Activities
Flow rates and activities are calculated using the waste volumes and activities given in NUREG-0016, Table 1-2, "BWR Liquid Wastes" (Ref. 12).

These input flows are supplemented by the use of expected flows and activities more specific to the plant design as given in the SAR/ER. The inlet streams are combined to form the principal waste streams (drain wastes and regenerant wastes) considered in this guide, based on the radwaste treatment system described in the SAR/ER.

Input activities are based on the weighted average activity of the composite stream entering the waste collection tanks.

b. Tank Factors
The tank factors indicate the type of processing the waste stream has undergone prior to its entry into the tank. The tank factors provide the capability to consider radionuclide removal by demineralizers prior to the waste stream input into the tank. For evaporator bottoms tanks, the tank factors provide the capability to consider the effects of radionuclide concentration in the evaporator. Therefore, in determining

the radionuclide concentration in a tank, the type of processing upstream of the tank must be considered and entered as tank factors on CARDS 13 and 17.

The following factors are considered in calculating overall tank factors for the systems:

(1) TFs are categorized by radionuclides.
    Halogens
    Cs, Rb
    Other Nuclides
    Note: TF of 1 is assumed for tritium.

(2) The system TF is the product of the individual equipment TF in each of the systems, e.g., the effect of the demineralizer removal, if any, is multiplied by the effect of the evaporator concentration, if any.

(3) Tank Factors for Demineralizers
    The tank factors for demineralizers are entered in the same manner as decontamination factors (DFs) are entered in the BWR-GALE Code. Therefore, the values used for TFs for demineralizers are the same as those given in NUREG-0016, Table 1-3, "Decontamination Factors for BWR Liquid Waste Treatment Systems" (Ref. 11).

(4) Tank Factors for Evaporators
    The tank factors for evaporators express the increase in concentration of radionuclides in the evaporator bottoms resulting from evaporator operation. The values entered on the cards are the ratio of the evaporator bottoms stream flow to the evaporator inlet stream flow. Therefore, the TFs for evaporators are entered as follows:

Evaporator	All Nuclides
Waste Drain Stream	0.01
Regenerant Waste Stream	0.05

NRC FORM 53A
(12-75)

U.S. NUCLEAR REGULATORY COMMISSION
ADP TRANSCRIPTION SHEET

INPUT DATA BWR-RATAFR CODE

Card	Label	Description
CARD 1	REACTR	NAME OF REACTOR [ ]
CARD 2	POW1	THERMAL POWER LEVEL (MEGAWATTS) [ ]
CARD 3	STMFR	TOTAL STEAM FLOW (MILLION LBS/HR) [ ]
CARD 4	PCVOL	MASS OF WATER IN REACTOR VESSEL (MILLION LBS) [ ]
CARD 5	LETDWN	CLEAN-UP DEMINERALIZER FLOW (MILLION LBS/HR) [ ]
CARD 6	REGENT	CONDENSATE DEMINERALIZER REGENERATION TIME (DAYS) [ ]
CARD 7	FFCDM	FRACTION FEEDWATER THROUGH CONDENSATE DEMIN [ ]
CARD 8	HYTRTM	HYDROLOGICAL TRAVEL TIME (DAYS) [ ]
CARD 9	HYDF	HYDROLOGICAL DILUTION FACTOR [ ]
CARD 10	CWFLR	HIGH PURITY WASTE INPUT [ ] GPD AT [ ] PCA [ ]
CARD 11	CWTANK	TANK NAME [ ] TANK VOLUME [ ] GAL
CARD 12	KEVBTC	IS TANK IN SYSTEM A BOTTOMS TANK? 0 IF NO, 1 IF YES [ ]
CARD 13	TFI= [ ]	TFCS= [ ] TFI=[ ]
CARD 14	RGWFR	REGENERANT WASTE INPUT [ ] GPD
CARD 15	RGTANK	TANK NAME [ ] TANK VOLUME [ ] GAL
CARD 16	KEVBTR	IS TANK IN SYSTEM A BOTTOMS TANK? 0 IF NO, 1 IF YES [ ]
CARD 17	DFI= [ ]	DFCS= [ ] DFI=[ ]

TYPE = [ ]

BWR

			4/78	TYPE = BWR
CARD 1	NAME	NAME OF REACTOR SAMPLE CASE BWR		
CARD 2	POWTH	THERMAL POWER LEVEL (MEGAWATTS)		3440.
CARD 3	GTO	TOTAL STEAM FLOW (MILLION LBS/HR)		14.166
CARD 4	WLIQ	MASS OF WATER IN REACTOR VESSEL (MILLION LBS)		0.588
CARD 5	GDE	CLEAN-UP DEMINERALIZER FLOW (MILLION LBS/HR)		0.135
CARD 6	REGENT	CONDENSATE DEMINERALIZER REGENERATION TIME (DAYS)		36.75
CARD 7	FFCDM	FRACTION FEED WATER THROUGH CONDENSATE DEMIN		1.
CARD 8	HYTRTM	HYDROLOGICAL TRAVEL TIME (DAYS)		2.0
CARD 9	HYDF	HYDROLOGICAL DILUTION FACTOR		200000.
CARD 10		HIGH PURITY WASTE INPUT 27800. GPD AT .164 PCA		
CARD 11		TANK NAME WASTE COLLECTION TANK VOLUME 30000. GAL		0
CARD 12		IS TANK IN SYSTEM A BOTTOMS TANK 0 IF NO 1 IF YES		
CARD 13		DFI= 1.0E-00DFCS= 1.0E-03DF0 = 1.0E-00		
CARD 14		REGENERATION SOLTNS INPUT 2550. GPD		
CARD 15		TANK NAME CONCENTRATOR WASTE TANK VOLUME 5000. GAL		1
CARD 16		IS TANK IN SYSTEM A BOTTOMS TANK 0 IF NO 1 IF YES		
CARD 17		DFI= 5.0E-02DFCS= 5.0E-02DF0 = 5.0E-02		

1.
2.
3.
4.
5.
6.
7.
8.
9.
10.
11.
12.
13.
14.
15.
16.
17.

```
                SAMPLE CASE BWR        4/78          BWR
THERMAL POWER LEVEL (MEGAWATTS)                   3440.0000
PLANT CAPACITY FACTOR                                0.80
TOTAL STEAM FLOW (MILLION LBS/HR)                   14.1660
MASS OF WATER IN REACTOR VESSEL (MILLION LBS)        0.5880
OFF-GAS RELEASE RATE(UC/SEC)                     350000.
FISSION PRODUCT CARRY-OVER FRACTION                  0.0010
HALOGEN CARRY-OVER FRACTION                          0.0200
CLEAN-UP DEMINERALIZER FLOW (MILLION LBS/HR)         0.1350
CONDENSATE DEMINERALIZER REGENERATION TIME (DAYS)   36.7500
FRACTION FEED WATER THROUGH CONDENSATE DEMIN         1.0000
HYDROLOGICAL TRAVEL TIME (DAYS)                      2.00
HYDROLOGICAL DILUTION FACTOR                    200000.
HIGH PURITY WASTE INPUT GPD                          2.78E+04
REGENERATION SOLTNS INPU GPD                         2.55E+03

FAILED TANK PARAMETERS

                                                      TANK FACTORS
                          VOLUME        I          CS         OTHERS
FAILED TANK
WASTE COLLECTION          30000.     1.00E+00    1.00E+00    1.00E+00
CONCENTRATOR WASTE         5000.     5.00E-02    5.00E-02    5.00E-02
```

SAMPLE CASE BWR   4/78   LIQUID TANK FAILURE
NAME OF TANK FAILED: WASTE COLLECTION
VOLUME OF TANK FAILED: 24000. GAL. (80% OF TANK CAPACITY)
HYDROLOGICAL TRAVEL TIME (DAYS):   2.00
HYDROLOGICAL DILUTION FACTOR: 200000.

NUCLIDE	HALF-LIFE (DAYS)	PRIMARY COOLANT CONC. (UCI/ML)	10CFR20 LIMITS (UCI/ML)	FAILED TANK CONC. (UCI/ML)	CRITICAL RECEPTOR CONC. (UCI/ML)	FRACTION 10CFR20
CORROSION AND ACTIVATION PRODUCTS						
FISSION PRODUCTS						
I131	8.05E+00	2.84E-02	3.00E-07	4.50E-03	1.90E-08	0.0630
I133	8.75E-01	1.07E-01	1.00E-06	1.30E-02	1.30E-08	0.0130
ALL OTHERS		1.81E+00		4.90E-02	3.30E-08	0.0008
TOTAL EXCEPT TRITIUM		1.95E+00		6.60E-02	6.50E-08	0.0770

THE MAXIMUM QUANTITY OF TRITIUM IN THE TANK IS 5.0E+03 CURIES.

THE MAXIMUM QUANTITY OF CORROSION AND FISSION PRODUCTS (EXCLUDING TRITIUM) IN THE TANK IS 1.5E+01 CURIES.

SAMPLE CASE BWR 4/78   LIQUID TANK FAILURE
NAME OF TANK FAILED: CONCENTRATOR WASTE
VOLUME OF TANK FAILED: 4000. GAL. (80% OF TANK CAPACITY)
HYCROLOGICAL TRAVEL TIME (DAYS):   2.00
HYCROLOGICAL DILUTION FACTOR: 200000.

NUCLIDE	HALF-LIFE (DAYS)	PRIMARY COOLANT CONC. (UCI/ML)	10CFR20 LIMITS (UCI/ML)	FAILED TANK CONC. (UCI/ML)	CRITICAL RECEPTOR CONC. (UCI/ML)	FRACTION 10CFR20
CORROSION AND ACTIVATION PRODUCTS						
P 32	1.43E+01	1.96E-04	2.00E-05	2.00E-02	8.90E-08	0.0045
CR 51	2.78E+01	4.91E-03	2.00E-03	9.50E-01	4.50E-06	0.0023
MN 54	3.03E+02	5.90E-05	1.00E-04	2.30E-02	1.10E-07	0.0011
FE 55	9.50E+02	9.83E-04	8.00E-04	3.90E-01	2.00E-06	0.0025
CO 58	7.13E+01	1.97E-04	9.00E-05	6.00E-02	2.90E-07	0.0032
CO 60	1.92E+03	3.93E-04	3.00E-05	1.60E-01	8.00E-07	0.0270
ZN 65	2.45E+02	1.97E-04	1.00E-04	7.40E-02	3.70E-07	0.0037
FISSION PRODUCTS						
SR 89	5.20E+01	5.73E-04	3.00E-06	1.60E-01	7.60E-07	0.2500
SR 90	1.03E+04	3.44E-05	3.00E-07	1.40E-02	7.10E-08	0.2400
Y 90	2.67E+00	0.0	2.00E-05	1.40E-02	4.20E-08	0.0021
Y 91	5.88E+00	2.29E-04	3.00E-05	1.10E-02	5.20E-07	0.0170
MO 99	2.79E+00	1.13E-02	4.00E-05	1.80E-02	5.60E-08	0.0014
RU103	3.96E+01	1.15E-04	8.00E-05	2.70E-02	1.30E-07	0.0017
RU106	3.67E+02	1.72E-05	1.00E-05	6.70E-03	3.30E-08	0.0033
TE129M	3.40E+01	2.29E-04	2.00E-04	5.00E-02	2.40E-07	0.0120
I131	8.05E+00	2.84E-02	3.00E-07	2.20E+01	9.40E-05	310.0000
CS134	7.49E+02	1.72E-04	9.00E-06	3.80E-02	1.90E-07	0.0210
CS137	1.10E+04	4.02E-04	2.00E-05	9.10E-02	4.60E-07	0.0230
BA140	1.28E+01	2.29E-03	2.00E-05	2.30E-01	8.90E-07	0.0440
LA140	1.67E+00	0.0	2.00E-05	2.30E-02	5.00E-07	0.0250
CE141	3.24E+01	1.72E-04	9.00E-05	4.00E-02	1.90E-07	0.0021
PR143	1.37E+01	2.29E-04	5.00E-05	2.40E-02	1.10E-07	0.0021
CE144	2.84E+02	1.72E-05	1.00E-05	6.50E-03	3.30E-08	0.0033
ALL OTHERS		1.90E+00		2.50E-01	2.90E-07	0.0046
TOTAL EXCEPT TRITIUM		1.95E+00		2.50E+01	1.10E-04	310.0000

THE MAXIMUM QUANTITY OF TRITIUM IN THE TANK IS 5.0E+03 CURIES.

THE MAXIMUM QUANTITY OF CORROSION AND FISSION PRODUCTS (EXCLUDING TRITIUM) IN THE TANK IS 1.2E+00 CURIES.

APPENDIX C

RATAFR LISTING

This appendix contains the program listing in FORTRAN for the RATAFR Code, applicable to PWR's and BWR's using the input data cards from Appendix A or B of this manual. The nuclear data library and subroutines are available in card deck form from the Effluent Treatment Systems Branch, USNRC, (301)492-7775. The remainder of this appendix contains the RATAFR program listing.

```
  1.  C    RATAF CODE FOR CALCULATING CONSEQUENCES OF RADIOACTIVE LIQUID
  2.  C    TANK FAILURES.  MODIFIED MARCH 1976 TO CALCULATE TANK ISOTOPIC
  3.  C    CONCENTRATIONS TO PROVIDE AS INPUT FOR DETERMINING CONCENTRATIONS
  4.  C    AT POTABLE WATER SUPPLIES.  BASES FOR CODE IS THE LIQUID GALE
  5.  C    CODE OF JULY 1975.                                            00000080
  6.
  7.       INTEGER*2 NAME(3),ELE(99),STA(2),LOC,NONC,KD
  8.       REAL*4 LETDWA,LETDWN,MCH3,MQH3,MCCFP,MQCFP
  9.       COMMON/LABEL/ ELE,STA
 10.       COMMON/MATRIX/A(2500),LOC(2500),NONO(800),KD(800)             00000190
 11.       COMMON/FLEX/FLUX(10),MMN,MOUT,INDEX,QXN,AXN,ERR,NOBLND,MZERO  00000200
 12.       COMMON/PROCSS/ MPROS,PRATE(8),NOPROS(8),NZPROS(8,20),PR(800)  00000210
 13.       COMMON/FG/XZFRO(800),XZH(800),XTEMP(800),XNEW(10,800),        00000220
 14.      1 B(800),D(800)                                                00000230
 15.       COMMON/FLUXN/T(20),POWER(10),TOCAP(800),FISS(100),DIS(800),ILITE, 00000240
 16.      1 IACT,IFP,IIOT,NON,INPT                                       00000250
 17.       COMMON/CUT/NUCL(800),TITLE(20),Q(800),FG(800),CUTOFF(7),      00000260
 18.      1 PCW,BUGIUP,FLUXJ,MSTAR,ALPHAN(100),SPONF(100),ABUND(500),    00000270
 19.      2 BASIS(10),TCONST,TUNIT                                       00000280
 20.       COMMON/MPC/APCTAB,AMPC(800),WMPC(800)                         00008120
 21.       COMMON/COYP/PWCONC(800)
 22.       COMMON /CONR/BCONC(800)
 23.       DIMENSION PCONC(800),DWCONC(800),CWCONC(800),CMCONC(800),
 24.      1 RIJV(800)
 25.       DIMENSION TKCONC(800),PER(800)
 26.       DIMENSION PWCON(800),FRAC(800)
 27.       DIMENSION SRTANK(6),DWTANK(6),CWTANK(6),RGTANK(6)
 28.       DIMENSION WORD26(14),WORD24(6),REACTR(7)
 29.       DATA PWR?/, PWR'/,'BWR'/ BWR'/
 30.  C    BCONC CONTAINS PRIMARY COOLANT CONCENTRATIONS FOR BWR'S.
 31.  C    PWCONC CONTAINS PRIMARY COOLANT CONCENTRATIONS FOR PWR'S.     00000570
 32.  C                                                                  00000580
 33.  C    READ NUCLEAR DATA AND CONSTRUCT TRANSITION MATRIX
 33.1      CALL NUDATA(NLIBE)
 34.  C
 44.       DO 20 I=2,IIOT                                                00000590
 45.       NONO(I)=NONO(I)+NONO(I-1)                                     00000610
 46.       KD(I)=KD(I)+NONO(I-1)                                         00000620
 47.    20 CONTINUE                                                      00000630
 48.    30 INDEX=0                                                       00000640
 49.       QXN=0.001
 50.       AXN=-ALOG(QXN)                                                00000680
 51.       TCONST=86400.                                                00000730
 52.       TRG=0.0                                                       00003640
 53.       TD=0.0                                                        00000740
 54.       TC=0.0
 55.       REGENT=0.0
 56.       HYTRTM=0.0
 57.       HYDF=0.0
 58.       DWFLR=0.0
 59.       RGWFR=0.0
 60.       EVAPS=1.0
 61.       EVAPO=1.0
 62.       EVAPC=1.0
 63.       EVAPR=1.0
 64.       DO 40 J=1,800                                                 00000840
```

```
 65.       PCONC(J)=0.0                                              00000850
 66.       DWCONC(J)=0.0                                             00000880
 67.       RINV(J)=0.0                                               00000890
 68.       CWCONC(J)=0.0                                             00000900
 69.       CMCONC(J)=0.0
 70.       TKCONC(J)=0.0
 71.       PWCON(J)=0.0
 72.       FRAC(J)=0.0
 73.       PER(J)=0.0
 74.       XZH(J)=0.0
 75.    40 CONTINUE
 76. C
 77. C   READ DESCRIPTION OF REACTOR AND RADWASTE TREATMENT PLANT
 78. C
 79.       PRINT 9026                                                00000910
 80.       READ 9010,REACTR,TYPE                                     00000920
 81.       PRINT 9010,RFACTR,TYPE                                    00000930
 82.       READ 9011,WORD56,POW1                                     00000940
 83.       PRINT 9011,WORD56,POW1                                    00000950
 84.       PF=0.80                                                   00000970
 85.       PRINT 9027                                                00000980
 86.       IF(TYPE.EQ.BWR) GO TO 50                                  00000990
 87. C   READ DATA FOR PWR NSSS PARAMETERS AND TANK PARAMETERS       00001000
 88.       READ 9022,WORD56,PCVOL                                    00001010
 89.       PRINT 9022,WORD56,PCVOL                                   00001020
 90.   700 FAILDB=1.0                                                00001030
 91.       FAILL4=0.12                                               00001040
 92.       FAILRA=FAILDR/FAILEA
 93.       PRINT 9028,FAILDB                                         00001050
 94.       READ 9022,WORD56,LETDWN                                   00001060
 95.       PRINT 9022,WORD56,LETDWN
 96.       READ 9022,WORD56,CBFLR
 97.       PRINT 9022,WORD56,CBFLR
 98.       READ 9085,WORD56,HYTRTM
 99.       PRINT 9085,WORD56,HYTRTM
100.       READ 9090,WORD56,HYDF
101.       PRINT 9070,WORD56,HYDF
102.       READ 9013,WORD24,SBLDR
103.       PRINT 9025,WORD24,SRLDR
104.       CWA=1.C
105.       READ 9013,WORD24,EDFLR,EDA
106.       PRINT 9025,WORD24,EDFLR
107.       READ 9C23,SRTANK,SBTKSZ
108.       READ 9086,KEV6TS
109.       IF (KEVBTS.EQ.1) EVAPS=0.02
110.       READ 9014,DFICM,DFCSCM,DFCM
111.       READ 9013,WORD24,DWFLR,DWA
112.       IF (DWFLR.EC.0.0)GO TO 4446
113.       PRINT 9025,WORD24,DWFLR
114.  4446 CONTINUE
115.       READ 9023,DWTANK,DWTKSZ
116.       READ 9086,KEVBTD
117.       IF (KEVBTD.EQ.1)EVAPD=0.02
118.       READ 9014,DFIDW,DFCSDW,DFDW
119.       K=1
120.       PRINT 9045                                                00001520
121.       PRINT 9016                                                00001560
122.       IF (SBTKSZ.EQ.0.0)GO TO 45
123.       PRINT 9024,SRTANK,SBTKSZ,DFICM,DFCSCM,DFCM
124.       GO TO 46
```

C-3

```
125.    45 K=2
126.    46 CONTINUE
127.       IF (DWTKSZ.EQ.0.0)GO TO 47
128.       PRINT 9024,DWTANK,DWTKSZ,DFIDW,DFCSDW,DFDW    00002300
129.    47 CONTINUE                                      00002310
130.    C                                                00002320
131.    C  CONVERSION OF UNITS
132.    C
133.       DFRG=1.0
134.       DFIRG=1.0
135.       DFCSRG=1.0
136.       GO TO 240                                     00002470
137.    C
138.    C  READ DATA FOR BWR NSSS PARAMETERS AND TANK PARAMETERS
139.    C
140.    50 READ 9022,WORD56,STMFR                        00002480
141.       PRINT 9022,WORD56,STMFR                       00002490
142.       READ 9022,WORD56,PCVOL                        00002500
143.       PRINT 9022,WORD56,PCVOL                       00002510
144.       OGDB=35000J.                                  00002520
145.       PRINT 9052,OGDB
146.       OGEA=60000.
147.       OGRTIO=OGDB/OGEA
148.       FPEF=0.001                                    00002530
149.       HEF=0.020
150.       PRINT 9030,FPEF,HEF                           00002550
151.       READ 9022,WORD56,LETDWN                       00002560
152.       PRINT 9022,WORD56,LETDWN                      00002570
153.       READ 9022,WORD56,REGENT                       00002650
154.       PRINT 9022,WORD56,REGENT                      00002660
155.       READ 9022,WORD56,FFCDM                        00002670
156.       PRINT 9022,WORD56,FFCDM                       00002680
157.       READ 9085,WORD56,HYTRTM
158.       PRINT 9085,WORD56,HYTRTM
159.       READ 9090,WORD56,HYDF
160.       PRINT 9090,WORD56,HYDF
161.       K=1
162.       READ 9013,WORD24,CWFLR,CWA
163.       READ 9023,CWTANK,CWTKSZ
164.       READ 9086,KEVBTC
165.       IF (KEVRTC.EQ.1)EVAPC=0.01
166.       READ 9014,DFICW,DFCSCW,DFCW
167.       IF (CWTKSZ.EQ.0.)GO TO 52
168.       PRINT 9025,WORD24,CWFLR                       00002710
169.       GO TO 54                                      00002750
170.    52 K=2
171.    54 CONTINUE
172.       READ 9013,WORD24,RGWFR
173.       READ 9023,RGTANK,RGTKSZ
174.       READ 9086,KEVBTR
175.       IF (KEVRTR.EQ.1)EVAPR=0.05
176.       READ 9014,DFIRG,DFCSRG,DFRG
177.       IF (RGTKSZ.EQ.0.) GO TO 56
178.       PRINT 9025,WORD24,RGWFR
179.    56 CONTINUE
180.       PRINT 9045
181.       PRINT 9016
182.       IF (CWTKSZ.EQ.0.0)GO TO 58
183.       PRINT 9024,CWTANK,CWTKSZ,DFICW,DFCSCW,DFCW
184.    58 CONTINUE
```

C-4

```
185.      IF (RGTKSZ.EQ.0.0)GO TO 60
186.      PRINT 9024,RGTANK,RGTKSZ,DFIRG,DFCSRG,DFRG
187.   60 CONTINUE
188.   77 DO 78 I=1,ITOT
189.      B(I)=0.0
190.   78 CONTINUE
191. C                                                              00003290
192.      DFIDW=1.0
193.      DFCSDW=1.0
194.      DFDW=1.0                                                  00004850
195.  240 CONTINUE                                                  00004860
196. C
197. C    CALCULATE PRIMARY COOLANT CONCENTRATIONS FOR PWRS         00004880
198. C
199.      IF(ITYPE.EQ.BWR)GO TO 251
200.      AFPTES=0.0
201.      DO 242 I=1,ITOT
202.  242 PCONC(I)=PWCONC(I)
203.      POWA=POW1
204.      PCVOA=PCVOL*1E3
205.      LETDWA=LETDWM*500.53
206.      SBLDA=SBLDR*.3476
207.      CBFLA=CBFLR*500.53
208. C    CHECK TO SEE IF PRIMARY PLANT PARAMETERS ARE WITHIN SPECIFIED
209. C    RANGES
210.      IF(ABS(POWA-3400).GT.400.1)GO TO 243
211.      IF(ABS(PCVOA-5.5E5).GT.0.5001E5)GO TO 243
212.      IF(ABS(LETDWA-3.7E4).GT.0.5001E4)GO TO 243
213.      IF(ABS(SBLDA-625.).GT.375.1)GO TO 243
214.      IF(ABS(CBFLA-3750.).GT.3750.1)GO TO 243
215.      GO TO 247
216. C    CALCULATE PWR PRIMARY COOLANT ADJUSTMENT FACTORS
217.  243 AFPTES=1.0
218.      RHAL2=(LETDWA*0.9+0.1*SOLDA)/PCVOA
219.      RCSRB2=(LETDWA*0.5+0.5*(SBLDA+CBFLA*0.9))/PCVOA
220.      RCFP2=(LETDWA*0.9+C.1*(SBLDA+CBFLA*0.9))/PCVOA
221.      RK2=161.76*POWA/PCVOA
222.      DO 246 J=1,ITOT
223.      IF(PCONC(J).EQ.0.0) GO TO 246
224.      NZ=NUCL(J)/10000
225.      DL=DIS(J)*3600.
226.      IF (NZ.EQ.1) GO TO 246
227.      IF(NZ.EQ.53.OR.NZ.EQ.35)GO TO 244
228.      IF(NZ.EQ.37.OR.NZ.EQ.55)GO TO 245
229.      PCONC(J)=PCONC(J)*RK2*(0.0612+DL)/(RCFP2+DL)
230.      GO TO 246
231.  244 PCONC(J)=PCONC(J)*RK2*(0.0606+DL)/(RHAL2+DL)
232.      GO TO 246
233.  245 PCONC(J)=PCONC(J)*RK2*(0.0371+DL)/(RCSRB2+DL)
234.  246 CONTINUE
235.  247 PCVOL=PCVOL*1000.*0.7/62.4
236.      DO 279 I=1,ITOT
237.      IF (PCONC(I).EQ.0.0)GO TO 279
238.      FAIL1=FAILRA
239.      IF (I.LE.ILITE)FAIL1=1.0
240.      PCONC(I)=PCONC(I)/(DIS(I)*1.6283E13)*FAIL1
241.  279 CONTINUE
242. C
243. C                                                              00005480
244.      GO TO 400
```

```
245.    C
246.    C  251  CONTINUE
247.    C       CALCULATE BWR PRIMARY COOLANT CONCENTRATIONS
248.          DO 2251 I=1,ITOT
249.    2251  PCONC(I)=BCONC(I)
250.          POWA=POW1
251.          PCVOA=PCVOL*1E6
252.          LETDWA=LETDWN*1E6
253.          STMFA=STMFR*1E6
254.          FFCDA=FFCDM
255.    C       CHECK TO SEE IF PLANT PARAMETERS ARE WITHIN SPECIFIED RANGES
256.          IF(ABS(POWA-3400).GT.400.1)GO TO 252
257.          IF(ABS(PCVOA-3.8E5).GT.0.4001E5)GO TO 252
258.          IF(ABS(LETDWA-1.3E5).GT.0.2001E5)GO TO 252
259.          IF(ABS(STMFA-1.5E7).GT.0.2001E7)GO TO 252
260.          IF(ABS(FFCDA-0.9).GT.0.1001)GO TO 252
261.          GO TO 256
262.    C       CALCULATE BWR ADJUSTMENT FACTORS
263.    252  RHAL2=(LETDWA*0.9+FFCDA*STMFA*0.018)/PCVOA
264.          RCSRB2=(LETDWA*0.5+FFCDA*STMFA*5E-4)/PCVOA
265.          RCFP2=(LETDWA*0.9+FFCDA*STMFA*9E-4)/PCVOA
266.          RK2=111.76*POWA/PCVOA
267.          DO 255 J=1,ITOT
268.          IF(PCONC(J).EQ.0.0) GO TO 255
269.          NZ=NUCL(J)/10000
270.          DL=DIS(J)*3600
271.          IF (NZ.EQ.1) GO TO 255
272.          IF (NZ.EQ.53.OR.NZ.EQ.35)GO TO 253
273.          IF (NZ.EQ.37.OR.NZ.EQ.55)GO TO 254
274.          PCONC(J)=PCONC(J)*RK2*(0.3434+DL)/(RCFP2+DL)
275.          GO TO 255
276.    253  PCONC(J)=PCONC(J)*RK2*(0.1908+DL)/(RCSRB2+DL)
277.          GO TO 255
278.    254  PCONC(J)=PCONC(J)*RK2*(0.1908+DL)/(RCSRB2+DL)
279.    255  CONTINUE
280.    256  PCVOL=PCVOL*100000G./62.4
281.          LETDWN=LETDWN*2000.
282.          STMFR=STMFR*2851.
283.          DO 2255 J=1,ITOT
284.          OGRTI=OGRTIO
285.          IF (J.LE.ILITE)OGRTI1=1.0
286.          IF(PCCNC(J).GT.0.0)PCONC(J)=PCONC(J)/(DIS(J)*1.6283E13)*OGRTI1     00003340
                                                                                 00003350
287.    2255  CONTINUE
288.          IF(REGENT.GT.0.0) GO TO 257
289.          GO TO 400
290.    C
291.    C       COMPUTE REMOVAL CONSTANT FOR CONDENSATE DEMINERALIZER IN BWR     00005120
292.    257  CCBDM=0.9*STMFR*FPEF/(PCVOL*7.48*60.)*FFCDM
293.          CSBDM=0.5*STMFR*FPEF/(PCVOL*7.48*60.)*FFCDM
294.          DO 258 I=1,ITOT
295.          NZ=NUCL(I)/10000
296.          PR(I)=CCBDM
297.          IF(NZ.EQ.53.OR.NZ.EQ.35)PR(I)=CCBDM*HEF/FPEF
298.          IF(NZ.EQ.37.OR.NZ.EQ.55)PR(I)=CSBDM
299.          XZHJ=PCCNC(I)*PR(I)*PCVOL*0.02832
300.          B(I)=XZHJ
301.          XZH(I)=XZHJ*86400).
302.    258  CONTINUE
303.          XZERO(I)=0.
304.    C       CALCULATE INVENTORIES ON BWR CONDENSATE RESINS                   00005130
```

```
305.     290 T(1)=REGENT                                                            00005420
306.         CALL SOLVE
307.         DO 295 I=1,ITOT
308.     295 RINV(I)=XTEMP(I)
309.   C
310.   C     THIS PORTION OF PROGRAM CALCULATES FAILED TANK CONCENTRATIONS
311.   C
312.     400 CONTINUE                                                               00008320
313.         RGWFRM=RGWFR*3785./1E6
314.         DO 410 I=1,ITOT
315.     410 D(I)=-DIS(I)
316.         DO 430 J=1,ITOT
317.     420 NZ=NUCL(J)/10000
318.         IF(NZ.EQ.36.OR.NZ.EQ.54) GO TO 430
319.         IF (TYPE.EQ.PWR)GO TO 425
320.         CWCONC(J)=PCONC(J)*CWA                                                 00008340
321.         IF (NZ.EQ.1) CWCONC(J)=PCONC(J)
322.         IF (RGWFR.EQ.0.0)GO TO 430
323.         RINV(J)=RINV(J)/(REGENT*RGWFRM)
324.         IF (NZ.EQ.1) RINV(J)=PCONC(J)
325.         GO TO 430
326.     425 DFCVCS=10.
327.         IF(NZ.EQ.1)DFCVCS=1.0
328.         IF(NZ.EQ.37.OR.NZ.EQ.55) DFCVCS=2.
329.         CWCONC(J)=PCONC(J)*(CWA*SBLDR/DFCVCS+EDA*EDFLR)/(SBLDR+EDFLR)          00008360
330.         DWCONC(J)=PCONC(J)*DWA
331.     430 CONTINUE                                                               00008470
332.   C
333.   C     CALCULATE RADIOACTIVITY AFTER COLLECTION AT A CONSTANT RATE            00008480
334.         IF (TYPE.EQ.BWR)GO TO 432
335.         IF (SBLDR.GT.0.0)TC=SBTKSZ*0.8/((SBLDR+EDFLR)*EVAPS)
336.         GO TO 434
337.     432 CONTINUE
338.         IF (CWFLR.GT.0.0)TC=CWTKSZ*0.8/(CWFLR*EVAPC)                           00008490
339.     434 CONTINUE                                                               00008500
340.         IF (DWFLR.GT.0.0)TC=DWTKSZ*0.8/(DWFLR*EVAPD)
341.         IF (RGWFR.GT.0.0)TRG=(RGTKSZ*0.8-11900.*EVAPR)/(RGWFR*2.*EVAPR)        00008520
342.         IF (TRG.LT.0.0) TRG=0.
343.   C
344.         CALL COLLECT(TC*86400.,CWCONC,ILITE,ITOT)
345.         CALL COLLECT(TD*86400.,DWCONC,ILITE,ITOT)
346.     440 IF (REGENT.LE.0.0)GO TO 450                                            00008580
347.         CALL STORAG(TRG*86400.,RINV,ILITE,ITOT)
348.     450 DO 500 I=1,ITOT
349.         NZ=NUCL(I)/10000
350.         IF (NZ.EQ.1) GO TO 500
351.         IF (NZ.EQ.35.OR.NZ.EQ.53)GO TO 460
352.         IF (NZ.EQ.37.OR.NZ.EQ.55)GO TO 470
353.   C
354.   C     CHEMICAL TREATMENT FOR OTHER CATIONS
355.   C
356.         CWCONC(I)=CWCONC(I)/DFCW                                               00008650
357.         DWCONC(I)=DWCONC(I)/DFDW                                               00008660
358.         RINV (I)=RINV (I)/DFRG                                                 00008670
359.         GO TO 500                                                              00008680
360.   C
361.   C     CHEMICAL TREATMENT FOR ANIONS                                          00008700
362.   C
363.     460 CWCONC(I)=CWCONC(I)/DFICW                                              00008790
364.         DWCONC(I)=DWCONC(I)/DFIDW                                              00008800
```

```
365.      RINV (I)=RINV (I)/DFIRG
366.      GO TO 500
367.  C
368.  C   CHEMICAL TREATMENT FOR R8 AND CS
369.  C
370.  470 CWCONC(I)=CWCONC(I)/DFCSCW              00008910
371.      DWCONC(I)=DWCONC(I)/DFCSDW              00008920
372.      RINV (I)=RINV (I)/DFCSRG                00008930
373.  500 CONTINUE
374.  C
375.      STS=S8TKSZ*0.8
376.      DTS=DWTKSZ*0.8
377.      CTS=CWTKSZ*0.8
378.      RTS=RGTKSZ*0.8
379.  C
380.      IF(REGENT.LT.0.001)GO TO 503            00008960
381.      DO 502 I=1,ITOT
382.      CMCONC(I)=RINV(I)
383.  502 CONTINUE
384.  503 CONTINUE
385.      IF (K.EQ.2) GO TO 508
386.      CTKSZ=STS
387.      IF (TYPE.EQ.BWR) CTKSZ=CTS              00009410
388.      DO 507 I=1,ITOT
389.  507 TKCONC(I)=CWCONC(I)
390.      GO TO 512
391.  508 DAN=1.6
392.      IF(TYPE.EQ.BWR)GO TO 510
393.      CTKSZ=DTS
394.      DO 509 I=1,ITOT
395.  509 TKCONC(I)=DWCONC(I)
396.      GO TO 512
397.  510 KATH=4.7
398.      CTKSZ=RTS
399.      DO 511 I=1,ITOT
400.  511 TKCONC(I)=CMCONC(I)
401.  512 CONTINUE
402.      DO 540 I=1,ITOT
403.      NZ=NUCL(I)/10000
404.      IF(NZ.EQ.36.OR.NZ.EQ.54) GO TO 540      00009600
405.      DISI=DIS(I)*1.6283E13
406.      TKCONC(I)=TKCONC(I)*DISI                00009620
407.      IF (TKCONC(I).GT.0.0) GO TO 535
408.      PWCON(I)=0.0
409.      GO TO 540
410.  535 V=DIS(I)*HYTRTM*86400.
411.      IF (V.GT.75.) V=75.
412.      PWCON(I)=(TKCONC(I)/HYDF)*EXP(-V)
413.  540 CONTINUE
414.      DO 545 I=1,ITOT
415.  545 FRAC(I)=PWCON(I)/WMPC(I)
416.  550 SAPRIM=0.0
417.      STANK=0.0
418.      SCRECN=0.0
419.      SFRACT=0.0
420.      PAPRIM=0.0
421.      PTANK=0.0
422.      PCRECN=0.0
423.      PFRACT=0.0
424.      MCH3=TKCONC(3)/FRAC(3)                  00010010
```

C-8

```
425.      MQH3=MCH3*CTKS2*3785./1.0E6
426.      IF (MQH3.GT.5000.) MQH3=5000.
427.      IF (TYPE.EQ.BWR) GO TO 553
428.      IF (K.EQ.1) PRINT 9076,REACTR,SBTANK,STS,HYTRTM,HYDF      00010170
429.      IF (K.EQ.2) PRINT 9076,REACTR,DWTANK,DTS,HYTRTM,HYDF      00010180
430.      GO TO 555                                                 00010190
431.  553 CONTINUE
432.      IF (K.EQ.1) PRINT 9076,REACTR,CWTANK,CTS,HYTRTM,HYDF
433.      IF (K.EQ.2) PRINT 9076,REACTR,RGTANK,RTS,HYTRTM,HYDF
434.  555 CONTINUE
435.      PRINT 9077                                                00010220
436.      PRINT 9081
437.      KOUNTR=1
438.      I1=ILITE+IACT+1                                           00010250
439.      L=1                                                       00010260
440.      DO 580 I=1,ITOT
441.      IF (I1.EQ.I1)PRINT 9082
442.      NZ=NUCL(I)/10000
443.      IF (NZ.EQ.36.OR.NZ.EQ.54)GO TO 580
444.      DISI=DIS(I)*1.6283E+13
445.      APRIM=PCONC(I)*DISI                                       00010350
446.      WMPC1=WMPC(I)
447.      TANK=TKCONC(I)
448.      CRECN=PWCON(I)
449.      FRACT=FRAC(I)
450.      NUCL1=NUCL(I)
451.      L=L+1                                                     00010470
452.      IF(NZ.EQ.1) GO TO 560
453.      SAPRIM=SAPRIM+APRIM
454.      STANK=STANK+TANK
455.      SCRECN=SCRECN+CRECN
456.      SFRACT=SFRACT+FRACT
457.  560 IF (FRACT.LT.0.001) GO TO 580
458.      IF (MOD(KOUNTR,50).NE.0) GO TO 570
459.      PRINT 9084,          REACTR                               00010650
460.      PRINT 9077
461.  570 CALL NGAH(NUCL(I),NAME)
462.      THALF=8.0225E-6/DIS(I)
463.      ISUB=2
464.      IF (TANK.GT.1.) ISUB=1
465.      DIV=10.**(INT(ALOG10(TANK))-ISUB)
466.      TANK1=AINT(TANK/DIV+0.5)*DIV
467.      ISUB=2
468.      IF (CRECN.GT.1.0) ISUB=1
469.      DIV=10.**(INT(ALOG10(CRECN))-ISUB)
470.      CRECN1=AINT(CRECN/DIV+0.5)*DIV
471.      ISUB=2
472.      IF (FRACT.GT.1.0) ISUB=1
473.      DIV=10.**(INT(ALOG10(FRACT))-ISUB)
474.      FRACT1=AINT(FRACT/DIV+0.5)*DIV
475.      ISUB1=1
476.      PRINT 9078,    NAME,THALF,APRIM,WMPC1,TANK1,CRECN1,FRACT1  00010700
477.      KOUNTR=KOUNTR+1
478.      IF(NZ.EQ.1) GO TO 580                                     00010720
479.      PAPRIM=PAPRIM+APRIM
480.      PTANK=PTANK+TANK
481.      PCRECN=PCRECN+CRECN
482.      PFRACT=PFRACT+FRACT
483.  580 CONTINUE                                                  00010830
484.      PAPRIM=SAPRIM-PAPRIM
```

```
      PTANK=STANK-PTANK
      PCRECN=SCRECN-PCRECN
      PFRACT=SFRACT-PFRACT
      MCCFP=STANK/SFRACT
      MQCFP=MCCFP*CTKSZ*3785./1.0E6
      IF (MQCFP.GT.15.) MQCFP=15.
      ISUBP=2
      IF (PTANK.GT.1.0) ISUBP=1
      DIV=10.**(INT(ALOG10(PTANK))-ISUBP)
      PTANK=AINT(PTANK/DIV+0.5)*DIV
      ISUBP=2
      IF (PCRECN.GT.1.0) ISUBP=1
      DIV=10.**(INT(ALOG10(PCRECN))-ISUBP)
      PCRECN=AINT(PCRECN/DIV+0.5)*DIV
      IF (PFRACT.EQ.0.0) GO TO 585
      ISUBP=2
      IF (PFRACT.GT.1.0) ISUBP=1
      DIV=10.**(INT(ALOG10(PFRACT))-ISUBP)
      PFRACT=AINT(PFRACT/DIV+0.5)*DIV
  585 ISU3S=1
      IF (STANK.LT.1.0) ISUBS=2
      DIV=10.**(INT(ALOG10(STANK))-ISUBS)
      STANK=AINT(STANK/DIV+0.5)*DIV
      ISUBS=1
      IF (SCRECN.LT.1.0) ISUBS=2
      DIV=10.**(INT(ALOG10(SCRECN))-ISUBS)
      SCRECN=AINT(SCRECN/DIV+0.5)*DIV
      ISUBS=1
      IF (SFRACT.LT.1.0) ISUBS=2
      DIV=10.**(INT(ALOG10(SFRACT))-ISUBS)
      SFRACT=AINT(SFRACT/DIV+0.5)*DIV
      PRINT 9070,    PAPRIM,PTANK,PCRECN,PFRACT
      PRINT 9080,    SAPRIM,STANK,SCRECN,SFRACT
      PRINT 9100,    MQH3,MQCFP
      IF(TYPE.EQ.BWR)GO TO 600
      IF(K.EQ.2.OR.DWTKSZ.EQ.0.0)GO TO 30
      GO TO 610
  600 CONTINUE
      IF(K.EQ.2.OR.RGTKSZ.EQ.0.0)GO TO 30
  610 K=K+1
      GO TO 503
C
C                                         FORMATS                          00005630
C                                                                          00005640
 9010 FORMAT(32X,7A4,16X,A4)                                               00005650
 9011 FORMAT(16X,13A4,A3,F9.4)                                            00005760
 9012 FORMAT(16X,14A4,F8.4)                                               00005770
 9013 FORMAT(16X,6A4,1X,F8.0,7X,F5.3)                                     00005780
 9014 FORMAT(20X,F9.0,2(5X,F8.0))
 9016 FORMAT('0',70X,'TANK FACTORS'/34X,'FAILED TANK',13X,'VOLUME',6X,     00005890
     1           'I',9X,'CS',7X,'OTHERS')
 9022 FORMAT(16X,14A4,F8.4)
 9023 FORMAT(26X,6A4,14X,F9.0)
 9024 FORMAT(30X,6A4,3X,F9.0,2X,3(1PE9.2,1X))
 9025 FORMAT(16X,6A4,' GPD',28X,1PE8.2)
 9026 FORMAT(1H1)
 9027 FORMAT(16X,'PLANT CAPACITY FACTOR',T75,'0.80')                       00006010
 9028 FORMAT(16X,'PERCENT FUEL WITH CLADDING DEFECTS',T75,F6.4)            00006020
 9030 FORMAT(16X,'FISSION PRODUCT CARRY-OVER FRACTION',T75,F6.4/16X,       00006030
     1'HALOGEN CARRY-OVER FRACTION',T75,F6.4)                              00006060
                                                                          00006070
```

```
9045 FORMAT(/,15X,'FAILED TANK PARAMETERS')
9052 FORMAT(16X,'OFF-GAS RELEASE RATE(UC/SEC)',28X,F8.0)
9076 FORMAT (1H1,20X,7A4,' LIQUID TANK FAILURE'/1H ,21X,'NAME OF TANK F
     1AILED: ',6A4/1H ,21X,'VOLUME OF TANK FAILED: ',F9.0,' GAL. (80
     2% OF TANK CAPACITY)'/1H ,21X,'HYDROLOGICAL TRAVEL TIME (DAYS):
     3',F8.2/1H ,21X,'HYDROLOGICAL DILUTION FACTOR: ',F8.0)
9077 FORMAT (1H0,28X,'PRIMARY',22X,'FAILED',7X,'CRITICAL'/29X,'COOLANT'
     1,7X,'ICCFR20',9X,'TANK',8X,'RECEPTOR',6X,'FRACTION'/4X,'NUCLIDE',
     24X,'HALF-LIFE',5X,'CONC.',9X,'LIMITS',10X,'CONC.',7X,'CONC.',9X,
     3'10CFR20'/15X,'(DAYS)',2X,4(6X,'(UCI/ML)'))
9078 FORMAT (4X,A2,I3,A1,4X,1PE9.2/(5X,1PE9.2),3X,0PF12.4)
9079 FORMAT (4X,'ALL OTHERS',14X,1PE9.2,19X,1PE9.2,5X,1PE9.2,3X,0PF12.4
     1)
9080 FORMAT (4X,'TOTAL'/4X,'EXCEPT TRITIUM',10X,1PE9.2,19X,1PE9.2,5X,1P
     1E9.2,3X,0PF12.4)
9081 FORMAT (4X,'CORROSION AND ACTIVATION PRODUCTS')
9082 FORMAT (1H0,4X,'FISSION PRODUCTS')
9084 FORMAT (1H1,20X,7A4,' LIQUID TANK FAILURE (CONTINUED)')
9085 FORMAT(16X,14A4,F8.2)
9086 FORMAT (79X,I1)
9090 FORMAT(16X,14A4,F8.0)
9100 FORMAT (1H0,3X,'THE MAXIMUM QUANTITY OF TRITIUM IN THE TANK IS ',1
     1PE7.1,' CURIES.'/1H0,3X,'THE MAXIMUM QUANTITY OF CORROSION AND FIS
     2SION PRODUCTS (EXCLUDING TRITIUM) IN THE TANK IS ',1PE7.1,' CURIES
     3.')
     END
     BLOCK DATA                                                          00006230
     COMMON /CONB/BCONC(800)
     COMMON/CONP/PWCONC(800)
     DATA BCONC/2*0.0,01,33*0,
     1                      9E-3,13*0,2E-4,53*0,5E-3,4*0,6E-5,0.0,5E-2,3*0,
     1IE-3,3*0,3E-5,0.0,2E-4,2*0,4E-4,7*0,1E-6,0.0,3E-4,2*0,3E-2,4*0,
     22E-4,3*0,2E-3,98*0,4E-4,64*0,7E-3,63*0,3E-3,4*0,5E-3,2*0,3E-3,
     319*0,5E-3,1E-4,3*0,6E-6,5*0,4E-3,0.0,4E-5,3*0,1E-2,6E-3,4*0,4E-3,
     411*0,7E-6,0.0,7E-6,6*0,5E-6,5*0,2E-3,4*0,3E-6,21*0,1E-6,104*0,4E-5,13*0,1E-4,
     552E-5,3*0,8E-2,6*0,2E-3,4*0,3E-6,2*0,2E-5,2*0,2E-2,5*0,7E-2,2*0,2E-2,8*0,
     660.0,5E-3,5*0,1E-5,3E-2,4*0,1E-2,3*0,4E-4,4*0,1E-2,0.0,3E-5,3*0,
     772E-5,3*0,7E-5,4*0,1E-2,5*0,3E-6,10*0,3E-6,81*0/
     86E-3,5E-3,7*0,3E-5,4E-5,2*0,3E-6,10*0,3E-6,81*0/
     DATA PWCONC/2*0,1.0,1C1*0,
     1                      1.9F-3,4*0.3.1E-4,5*0,1.6E-3,3*0.0..016,
     12*0,2E-3,185*0,1.2E-3,63*0,4.8E-3,4*0,2.6E-3,2*0,3E-4,6*0,8.5E-5,
     28*0.,2.4*0.3.5E-4,3*0,1E-5,0.0,1.2E-6,3*0,6.5E-4,3.6E-4,6.4E-5,9*000010680
     33,3.4E-5,11*0,6.6E-5,0.,5E-5,15*0,.086,,048,16*0,4.5E-5,4.5E-5,14*0,      00010690
     41E-5,5.0,1E-5,1C3*C,2.9E-5,8*0,2.8E-4,8.5E-4,10*0,1.4E-3,1.6E-3,
     558*0,2.1E-3,3*0,2.5E-3,1.1E-3,27,5*0,.027,.1,4*0,.38,5*0,.047,2*0,
     66.025,2*0,.19,8*0,.013,3*0,.018,.016,12*0,2.2E-4,1.5E-4,5*0,7E-5,
     712*0,4E-5,5E-5,2*0,3.3E-5,3.3E-5,91*0/
     END
     SUBROUTINE SOLVE                                                    00010990
     COMMON/EG/XZFRO(800), XZH(800),XTEMP(800),XNEW(10,800),             00011000
     1  B(800),D(800)                                                    00011010
     COMMON/FLEX/FLUX(10),MMN,MOUT,INDEX,QXN,AXN,ERR,NOBLND,MZERO        00011020
     COMMON/PROCSS/ MPROS,PRATE(8),NOPROS(8),NZPROS(8,20),PR(800)        00011030
     COMMON/FLUXW/TI(20),POWCR(10),TOCAP(800),FISS(100),DIS(800),ILITE,  00011040
     1 IACT,IFP,IIOT,NON,INPT                                            00011050
     COMMON/OUT/NUCL(800),TITLE(20),Q(800),FG(800),CUTOFF(7),            00011060
     1 POW,BURNUP,FLUXB,MSTAR,ALPHAN(100),SPONF(100),ABUND(500),         00011070
     2 BASIS(10),ICONST,TUNIT                                            00011080
     DO 10 I=1,IIOT                                                      00011090
```

```fortran
605.        D(I)=-DIS(I)
606.     10 XTEMP(I)=0.0
607.        DELT=T(I)*TCONST
608.        CALL DECAY(1,DELT,ITOT)
609.        CALL TERM(DELT,1,ILITE,ITOT)
610.        CALL EQUIL(1,ITOT)
611.        DO 30 I=1,ITOT
612.     30 XTEMP(I)=XNEW(1,I)
613.        RETURN
614.        END
615.        SUBROUTINE TERM(T,M,ILITE,ITOT)
616.   C
617.   C    TERM ADDS ONE TERM TO EACH ELEMENT OF THE SOLUTION VECTOR
618.   C    CSUM(J) IS THE CURRENT APPROXIMATION TO XNEW(M,J)
619.   C    CIMO(J) IS THE VECTOR CONTAINING THE LAST TERM ADDED TO EACH
620.   C    ELEMENT OF CSUM(J)
621.   C    CIMN(J) IS THE VECTOR CONTAINING 1/TON TIMES THE NEW TERM TO BE
622.   C    ADDED TO CSUM(J)
623.   C    CIMN(J) IS GENERATED FROM CIMO(J) BY A RECURSION RELATION:
624.   C        CIMN(J)= SUM OVER L OF (AP(J,L)*CIMO(L))
625.   C    AP(I,J) IS THE REDUCED TRANSITION MATRIX FOR THE LONG-LIVED
626.   C    NUCLIDES
627.   C
628.        LOGICAL*1 LONG
629.        INTEGER*2 LOC,NONO,KD
630.        INTEGER*2 LOCP(2500)
631.        INTEGER*2 NOYP(800)
632.        INTEGER*2 NQ,NQU,NQUEUE
633.        REAL*8 BATE,RATM
634.        REAL*8 CIMN(800),CSUM(800),CIMNI
635.        DIMENSION AP(2500),CIMB(800),CIMO(800)
636.        DIMENSION QUR(50)
637.        COMMON/SERIES/ XP(800),XPAR(800),LONG(800)
638.        COMMON/DEBUGG/AP
639.        COMMON/FLEX/FLUX(1C),MMN,MOUT,INDEX,QXN,AXN,ERR,NOBLND,MZERO
640.        COMMON/EQ/XZERO(800),XZH(800),XTEMP(800),XNEW(10,800),
641.       1      B(800),D(800)
642.        COMMON/MATRIX/A(2500),LOC(2500),NONO(800),KD(800)
643.        COMMON/DEBUGG/AP
644.        COMMON/TERMD/DD(100),DXP(100),QUEUE(50),NQU(50),NQUEUE(50),NQ(800),
645.        NUL=0
646.        NN=0
647.   C    FIRST CONSTRUCT REDUCED TRANSITION MATRIX FOR LONG-LIVED ISOTOPES
648.        DO 220 L=1,ITOT
649.        IF(.NOT.LONG(L)) GO TO 210
650.        NUM=NONO(L)
651.        IF(M.GT.MMN.OR.M.EQ.MZERO)  NUM=KD(L)
652.        CIMB(L)=B(L)
653.        IF(NUM.LE.NUL) GO TO 210
654.        NS=NN+1
655.        N=NUL
656.        NL=NUM-NUL
657.        DO 200 N1=1,NL
658.        N=N+1
659.        J=LOC(N)
660.        DJ=-D(J)
661.   C
662.   C    THIS IS A TEST TO SEE IF ONE OF THE ASSYMPTOTIC SOLUTIONS APPLIES
663.   C
664.        IF(.NOT.LONG(J)) GO TO 10
           NN=NN+1
```

Sequence numbers (right margin): 00011100 through 00011690

```
665.           AP(NN)=A(N)                                          00011700
666.           LOCP(NN)=J                                           00011710
667.           GO TO 200                                            00011720
668.   C                                                            00011730
669.   C    GOING BACK UP THE CHAIN TO FIND A PARENT WHICH IS NOT IN 00011740
670.   C    EQUILIBRIUM                                             00011750
671.   10      NSAVE=0                                              00011760
672.           QUE=A(N)/DJ                                          00011770
673.           DRB=1.0                                              00011780
674.           CIMB(L)=CIMB(L)+QUE*B(J)                             00011790
675.           NQ(L)=0                                              00011800
676.           NQ(J)=L                                              00011810
677.   20      NUX=NONO(J)                                          00011820
678.           IF(M.GT.MMN.OR.M.EQ.MZERO)  NUX=KD(J)                00011830
679.           NUF=0                                                00011840
680.           IF(J.GT.1)  NUF=NONO(J-1)                            00011850
681.           NX=NUX-NUF                                           00011860
682.           IF(NX.LT.1)  GO TO 190                               00011870
683.           K=NUF                                                00011880
684.           DO 180 KK=1,NX                                       00011890
685.           K=K +1                                               00011900
686.           J1=LOC(K)                                            00011910
687.           CJ=-D(J1)                                            00011920
688.           KP=J                                                 00011930
689.   30      IF(J1.EQ.NQ(KP))  GO TO 180                          00011940
690.           KP=NQ(KP)                                            00011950
691.           IF(KP.NE.0)  GO TO 30                                00011960
692.           AKDJQ=QUE*A(K)/DJ                                    00011970
693.           IF(.NOT.LONG(J1))  GO TO 160                         00011980
694.           TRM=1.0-XP(J1)                                       00011990
695.           IF(TRM.LT.1.0E-6)  GO TO 120                         00012000
696.           NQ(J1)=J                                             00012010
697.           I=1                                                  00012020
698.           KP=J1                                                00012030
699.   40      DD(I)=-D(KP)                                         00012040
700.           DXP(I)=XP(KP)                                        00012050
701.           KP=NQ(KP)                                            00012060
702.           IF(KP.EQ.0)  GO TO 50                                00012070
703.           I=I+1                                                00012080
704.           IF(I.LE.100)  GO TO 40                               00012090
705.   C    IF QUEUE OF SHORT-LIVED NUCLIDES EXCEEDS 100 ISOTOPES, TERMINATE 00012100
706.   C    CHAIN AND WRITE MESSAGE                                 00012110
707.           PRINT 9000,   M,L,J1,J,AKDJQ                         00012120
708.   9000    FORMAT('1TOO LONG A QUEUE HAS BEEN FORMED IN TERM',4I5,E12.5) 00012130
709.           GO TO 190                                            00012140
710.   50      BATM=0.D0                                            00012150
711.           IM=I-1                                               00012160
712.           DO 110 I=2,IM                                        00012170
713.           DL=DD(I)                                             00012180
714.           XPL=DXP(I)                                           00012190
715.           BATE=0.D0                                            00012200
716.           I1=I-1                                               00012210
717.   C    D R VONDY FORM OF BATEMAN EQUATIONS -- ORNL-TM-361      00012220
718.           DO 100 KB=1,I1                                       00012230
719.           XPJ=DXP(KB)                                          00012240
720.           IF(XPL+XPJ.LT.ERR)  GO TO 100                        00012250
721.           DK=DD(KB)                                            00012260
722.           PROD=(DL/DK-1.0)                                     00012270
723.           DKR=PROD                                             00012280
724.                                                                00012290
```

```
      IF( ABS(PROD).GT.1.E-4) GO TO 60                                   00012300
C     USE THIS FORM FOR TWO NEARLY EQUAL HALF-LIVES                      00012310
      PROD=T*DK*XPJ*(1.0-0.5*(DL-DJ)*T)                                  00012320
      GO TO 70                                                           00012330
60    PROD=(XPJ-XPL)/PROD                                               00012340
      PROI=XPJ/DKR                                                       00012350
70    S1=2./(DK*T)                                                       00012360
      DO 90 JK=1,I1                                                      00012370
      IF(JK.EQ.KB) GO TO 90                                             00012380
      S=1.0-CK/CD(JK)                                                    00012390
      IF( ABS(S).GT.1.E-4) GO TO 80    PROD=PROI                        00012400
      IF(ABS(DKR).GT.1.0E-4) PROD=PROI                                  00012410
      S=S1                                                               00012420
80    PI=PI*S                                                            00012430
      IF(ABS(PI).GT.1.E25)   GO TO 100                                  00012440
90    CONTINUE                                                           00012450
      BATE=BATE+PROD/PI                                                  00012460
100   CONTINUE                                                           00012470
C     IF SUMMATION IS NEGATIVE, SET EQUAL TO ZERO AND PRINT MESSAGE     00012480
      IF(BATE.LT.0.D0)   PRINT 9001,  L,IM,BATE,BATM                     00012490
9001  FORMAT('IBATE IS NEGATIVE IN TERM. THERE ARE MORE THAN TWO SHORT-L00012500
     1IVED NUCLIDES IN A CHAIN WITH NEARLY EQUAL DIAGONAL ELEMENTS'/     00012510
     2' L,IM,BATE,BATM = ',2I5,1P2E12.5)                                 00012520
      IF(BATE.LT.0.D0)   BATE=0.D0                                       00012530
      BATM=BATM+BATE                                                     00012540
110   CONTINUE                                                           00012550
      DRA=AKDJQ*DJ*(TRM-BATM)/TRM                                        00012560
      GO TO 130                                                          00012570
120   DRA=AKDJQ*AMAX1(DRB,0.0)*DJ                                        00012580
130   IF(NS.GT.NN) GO TO 150                                            00012590
      DO 140 LJ=NS,NN                                                    00012600
      IF(LOCP(LJ).NE.J1)   GO TO 140                                    00012610
      AP(LJ)=AP(LJ)+DRA                                                  00012620
      GO TO 180                                                          00012630
140   CONTINUE                                                           00012640
150   NN=NN+1                                                            00012650
      AP(NN)=DRA                                                         00012660
      LOCP(NN)=J1                                                        00012670
      GO TO 180                                                          00012680
160   IF(AKDJQ.LE.1.0E-06)   GO TO 180                                  00012690
      IF(NSAVE.GE.50) GO TO 180                                         00012700
170   NSAVE=NSAVE+1                                                      00012710
      NQUEUE(NSAVE)=J1                                                   00012720
      QUEUE(NSAVE)=AKDJQ                                                 00012730
      NQU(NSAVE)=J                                                       00012740
      QUB(NSAVE)=DRB-1./(DJ*T)                                          00012750
      GO TO 180                                                          00012760
180   CONTINUE                                                           00012770
190   IF(NSAVE.LE.0) GO TO 200                                          00012780
      J=NQUEUE(NSAVE)                                                    00012790
      QUE=QUEUE(NSAVE)                                                   00012800
      NQ(J)=NQU(NSAVE)                                                   00012810
      DRB=QUB(NSAVE)                                                     00012820
      CIMB(L)=CIMB(L)+QUE*B(J)*AMAX1(DRB,0.0)                           00012830
      NSAVE=NSAVE-1                                                      00012840
      GO TO 20                                                           00012850
200   CONTINUE                                                           00012860
210   NUL=NGNO(L)                                                        00012870
      NQUP(L)=NN                                                         00012880
220   CONTINUE                                                           00012890
```

C-14

```
785.  C    FIND NORM OF MATRIX AND ESTIMATE ERROR AS DESCRIBED IN LAPIDUS     00012900
786.  C    AND LUUS, OPTIMAL CONTROL OF ENGINEERING PROCESSES BLAISDELL 1967  00012910
787.  C    FIND THE MINIMUM OF THE MAXIMUM ROW SUM AND THE MAXIMUM COLUMN SUM 00012920
788.       ASUM =0.0                                                         00012930
789.       ASUMJ=0.0                                                         00012940
790.       NUL=1                                                             00012950
791.       DO 250 I=1,ITOT                                                   00012960
792.       IF(.NGT.LONG(I)) GC TO 250                                        00012970
793.       DI=-D(I)*T                                                        00012980
794.       AJ=DI                                                             00012990
795.       NUM=NCNP(I)                                                       00013000
796.       IF(NUL.GT.NUM) GO TO 240                                          00013010
797.       DO 230 N=NUL,NUM                                                  00013020
798.  230  AJ=AJ+AP(N)                                                       00013030
799.  240  AI=DI+DI                                                          00013040
800.       IF(AI.GT.ASUM )    ASUM =AI                                       00013050
801.       IF(AJ.GT.ASUMJ)    ASUMJ=AJ                                       00013060
802.  250  NUL=NCNP(I)+1                                                     00013070
803.       IF(ASUMJ.LT.ASUM)  ASUM=ASUMJ                                     00013080
804.  C    USE ASUM TO DECIDE HOW MANY TERMS ARE REQUIRED AND ESTIMATE ERROR 00013090
805.       NLARGE=3.5*ASUM +5.                                              00013100
806.       XLARGE=NLARGE                                                     00013110
807.       ERRI=EXP(ASUM )*(ASUM )*(ASUM *2.71828/XLARGE)**NLARGE/SORT(6.2832*XLARGE) 00013120
808.       IF(ERRI.GT.1.E-3)  PRINT 9002,    ERR1.ASUM ,NLARGE              00013130
809.  9002 FORMAT('0MAXIMUM ERROR GT 0.001,  =*F10.6,' TRACE = 'F10.4,      00013140
810.      1  ' NLARGE = '16)                                                00013150
811.  C    NEXT GENERATE MATRIX EXPONENTIAL SOLUTION                         00013160
812.       DO 260 I=1,ITOT                                                   00013170
813.       CSUM(I)=XTEMP(I)                                                  00013180
814.       CIMN(I)=XTEMP(I)                                                  00013190
815.  260  CONTINUE                                                          00013200
816.       ERR3=0.C01*EPR                                                    00013210
817.       DO 310 NT=1,NLARGE                                                00013220
818.       DO 270 I=1,ITOT                                                   00013230
819.       CIM0(I)=CIMN(I)                                                   00013240
820.  270  CONTINUE                                                          00013250
821.       TDN=T/NT                                                          00013260
822.       NUL=1                                                             00013270
823.       DO 300 I=1,ITOT                                                   00013280
824.       IF(.NGT.LONG(I)) GO TO 300                                        00013290
325.       NUM=NUNP(I)                                                       00013300
326.       CIMNI=0.0                                                         00013310
327.       IF(NT.EC.1) CIMNI=CIM3(I)                                         00013320
328.       IF(NUL.GT.NUM) GO TO 290                                          00013330
329.       DO 280 N=NUL,NUM                                                  00013340
330.       J=LOCP(N)                                                         00013350
331.  280  CIMNI=CIMNI+AP(N)*CIM0(J)                                         00013360
332.  290  CIMNI=CIMNI+D(I)*CIM0(I)                                          00013370
333.       CIMNI=TDN*CIMNI                                                   00013380
334.       IF(DADS(CIMNI).LT.ERR3)    CIMNI=0.DO                             00013390
335.       CIMN(I)=CIMNI                                                     00013400
336.       CSUM(I)=CSUM(I)+CIMNI                                             00013410
337.       NUL=NCNP(I)+1                                                     00013420
338.  300  CONTINUE                                                          00013430
339.  310  CONTINUE                                                          00013440
340.       DO 320 I=1,ITOT                                                   00013450
341.       IF(CSUM(I).LT.ERR)  CSUM(I)=0.0                                   00013460
342.       IF(CLONG(I)) XNEW(M,I)=CSUM(I)                                    00013470
343.  320  CONTINUE                                                          00013480
843.       RETURN                                                            
844.       END                                                               00013490
```

```
      SUBROUTINE DECAY(M,T,ITOT)
C     DECAY TREATS SHORT-LIVED ISOTOPES AT BEGINNING OF CHAINS USING
C     BATEMAN EQUATIONS
      LOGICAL*1 LONG
      REAL*8 BATE
      INTEGER*2 LOC,NONO,KD
      INTEGER*2 NQ,NQU,NQUEUE
      COMMON/DEBUGG/AP(2500)
      COMMON/SERIES/ XP(800),XPAR(800),LONG(800)
      COMMON/FLEX/FLUX(1C),MMN,MOUT,INDEX,QXN,AXN,ERR,NOBLND,MZERO
      COMMUN/SQ/XZFRQ(800),XZH(800),XTEMP(800),XNEW(10,800),
     1  B(800),D(800)
      COMMON/MATRIX/A(25G0),LOC(2500),NONO(800),KD(800)
      CQMMQ/FTERMD/DD(10G),DXP(100),QUEUE(50),NQU(50),NQUEUE(50),NQ(800)
      DO 10 I=1,ITOT
      XPAR(I)=C.0
      LONG(I)=.FALSE.
      XPI=0.0
      DT=D(I)*T
      IF(DT.LT.-50.) GO TO 10
      IF(ABS(DT).LF.AXN) LONG(I)=.TRUE.
      XPI=EXP(OT)
   10 XP(I)=XPI
      NUL=1
      DO 160 L=1,ITOT
      XTEM=0.0
      DL=-D(L)
      NUM=NONO(1L)
      IF(M.GT.MMN.OR.M.EQ.MZERO)  NUM=KD(L)
      IF(NUM.LT.NUL) GO TO 150
      DO 140 N=NUL,NUM
      J=LOC(N)
      DJ=-D(J)
      IF(LONG(JJ) GO TO 140
C     USC THIS FORM FOR TWO NEARLY EQUAL HALF-LIVES
      IF(ABS(DL/DJ-1.0).LE.1.0E-5)  XTEM=XTEM+XTEMP(J)*A(N)*XP(J)*T
      IF(ABS(DL/DJ-1.0).GT.1.0E-5)
     1   XTEM=XTEM+XTEMP(J)*A(N)*(XP(J)-XP(L))/(DL-DJ)
      QUE=A(N)/DJ
      NQ(L)=0
      NQ(J)=L
      NSAVE=0
   20 NUX=NONO(J)
      IF(M.GT.MMN.OR.M.EQ.MZERO)  NUX=KD(J)
      NUF=1
      IF(J.GT.1)  NUF=NONO(J-1)+1
      IF(NUF.GT.NUX)  GO TO 130
      DO 120 K=NUF,NUX
      J1=LOC(K)
      IF(LONG(J1)) GO TO 120
      KP=J
   30 IF(J1.EQ.NQ(KP))  GO TO 120
      KP=NQ(KP)
      IF(KP.NE.0)  GO TO 30
      DJ=-D(J1)
      AKDJQ=A(K)/DJ*QUE
      IF(AKDJQ.LE.1.0E-06)  GO TO 120
      I=1
      NQ(J1)=J
      KP=J1
```

```
40    DD(I)=-D(KP)                                                    00014100
      DXP(I)=XP(KP)                                                   00014110
      KP=NQ(KP)                                                       00014120
      IF(KP.EQ.0) GO TO 50                                            00014130
      I=I+1                                                           00014140
      IF(I.LE.100) GO TO 40                                           00014150
      PRINT 9000, M,L,J1,J,AKDJQ                                      00014160
9000  FORMAT('1',4I5,E12.5)                                           00014170
      GO TO 130                                                       00014180
50    BATE=0.D0                                                       00014190
      I1=I-1                                                          00014200
      XPL=XP(L)                                                       00014210
C   D R VONDY FORM OF BATEMAN EQUATIONS -- ORNL-TM-361               00014220
      DO 100 KB=1,I1                                                  00014230
      XPJ=DXP(KB)                                                     00014240
      IF(XPL+XPJ.LT.ERR) GO TO 100                                    00014250
      DK=DD(KB)                                                       00014260
      PROD=(DL/DK-1.0)                                                00014270
      DKR=PRCD                                                        00014280
      IF( ABS(PROD).GT.1.E-4) GO TO 60                                00014290
      PROD=T*DK*XPJ*(1.0-0.5*(DL-DJ)*T)                               00014300
      GO TO 70                                                        00014310
60    PROD=(XPJ-XPL)/PROD                                             00014320
      PROL=XPJ/DKR                                                    00014330
70    PI=1.0                                                          00014340
      S1=2./(DK*T)                                                    00014350
      DO 90 JK=1,I1                                                   00014360
      IF(JK.EQ.KB) GO TO 90                                           00014370
      S=1.0-DK/DD(JK)                                                 00014380
      IF( ABS(S).GT.1.E-4) GO TO 80                                   00014390
C   USE THIS FORM FOR TWO NEARLY EQUAL HALF-LIVES                    00014400
      IF(ABS(DKR).GT.1.0E-4) PROD=PRO1                                00014410
      S=S1                                                            00014420
80    PI=PI*S                                                         00014430
      IF(ABS(PI).GT.1.E25) GO TO 100                                  00014440
90    CONTINUE                                                        00014450
100   BATE=BATE+PROD/PI                                               00014460
      CONTINUE                                                        00014470
      IF(BATE.LT.0.D0) PRINT 9001, L,I,BATE,XTEM,XTEM,XTEMP(J1),AKDJQ 00014480
9001  FORMAT(' L,I,BATE,XTEM,XTEM,XTEMP(J1),AKDJQ = ',2I5,1P4E12.5)   00014490
      IF(BATE.LT.0.D0) BATE=0.D0                                      00014500
      XTEM=XTEM+XTEMP(J1)*AKDJQ*BATE                                  00014510
      IF(NSAVE.GE.50) GO TO 120                                       00014520
110   NSAVE=NSAVE+1                                                   00014530
      NQUEUE(NSAVE)=J1                                                00014540
      QUEUE(NSAVE)=AKDJQ                                              00014550
      NQU(NSAVE)=J                                                    00014560
120   CONTINUE                                                        00014570
130   IF(NSAVE.LE.0) GO TO 140                                        00014580
      J=NQUEUE(NSAVE)                                                 00014590
      QUE=QUEUE(NSAVE)                                                00014600
      NQ(J)=NQU(NSAVE)                                                00014610
      NSAVE=NSAVE-1                                                   00014620
      GO TO 20                                                        00014630
140   CONTINUE                                                        00014640
      IF(LONG(L)) XPAR(L)=XTEM/XP(L)                                  00014650
150   NUL=NONO(L)+1                                                   00014660
      IF(.NOT.LONG(L)) XNEW(M,L)=XTEM+XTEMP(L)*XP(L)                  00014670
160   CONTINUE                                                        00014680
      DO 170 I=1,ITOT                                                 00014690
```

905.
906.
907.
908.
909.
910.
911.
912.
913.
914.
915.
916.
917.
918.
919.
920.
921.
922.
923.
924.
925.
926.
927.
928.
929.
930.
931.
932.
933.
934.
935.
936.
937.
938.
939.
940.
941.
942.
943.
944.
945.
946.
947.
948.
949.
950.
951.
952.
953.
954.
955.
956.
957.
958.
959.
960.
961.
962.
963.
964.

```
        IF(LONG(I)) XTEMP(I)=XTEMP(I)+XPAR(I)                              00014700
        IF(.NOT.LONG(I)) XTEMP(I)=0.0                                      00014710
170     CONTINUE                                                          00014720
        RETURN                                                            00014730
        END                                                               00014740
        SUBROUTINE EQUIL(M,ITOT)                                          00014750
C                                                                         00014760
C   EQUIL PUTS SHORT-LIVED DAUGHTERS IN EQUILIBRIUM WITH PARENTS          00014770
C   EQUIL USES GAUSS-SEICEL ITERATION TO GENERATE STEADY STATE            00014780
C   CONCENTRATIONS                                                        00014790
C                                                                         00014800
        LOGICAL*1 LONG                                                    00014810
        INTEGER*2 LOC,NONO,KD                                             00014820
        COMMON/EQ/XZFRD(800),XZH(800),XTEMP(800),XNEW(10,800),            00014830
       1 B(800),D(800)                                                    00014840
        COMMON/MATRIX/A(25CO),LOC(2500),NONO(800),KD(800)                 00014850
        COMMON/FLEX/FLUX(10),MMN,MOUT,INDEX,QXN,AXN,ERR,NOBLND,MZERO      00014860
        COMMON/SERIES/ XP(800),XPAR(800),LONG(800)                       00014870
        DO 10 I=1,ITOT                                                    00014880
        XPAR(I)=0.0                                                       00014890
        IF(.NOT.LONG(I)) GO TO 10                                         00014900
        XTEMP(I)=XTEMP(I)*XP(I)                                           00014910
        XPAR(I)=AMAX1(XNEW(M,I)-XTEMP(I),0.0)                            00014920
10      CONTINUE                                                          00014930
        ITER=1                                                            00014940
20      N=0                                                               00014950
        BIG=0.0                                                           00014960
        DO 60 I=1,ITOT                                                    00014970
        NUM=NONO(I)-N                                                     00014980
        DI=-D(I)                                                          00014990
        IF(LONG(I)) GO TO 50                                             00015000
        XNW=B(I)                                                          00015010
        IF(M.GT.MMN.OR.M.EQ.MZERO)  NUM=KD(I)-N                           00015020
        IF(NUM.EQ.0) GO TO 31                                             00015030
        DO 30 K=1,NUM                                                     00015040
        N=N+1                                                             00015050
        J=LOC(N)                                                          00015060
        DJ=-D(J)                                                          00015070
        XJ=XPAR(J)                                                        00015080
        IF(LONG(J)) XJ=XJ+XTEMP(J)/(1.0-DJ/DI)                           00015090
        XNW=XNW+A(N)*XJ                                                   00015100
30      CONTINUE                                                          00015110
31      XNW=XNW/DI                                                        00015120
        IF(XNW.LT.1.0E-50) GO TO 40                                       00015130
        ARG=ABS((XNW-XPAR(I))/XNW)                                       00015140
        IF(ARG.GT.BIG) BIG=ARG                                           00015150
40      XPAR(I)=XNW                                                       00015160
50      N=NONO(I)                                                         00015170
60      CONTINUE                                                          00015180
        IF(BIG.LT.QXN )   GOTO 70                                         00015190
        ITER=ITER+1                                                       00015200
        IF(ITER.LT.100) GO TO 20                                          00015210
        PRINT 9000                                                        00015220
        STOP                                                              00015230
70      DO 80 I=1,ITOT                                                    00015240
        IF(.NOT.LONG(I)) XNEW(M,I)=XNEW(M,I)+XPAR(I)                      00015250
80      CONTINUE                                                          00015260
        RETURN                                                            00015270
9000    FORMAT(' GAUSS SEICEL ITERATION DID NOT CONVERGE IN EQUIL')       00015280
        END                                                               00015290
```

```
      SUBROUTINE NUDATA(NLIBE)                                        00015300
C  NUDATA VERSION TO HANDLE THREE TYPES OF NUCLEAR DATA LIBRARIES     00015310
C  HAS POINTER, NLIBE.  = 1 FOR HTGR                                  00015320
C                       = 2 FOR LIGHT WATER REACTOR                   00015330
C                       = 3 FOR LMFBR                                 00015340
C                       = 4 FOR MSBR                                  00015350
C                                                                     00015360
      INTEGER*2 LOC,NONO,KD                                          00015370
      INTEGER*2 ELF(99),STA(2)                                       00015380
      INTEGER*2 KAP(800),MMAX(800)                                   00015390
      INTEGER*2 NAME(3)                                              00015400
      DIMENSION COEFF(7,800),NPROD(7,800),CAPT(6),                    00015410
     1 NUCAL(6),NSNRS(5),            YIELD(5,500),TYLD(5)             00015420
      DIMENSION Y(5)                                                 00015430
      DIMENSION SKIP(20)                                             00015440
      DIMENSION MSRS(20)                                             00015450
      COMMON/LABEL/ELE,STA                                           00015460
      COMMON/FLEX/FLUX(1G),MMN,MOUT,INDEX,QXN,AXN,ERR,NOBLND,MZERO    00015470
      COMMON/EQ/XZERO(800),XZH(800),XTEMP(800),XNEW(10,800),          00015480
     1 8(800),D(800)                                                 00015490
      COMMON/MPC/MPCTAB,AMPC(800),MMPC(800)                          00015500
      COMMON/FLUXN/T(22),POWER(10),TOCAP(800),FISS(100),DIS(800),ILITE, 00015510
     1 IACT,IFP,ITOT,NON,INPT                                        00015520
      COMMON/CUT/NUCL(80C),TITLE(20),Q(800),FG(800),CUTOFF(7),       00015530
     1 POW,BURNUP,FLUX8,MSTAR,ALPHAN(100),SPONF(100),ABUND(500),      00015540
     2 BASIS(10),ICONSI,IUNIT                                        00015550
      COMMON/MATRIX/A(2500),LOC(2500),KAP(1),(XZERO(401),MMAX(1),     00015560
      EQUIVALENCE (XZH(1),COEFF(1,1)),(XNEW(1,401),NPROD(1,1))        00015570
     1           ( XZH(1),COEFF(1,1)),(XNEW(1,401),NPROD(1,1))        00015580
      EQUIVALENCE (AI,DLAM)                                          00015590
      DATA NUCAL/-20030,-10000,10,11,-10,-9/                         00015600
      DATA MSRS/92330,922350,902320,922380,942390,922350,942410,     00015610
     1 927380,942390,942410,922350,942400,922380,942390,922330,      00015620
     2 922350,9C2320,922380,942390/                                  00015630
C                                                                     00015640
C  PROGRAM TO COMPUTE A MATRIX (TRANSITION MATRIX) FROM NUCLEAR DATA  00015650
C                                                                     00015660
      READ 9011,          (TITLE(I),I=1,18),NLIBE                     00015670
      IF(NLIBE.LT.0) PROGRAM WILL READ TAPE IN CASDAR FORMAT          00015680
      IGWC=0                                                         00015690
      IF(NLIBE.GT.0) GO TO 10                                        00015700
      IGWC=1                                                         00015710
      NLIBE=-NLIBE                                                   00015720
      PRINT 9000                                                    00015730
 9000 FORMAT(1HO,'WILL READ TAPE GENERATED BY CASDAR')               00015740
 10   NI=4-NLIBE                                                     00015750
 20   READ 9001,      THERM,RES,FAST,ERR,NMO,NDAY,NYR,MPCTAB,INPT,IR  00015760
      PRINT 9005,        NMO,NDAY,NYR                                 00015770
      PRINT 9006                                                    00015780
      PRINT 9007                                                    00015790
      PRINT 9008                                                    00015800
      PRINT 9009                                                    00015810
      PRINT 9010                                                    00015820
      PRINT 9013                                                    00015830
      PRINT 9014                                                    00015840
C                                                                     00015850
C  THERM = RATIO OF THERMAL FLUX TO TOTAL FLUX                        00015860
C  RES = RATIO OF RESONANCE FLUX TO TOTAL FLUX                        00015870
C  FAST = RATIO OF FAST FLUX TO TOTAL FLUX                            00015880
C  ERR = TRUNCATION ERROR LIMIT                                       00015890
```

```
C       READ DATA FOR LIGHT ELEMENTS                                            00015900
C                                                                               00015910
        K=5*(NLIBE-1)                                                           00015920
        DO 30 K1=1,5                                                            00015930
        K2=K+K1                                                                 00015940
30      NSORS(K1)=MSRS(K2)                                                      00015950
        PRINT 9018,   THERM,RES,FAST,(NSORS(K),K=1,5),NLIBE                     00015960
        I=0                                                                     00015970
        NUTAPE=0                                                                00015980
40      I=I+1                                                                   00015990
50      READ(8,9034,END=260)NUCL(I),DLAM,IU,FB1,FP,FP1,FT,FA,FSF,              00016000
       1Q(I),FG(I),ABUND(I),WMPC(I),AMPC(I)                                     00016010
        IF(IGWC.GT.0)   GO TO 70                                                00016020
        DO 60 N=1,NLIBE                                                         00016030
60      READ(8,9035) SIGTH,FNG1,FNA,FNP,RITH,FINA,FINP,SIGMEV,FN2N1,FFNA,      00016040
       1             FFNP,IT                                                    00016050
        GO TO 90                                                                00016060
70      DO 80 N=1,NLIBE                                                         00016070
80      READ(8,9040) SIGTH,FNG1,FNA,FNP,RITH,FINA,FINP,SIGMEV,FN2N1,FFNA,      00016080
       1             FFNP,IT                                                    00016090
90      IF(N1.EQ.0)GO TO 110                                                    00016100
        DO 100 N=1,N1                                                           00016110
100     READ(8,9036)   SKIP                                                     00016120
110     IF(IT.EQ.0) GO TO 50                                                    00016130
120     M=0                                                                     00016140
        CALL HALF(A1,IU)                                                        00016150
        NUCLI=NUCL(I)                                                           00016160
        IF(NUCLI.EQ.0)   GO TO 260                                              00016170
        CALL NOAH(NUCLI,NAME)                                                   00016180
        IF(MOD(I-1,50) .EQ. 0) PRINT 9012,      (TITLE (N),N=1,18'             00016190
        IF(MOD(I-1,50) .EQ. 0) PRINT 9016                                       00016200
        SIGTH=THERM*SIGTH                                                       00016210
        RITH=RES*RITH                                                           00016220
        SIGMEV=FAST*SIGMEV                                                      00016230
        SIGNA=SIGTH*FNA+RITH*FINA+SIGMEV*FFNA                                   00016240
        SIGNP=SIGTH*FNP+RITH*FINP+SIGMEV*FFNP                                   00016250
        FNG=1.0-FNA-FNP                                                         00016260
        IF(FNG.LT.1.0E-4)FNG=0.                                                 00016270
        FING=1.0-FINA-FINP                                                      00016280
        IF(FING.LT.1.0E-4)FING=0.                                              00016290
       -FN2N=1.0-FFNA-FFNP                                                      00016300
        IF(FN2N.LT.1.0E-4)FN2N=0.                                              00016310
        SIGNG=SIGTH*FNG+RITH*FING                                              00016320
        SIGN2N=SIGMEV*FN2N                                                      00016330
130     PRINT 9033,      NAME,       DLAM,FB1,FP,FP1,FT,FA,SIGNG,             00016340
       1             FNG1,SIGN2N,FN2N1,SIGNA,SIGNP,Q(I),FG(I),ABUND(I)         00016350
C       TEST RADIOACTIVITY                                                      00016360
C                                                                               00016370
140     IF(A1.LE.ERR)   GO TO 180                                               00016380
        ABETA=1.0                                                               00016390
C                                                                               00016400
C       TEST POSITRON EMISSION                                                  00016410
C                                                                               00016420
        IF(FP .LT. ERR) GO TO 150                                              00016430
        M=M+1                                                                   00016440
        COEFF(M,I)=FP*A1                                                        00016450
        NPROD(M,I)=NUCLI-10000                                                 00016460
        ABETA=ABETA-FP                                                         00016470
C                                                                               00016480
C       TEST POSITRON EMISSION TO EXCITED STATE OF PRODUCT NUCLIDE             00016490
```

```
C           IF(FP1 .LT. ERR) GO TO 150                                    00016500
            M=M+1                                                         00016510
            COEFF(M,I)=FP1*COEFF(M-1,I)                                   00016520
            NPROD(M,I)=NPROD(M-1,I)+1                                     00016530
            COEFF(M-1,I)=COEFF(M-1,I)-COEFF(M,I)                          00016540
C                                                                         00016550
C           TEST ISOMERIC TRANSITION                                      00016560
C                                                                         00016570
150         IF(FT .LT.ERR) GO TO 160                                      00016580
            M=M+1                                                         00016590
            COEFF(M,I)=FT*AI                                              00016600
            NPROD(M,I)=NUCLI                                              00016610
            ABETA=ABETA-FT                                                00016620
C                                                                         00016630
C           TEST ALPHA EMISSION                                          00016640
C                                                                         00016650
160         IF(FA .LT. ERR) GO TO 170                                     00016660
            M=M+1                                                         00016670
            COEFF(M,I)=FA*AI                                              00016680
            NPROD(M,I)=NUCLI-20040                                        00016690
            M=M+1                                                         00016700
            COEFF(M,I)=COEFF(M-1,I)                                       00016710
            NPROD(M,I)=20040                                              00016720
            ABETA=ABETA-FA                                                00016730
C                                                                         00016740
C           TEST NEGATRON EMISSION                                        00016750
C                                                                         00016760
170         IF(ABETA.LT.1.E-4) GO TO 180                                  00016770
            M=M+1                                                         00016780
            COEFF(M,I)=ABETA*AI                                           00016790
            NPROD(M,I)=NUCLI+10000                                        00016800
C                                                                         00016810
C           TEST NEGATRON EMISSION TO EXCITED STATE OF PRODUCT NUCLIDE    00016820
C                                                                         00016830
            IF(FB1 .LT. ERR)GO TO 180                                     00016840
            M=M+1                                                         00016850
            COEFF(M,I)=FB1*COEFF(M-1,I)                                   00016860
            NPROD(M,I)=NPROD(M-1,I)+1                                     00016870
            COEFF(M-1,I)=COEFF(M-1,I)-COEFF(M,I)                          00016880
C                                                                         00016890
C           COMPUTE NEUTRON CAPTURE CROSS SECTIONS IN THREE REGIONS       00016900
C                                                                         00016910
180         KAP(I)=M                                                      00016920
            DO 190 KI=1,6                                                 00016930
190         CAPT(KI) =0.0                                                 00016940
            CAPT(1)=SIGNA                                                 00016950
            CAPT(2)=SIGNP                                                 00016960
            CAPT(4)=SIGNG*FNG1                                            00016970
            CAPT(3)=SIGNG-CAPT(4)                                         00016980
            CAPT(6)=SIGN2N*FN2N1                                          00016990
            CAPT(5)=SIGN2N-CAPT(6)                                        00017010
200         TOCAP(I)=0.0                                                  00017020
C                                                                         00017030
C           TOTAL NEUTRON CROSS SECTION FOR NUCLIDE(I)                    00017040
            DO 220 K=1,6                                                  00017050
            CAPK(I)=CAPT(K)                                               00017060
            IF(CAPKI.LT.ERR)  GO TO 220                                   00017070
            M=M+1                                                         00017080
            NPROD(M,I)=NUCLI+NUCAL(K)                                     00017090
            COEFF(M,I)=CAPKI
```

C-21

```
        TOCAP(I)=TOCAP(I)+CAPKI                                              00017100
        IF(K.NE.1) GO TO 210                                                 00017110
        M=M+1                                                                00017120
        COEFF(M,I)=COEFF(M-1,I)                                              00017130
        NPROD(M,I)=20040                                                     00017140
210     IF(K.NE.2) GO TO 220                                                 00017150
        M=M+1                                                                00017160
        COEFF(M,I)=COEFF(M-1,I)                                              00017170
        NPROD(M,I)=10010                                                     00017180
220     CONTINUE                                                             00017190
230     IF(MOD(NUCLI,  10).EQ.0) GO TO 250                                   00017200
        DO 240 K=1,M                                                         00017210
240     NPROD(K,I)=NPROD(K,I)-1                                              00017220
250     MMAX(I) =M                                                          00017230
        IF(M.GT.7)    PRINT 9039, M                                         00017240
        DIS(I)=A1                                                            00017250
        GO TO 40                                                             00017260
260     ILITE = I-1                                                         00017270
        IACT=0                                                               00017280
C                                                                            00017290
C       READ DATA ON ACTINIDES                                              00017300
C                                                                            00017310
270     READ(8,9034,END=450)NUCL(II),DLAM,IU,FB1,FP,FP1,FT,FA,FSF,          00017320
       1Q(II),FG(II),DUMMY,WMPC(II),AMPC(II)                                00017330
        DO 280 N=1,NLIBE                                                     00017340
        READ(8,9037) SIGNG,RING,FNG1,SIGF,RIF,SIGFF,SIGN2N,FN2N1,SIGN3N,IT  00017350
280     CONTINUE                                                             00017360
        IF(N1.EQ.0) GO TO 300                                               00017370
        DO 290 N=1,N1                                                        00017380
290     READ(8,9036)   SKIP                                                  00017390
300     IF(IT .EQ. 0) GO TO 270                                             00017400
310     M=0                                                                 00017410
        NUCLI=NUCL(I)                                                        00017420
        IF(NUCLI.EQ.0)    GO TO 450                                         00017430
        DO 320 K=1,5                                                         00017440
        IF(NUCLI.EQ.NSORS(K)) NSORS(K)=I                                     00017450
320     CONTINUE                                                             00017460
        CALL HALF(A1,IU)                                                     00017470
        CALL NOAH(NUCLI,NAME)                                                00017480
        SIGNG=THERM*SIGNG+RES*RING                                           00017490
        SIGF =THERM*SIGF +RES*RIF +FAST*SIGFF                                00017500
        SIGN2N=SIGN2N*FAST                                                   00017510
        SIGN3N=SIGN3N*FAST                                                   0C017520
        IF(MOD(IACT,50).EQ.0)    PRINT 9012,        (TITLE (N),N=1,18)       00017530
        IF(MOD(IACT,50).EQ.0) PRINT 9024                                     00017540
        PRINT 9026,      NAME,    DLAM,FB1,FP,FP1,FT,FA,FSF,SIGNG,00017550
       1                          FNG1,SIGF,SIGN2N,SIGN3N,Q(II),FG(II)      00017560
340     IACT=IACT+1                                                         00017570
C                                                                            00017580
C       TEST RADIOACTIVITY                                                  00017590
C                                                                            00017600
        IF(A1.LT.ERR)   GO TO 380                                           00017610
        ABETA=1.0                                                           00017620
C       TEST POSITRON EMISSION                                              00017630
        IF(FP .LT. ERR) GO TO 350                                           00017640
        ABETA=ABETA-FP                                                      00017650
        M=M+1                                                               00017660
        COEFF(M,I)=FP*A1                                                    00017670
        NPROD(M,I)=NUCLI-10000                                              00017680
C       POSITRON EMISSION TO EXCITED STATE                                 00017690
```

```
          IF(FP1 .LT. ERR)GO TO 350                              00017700
          M=M+1                                                  00017710
          COEFF(M,I)=FP1*COEFF(M-1,I)                            00017720
          NPROD(M,I)=NPROD(M-1,I)+1                              00017730
          COEFF(M-1,I)=COEFF(M-1,I)-COEFF(M,I)                   00017740
C         ISOMERIC TRANSITION                                    00017750
          IF(FT .LT.ERR)GO TO 360                                00017760
          M=M+1                                                  00017770
          COEFF(M,I)=FT*A1                                       00017780
          NPROD(M,I)=NUCLI                                       00017790
          ABETA=ABETA-FT                                         00017800
C         ALPHA EMISSION                                         00017810
  360     IF(FA .LT.ERR)GO TO 370                                00017820
          M=M+1                                                  00017830
          COEFF(M,I)=FA*A1                                       00017840
          NPROD(M,I)=NUCLI-20040                                 00017850
          M=M+1                                                  00017860
          COEFF(M,I)=COEFF(M-1,I)                                00017870
          NPROD(M,I)=20040                                       00017880
          ABETA=ABETA-FA                                         00017890
C         BETA DECAY                                             00017900
  370     IF(ABETA.LT.1.E-4) GO TO 380                           00017910
          M=M+1                                                  00017920
          COEFF(M,I)=ABETA*A1                                    00017930
          NPROD(M,I)=NUCLI+10000                                 00017940
          IF(FB1 .LT. ERR)GO TO 380                              00017950
          M=M+1                                                  00017960
          COEFF(M,I)=COEFF(M-1,I)*FB1                            00017970
          COEFF(M-1,I)=COEFF(M-1,I)-COEFF(M,I)                   00017980
          NPROD(M,I)=NPROD(M-1,I)+1                              00017990
C                                                                00018000
C         NEUTRON CAPTURE CROSS SECTIONS                         00018010
C                                                                00018020
  380     KAP(I)=M                                               00018030
          DO 390 K=1,6                                           00018040
  390     CAPT(K )=0.0                                           00018050
          CAPT(2)=SIGNG*FNG1                                     00018060
          CAPT(1)=SIGNG-CAPT(2)                                  00018070
          CAPT(4)=SIGN2N*FN2N1                                   00018080
          CAPT(3)=SIGN2N-CAPT(4)                                 00018090
          FISS(IACT)=SIGF                                        00018100
          TOCAP(I)=0.0                                           00018110
          DO 410 K=1,4                                           00018120
          CAPKI=CAPT(K)                                          00018130
          IF(CAPKI.LT.ERR)  GO TO 410                            00018140
          M=M+1                                                  00018150
          TOCAP(I)=TOCAP(I)+CAPKI                                00018160
          COEFF(M,I)=CAPKI                                       00018170
          NPROD(M,I)=NUCLI+NUCAL(K+2)                            00018180
  410     CONTINUE                                               00018190
          TOCAP(I)=TOCAP(I)+FISS(IACT)                           00018200
C         N-3N CROSS SECTION                                     00018210
          A17=SIGN3N                                             00018220
          IF(A17.LT.ERR) GO TO 420                               00018230
          M=M+1                                                  00018240
          COEFF(M  ,I)= A17                                      00018250
          NPROD(M  ,I)= NUCLI-20                                 00018260
          TOCAP(I)=TOCAP(I)+A17                                  00018270
  420     IF(MOD(NUCLI,10).EQ.0) GO TO 440                       00018280
          DO 430 K=1,M                                           00018290
```

```
430      NPROD(K,I)=NPROD(K,I)-1                                          00018300
440      MMAX(I)=M                                                        00018310
         IF(M.GT.7)  PRINT 9039, M                                       00018320
         SPONF(IACT)=FSF*A1*6.023E23                                     00018330
         ALPHAN(IACT)=FA*A1*6.023E13*Q(I)*3.65                           00018340
         DIS(I)=A1                                                       00018350
         I=I+1                                                           00018360
         GO TO 270                                                       00018370
         IL=0                                                            00018380
450      DO 460 K=1,5                                                    00018390
460      TYLD(K)=0.0                                                     00018400
C                                                                        00018410
C        READ DATA FOR FISSION PRODUCTS                                  00018420
C                                                                        00018430
470      READ(8,9034,END=690)NUCL(I),DLAM,IU,FB1,FP,FP1,FT,FA,FSF,       00018440
        1Q(I),FG(I),DUMMY,WMPC(I),AMPC(I)                                00018450
         DO 480 N=1,NLIBE                                                00018460
480      READ(8,9038) SIGNG,RING,FNG1,Y,IT                               00018470
         IF(N1.EQ.0) GO TO 500                                           00018480
         DO 490 N=1,N1                                                   00018490
490      READ(8,9036)  SKIP                                              00018500
500      IF(IT .EQ. 0) GO TO 470                                         00018510
510      M=0                                                             00018520
         CALL HALF(A1,IU)                                                00018530
520      NUCLI=NUCL(I)                                                   00018540
         IF(NUCLI.EQ.0) GO TO 690                                        00018550
         CALL NOAH(NUCLI,NAME)                                           00018560
         IF(MOD(IL,50).EQ. 0)  PRINT 9012,      (TITLE (N),N=1,18)       00018570
         SIGNG=THERM*SIGNG+RES*RING                                      00018580
         IF(NLIBE.EQ.3) GO TO 540                                        00018590
530      IF(MOD(IL     ,50).EQ.0)  PRINT 9019                            00018600
         PRINT 9021,    NAME,          DLAM,FB1,FP,FP1,FT,SIGNG,         00018610
        1 FNG1,Y,Q(I),FG(I)                                              00018620
         GO TO 550                                                       00018630
540      IF(MOD(IL,50).EQ.0) PRINT 9020         DLAM,FB1,FP,FP1,FT,SIGNG,FNG1,  00018640
         PRINT 9022,    NAME  ,   Y(2),Y(4),Y(5),Q(I),FG(I)             00018650
        1                                                                00018660
C                                                                        00018670
C        TEST RADIOACTIVITY                                              00018680
C                                                                        00018690
550      IF(A1.LT.ERR)  GO TO 600                                        00018700
         ABETA=1.0                                                       00018710
C        POSITRGN EMISSION                                               00018720
         A3=FP                                                           00018730
         IF(A3.LT.ERR)  GO TO 570                                        00018740
         ABETA=ABETA-A3                                                  00018750
         AP1=A3*FP1                                                      00018760
         AP=A3-AP1                                                       00018770
         IF(AP.LT.ERR)  GO TO 560                                        00018780
         M=M+1                                                           00018790
         COEFF(M,I)=AP*A1                                                00018800
         NPROD(M,I)=NUCLI-10000                                          00018810
560      IF(AP1.LT.ERR)  GO TO 570                                       00018820
         M=M+1                                                           00018830
         COEFF(M,I)=AP1*A1                                               00018840
         NPROD(M,I)=NUCLI-9999                                           00018850
C        ISOMERIC TRANSITION                                             00018860
570      IF(FT .LT. ERR) GO TO 580                                       00018870
         M=M+1                                                           00018880
         COEFF(M,I)=FT*A1                                                00018890
```

```
        NPROD(M,I)=NUCLI
        ABETA=ABETA-FT
C       NEGATRCN EMISSION
580     IF(ABETA.LT.1.0E-4) GO TO 600
        A2=FB1
        AB1=ABETA*A2
        AB=ABETA-AB1
        IF(AB.LT.1.E-4) GO TO 590
        M=M+1
        COEFF(M,I)=AR*A1
        NPROD(M,I)=NUCLI+1C000
        IF(AB1.LT.1.E-6) GO TO 600
        M=M+1
        COEFF(M,I)=AR1*A1
590     NPROD(M,I)=NUCLI+1C001
C
C       NEUTRON CAPTURE CROSS SECTIONS FOR FISSION PRODUCTS USING THREE
C       REGION APPROXIMATICN
C
600     KAP(I)=M
        DO 610 K=1,6
610     CAPT(K)=0.0
        CAPT(2)=SIGNG*FNG1
        CAPT(1)=SIGNG-CAPT(2)
        TOCAP(I)=0.3
        DO 620 K=1,2
        CAPKI=CAPT(K)
        IF(CAPKI.LT.ERR)  GO TO 620
        M=M+1
        TOCAP(I)=TOCAP(I)+CAPKI
        COEFF(M,I)=CAPKI
        NPROD(M,I)=NUCLI+NUCAL(K+2)
620     CONTINUC
630     IF(MOC(NUCLI,101).EC.0) GO TO 650
        CO 640 K=1,M
        NPROD(K,I)=NPROD(K,I)-1
640     IL=IL+1
650     DO 660 J=1,5
        YJ=Y(J)*0.010
        TYLD(J)=TYLC(J)+YJ
        YIELD(J,IL)=YJ
        IF(NLIBE.EQ.1.OR.NLIBE.EQ.4) GO TO 680
        IF(NLIBE.EQ.3) YIELD(1,IL)=YJ
        YIELD(3,IL)=YJ
660     VMAX(I)=M
670     IF(M.GT.7)  PRINT 9039, M
680     CIS(I)=A1
        I=I+1
        GO TO 470
690     IFP=IL
C
C       ALL DATA ON NUCLIDES HAS BEEN READ, BEGIN TO COMPUTE MATRIX COEFF
C
        ITOT=I-1
C
C       FIND PRODUCT NUCLIDES FOR REACTIONS OF LIGHT ELEMENTS
C
        NON=0
700     DO 70G K=1,ITOT
        NONO(K)=0
```

```
1445.        IF(ILITE.LT.1) GO TO 760                                    00019500
1446.        DO 750 I=1,ILITE                                            00019510
1447.        NUCLI=NUCL(I)                                               00019520
1448.        DO 720 J=1,ILITE                                            00019530
1449.        KMAX=KAP(J)                                                 00019540
1450.        IF(KMAX.LT.1) GO TO 720                                     00019550
1451.        DO 710 M=1,KMAX                                             00019560
1452.        IF(NUCLI.NE.NPROD(M,J)) GO TO 710                           00019570
1453.        NONO(I)=NONO(I)+1                                           00019580
1454.        NON=NON+1                                                   00019590
1455.        IF(NON.GT.2500) PRINT 9041,     NON,NUCL(I)                 00019600
1456.        A(NON)=COEFF(M,J)                                           00019610
1457.        JT=J                                                        00019620
1458.        LOC(NON)=JT                                                 00019630
1459.  710   CONTINUE                                                    00019640
1460.  720   CONTINUE                                                    00019650
1461.        KD(I)=NONO(I)                                               00019660
1462.        DO 740  J=1,ILITE                                           00019670
1463.        K1=KAP(J)+1                                                 00019680
1464.        KMAX=MMAX(J)                                                00019690
1465.        IF(KMAX.LT.K1) GO TO 740                                    00019700
1466.        DO 730 M=K1,KMAX                                            00019710
1467.        IF(NUCLI.NE.NPROD(M,J)) GO TO 730                           00019720
1468.        NONO(I)=NONO(I)+1                                           00019730
1469.        NON=NON+1                                                   00019740
1470.        IF(NON.GT.2500) PRINT 9041,     NON,NUCL(I)                 00019750
1471.        A(NON)=COEFF(M,J)                                           00019760
1472.        JT=J                                                        00019770
1473.        LOC(NON)=JT                                                 00019780
1474.  730   CONTINUE                                                    00019790
1475.  740   CONTINUE                                                    00019800
1476.  750   CONTINUE                                                    00019810
1477. C                                                                  00019820
1478. C      NON ZERO MATRIX ELEMENTS FOR THE ACTINIDES                  00019830
1479. C                                                                  00019840
1480.  760   IF(IACT.LT.1) GO TO 820                                     00019850
1481.        IO=ILITE+1                                                  00019860
1482.        I1=ILITE+IACT                                               00019870
1483.        DO 810 I=IO,I1                                              00019880
1484.        NUCLI=NUCL(I)                                               00019890
1485.        DO 780 J=IO,I1                                              00019900
1486.        MAX=KAP(J)                                                  00019910
1487.        IF(MAX.LT.1) GO TO 780                                      00019920
1488.        DO 770 M=1,MAX                                              00019930
1489.        IF(NUCLI.NE.NPROD(M,J)) GO TO 770                           00019940
1490.        NONO(I)=NONO(I)+1                                           00019950
1491.        NON=NON+1                                                   00019960
1492.        IF(NON.GT.2500) PRINT 9041,     NON,NUCL(I)                 00019970
1493.        A(NON)=COEFF(M,J)                                           00019980
1494.        JT=J                                                        00019990
1495.        LOC(NON)=JT                                                 00020000
1496.  770   CONTINUE                                                    00020010
1497.  780   CONTINUE                                                    00020020
1498.        KD(I)=NONO(I)                                               00020030
1499.        DO 800 J=IO,I1                                              00020040
1500.        M1=KAP(J)+1                                                 00020050
1501.        M2=MMAX(J)                                                  00020060
1502.        IF(M2.LT.M1) GO TO 800                                      00020070
1503.        DO 790 M=M1,M2                                              00020080
1504.        IF(NUCLI.NE.NPROD(M,J)) GO TO 790                           00020090
```

```
      NONO(I)=NONO(I)+1
      NON=NON+1
      IF(NON.GT.2500) PRINT 9041,       NON,NUCL(I)
      A(NON)=COEFF(M,J)
      JT=J
  790 LOC(NON)=JT
  800 CONTINUE
  810 CONTINUE
C
C     MATRIX ELEMENTS FOR FISSION PRODUCTS
C
  820 IF(IFP.LT.1) GO TO 900
      IM=ILITE+IACT
      IO=IM+1
      IF(ITCT.LT.IO) GO TO 900
      DO 880 I=IO,ITOT
      NUCLI=NUCL(I)
      I2=MAX0(IO,I-10)
      I3=MINO(ITOT,I+10)
      DO 840 J=I2,I3
      KMAX=KAP(J)
      IF(KMAX.LT.1) GO TO 840
      DO 830 M=1,KMAX
      IF(NUCLI.NE.NPROD(M,J)) GO TO 830
      NONO(I)=NONO(I)+1
      NON=NCN+1
      IF(NON.GT.2500) PRINT 9041,       NON,NUCL(I)
      A(NON)=COEFF(M,J)
      JT=J
      LOC(NON)=JT
  830 CONTINUE
  840 CONTINUE
      KD(I)=NONO(I)
      DO 860 J=I2,I3
      K1=KAP(J)+1
      KMAX=KMAX(J)
      IF(KMAX.LT.K1) GO TO 860
      DO 850 M=K1,KMAX
      IF(NUCLI.NE.NPROD(M,J)) GO TO 850
      NONO(I)=NONO(I)+1
      NON=NCN+1
      IF(NCN.GT.2500) PRINT 9041,       NON,NUCL(I)
      A(NON)=COEFF(M,J)
      JT=J
  850 LOC(NON)=JT
  860 CONTINUE
      IF(IACT.LT.1) GO TO 880
      DO 870 K=1,5
      IL=I-IM
      IF(YIELD(K,IL).LT.ERR) GO TO 870
      NON=NCN+1
      IF(NON.GT.2500) PRINT 9041,       NON,NUCL(I)
      NONO(I)=NONO(I)+1
      KK=NSORS(K)
      LOC(NON)=KK
      KF=KK-ILITE
      A(NON)=YIELD(K,IL)*FISS(KF)
  870 CONTINUE
```

```
 880   CONTINUE                                                                    00020700
       IF(IFP.LE.0) GO TO 900                                                      00020710
       IF(NLIBE.NE.3) GO TO 890                                                    00020720
       PRINT 9027,     TYLD(2),TYLD(4),TYLD(5)                                     00020730
       GO TO 900                                                                   00020740
 890   PRINT 9030,     (TYLD(I),I=1,5)                                             00020750
                                                                                   00020760
C      ALL MATRIX ELEMENTS ARE NOW COMPUTED                                        00020770
C      BEGIN TRANSIENT SOLUTION                                                    00020780
C                                                                                  00020790
C                                                                                  00020800
C      TEMPORARILY WRITE OUT MATRIX ELEMENTS                                       00020810
C                                                                                  00020820
 900   IF(IR .EQ. 0) RETURN                                                        00020830
       PRINT 9029                                                                  00020840
       N=0                                                                         00020850
       DO 910 I=1,ITOT                                                             00020860
       NUM=NONO(I)                                                                 00020870
       IF(NUM.LE.0) GO TO 910                                                      00020880
       N1=N+NUM                                                                    00020890
       N=N+1                                                                       00020900
       PRINT 9028,      I,DIS (I),TOCAP(I),(A(K),LOC(K),K=N,N1)                    00020910
       N=N1                                                                        00020920
 910   CONTINUE                                                                    00020930
       RETURN                                                                      00020940
 920   STOP                                                                        00020950
C                                                                                  00020960
C      FORMATS      FORMATS      FORMATS      FORMATS                              00020970
C                                                                                  00020980
9001   FORMAT(4F10.5,6I2)                                                          00020990
9002   FORMAT(I6,F5.3,I1,5F3.3,E5.2,F3.3,          13X,E5.2,F3.3,2E5.2F3.3)        00021000
      1   ,F4.3,F3.3,F6.4)                                                         00021010
9003   FORMAT(I6,F5.3,I1,3X,4F3.3,2E5.2,F3.3,5E5.2,F4.3,F3.3)                      00021020
9004   FORMAT(I6,F5.3,I1,5F3.3,2E5.2,F3.3,4E5.2,F3.3,F4.3,F3.3,2E5.2)              00021030
9005   FORMAT(1H1,43X,'NUCLEAR TRANSMUTATION DATA    REVISED ',I2,'/',I2,'/',I2,'  00021040
      1/',I2,/,'ONUCL = NUCLIDE = 10000 * ATOMIC NO + 10 * MASS NO + ISOM          00021050
      2ERIC STATE (0 OR 1)',10X,'DLAM = DECAY CONSTANT (1/SEC).',/,' FB,            00021060
      3FP, FA, FT = FRACTIONAL DECAY BY BETA, POSITRON (OR ELECTRON CAPTU          00021070
      4RE), ALPHA, INTERNAL TRANSITION.   FB = 1 - FP - FA - FT',/,' FB1,          00021080
      5 FP1, FN01, FN2N1 = FRACTION OF BETA, POSITRON, N-GAMMA, N-2N TRAN          00021090
      6SITIONS TO EXCITED STATE OF PRODUCT NUCLIDE',/,' SIGTH, SIGNG, SIG          00021100
      7F, SIGNA, SIGNP = THERMAL CROSS SECTIONS (BARNS) FOR ABSORPTION, N          00021110
      8-GAMMA, FISSION, N-ALPHA, N-PROTON.')                                       00021120
9006   FORMAT('     SIGTH = SIGTH * (1 - FNA -FNP).  SIGNA = SIGTH * FNA.          00021130
      1SIGNP = SIGTH * FNP. FNA, FNP = FRACTION THERMAL N-ALPHA, N-PROTO           00021140
      2N.',/,' RITH, RING, RIF, RINA, RINP = RESONANCE INTEGRAL FOR ABSOR          00021150
      3PTION, N-GAMMA, FISSION, N-ALPHA, N-PROTON.',/,'   RING = RITH * (           00021160
      4I - FINA - FINP). RINA = RITH * FINA. RINP = RITH * FINP.  FINA, F          00021170
      5INP = FRACTION RESONANCE N-ALPHA, N-PROTON.',/,' SIGMEV, SIGFF, SI          00021180
      6GN2N, SIGNAF, SIGNPF = FAST CROSS SECTIONS (BARNS) FOR ABSORPTION,          00021190
      7FISSION, N-2N, N-ALPHA, N-PROTON.',/,'     SIGN2N = SIGMEV * (1 - F          00021200
      8NA - FFNP). SIGNAF = SIGMEV * FFNA.  SIGNPF = SIGMEV * FFNP.  FFNA           00021210
      9A, FFNP = FRACTION FAST N-ALPHA, N-P.')                                     00021220
9007   FORMAT(' Y23, Y25, YO2, Y28, Y49 = FISSION YIELD (PERCENT) FROM 230         00021230
      13-U, 235-U, 232-TH, 238-U, 239- PU.',/,' Q = HEAT PER DISINTEGRATI          00021240
      2CN.  FG = FRACTION OF HEAT IN GAMMAS OF ENERGY GREATER THAN 0.2 ME          00021250
      3V.',/,'O EFFECTIVE CROSS SECTIONS FOR A VOLUME AVERAGED THERMAL (L          00021260
      4T 0.876 EV) FLUX ARE AS FOLLOWS.',/,'     SIGF = SIGNG * THERM0          00021270
      5 + RING * RES.',/,'    FISSION -  SIGF * THERM + RIF * RES + SIGF          00021280
      6F * FAST.',10X,'THERM = 1/V CORRECTION FOR THERMAL SPECTRUM AND TE          00021290
```

```
          7MPERATURE.',/,'      N-2N      -   SIGN2N * FAST.',36X,'RES      = RATIO 00021300
          80F RESONANCE FLUX PER LETHARGY UNIT TO THERMAL FLUX.')             00021310
 9008     FORMAT('   N-ALPHA    -   SIGNA *THERM + RINA *RES + SIGNAF * FAST  00021320
          1.',7X,'FAST = 1.45 * RATIO OF FAST (GT 1.0 MEV) TO THERMAL FLUX ') 00021330
          2/,'   N-PROTON    -   SIGNP *THERM + RINP *RES + SIGNPF * FAST.')  00021340
 9009     FORMAT(1H0,59X,'REFERENCES',/,'  HALF LIVES, DECAY SCHEMES, AND     00021350
          1THERMAL POWER',/,' C M LEDERER, J M HOLLANDER, AND I PERLMAN,''TAB 00021360
          2LE OF ISOTOPES - SIXTH EDITION'' JOHN WILEY AND SONS, INC (1967)', 00021370
          3/,' B S DZHELEPOV AND L K PEKER ''DECAY SCHEMES OF RADIOACTIVE NUC 00021380
          4LEI'' PERGAMMON PRESS (1961)',/,' D T GOLDMAN AND JAMES R ROSSER   00021390
          5'CHART OF THE NUCLIDES'' NINTH EDITION GENERAL ELECTRIC CO (JULY   00021400
          61966)',/,' E D ARNOLD ''PROGRAM SPECTRA'' APPENDIX A OF ORNL-3576  00021410
          7(APRIL 1964)')                                                    00021420
 9010     FORMAT('   CROSS SECTIONS AND FLUX SPECTRA',/,' B E PRINCE ''NEUT   00021430
          1IRON REACTION RATES IN THE MSRE SPECTRUM'' ORNL-4119, PP 79-83 (JUL 00021440
          2Y 1967)',/,' B E PRINCE ''NEUTRON ENERGY SPECTRA IN MSRE AND MSBR''00021450
          3' ORNL-4191, PP 50-58 (DEC 1967)',/,' M D GOLDBERG ET AL ''NEUTRON 00021460
          4 CROSS SECTIONS'' BNL-325, SECOND ED, SUPP NO 2 (MAY 1964 - AUG 19 00021470
          56) ALSO EARLIER EDITIONS',/,' H T KERR, UNPUBLISHED ERC COMPILATIO 00021480
          60N (FEB 1968)',/, M K DRAKE ''A COMPILATION OF RESONANCE INTEGRAL  00021490
          7S'' NUCLEONICS, VOL 24, NO 8, PP 108-111 (AUG 1966)',/,' BNWL STAF 00021500
          8F ''INVESTIGATION OF N-2N CROSS SECTIONS'' BNWC-98, PP 44-98 (JUNE 00021510
          9 1965)')                                                          00021520
 9011     FORMAT(18A4,I3)                                                     00021530
 9012     FORMAT(1H1,20X,18A4)                                               00021540
 9013     FORMAT(' H ALTER AND C E WEBER ''PRODUCTION OF H AND HE IN METALS   00021550
          1DURING REACTOR IRRADIATION'' J NUCL MATLS, VOL 16, PP 68-73 (1965) 00021560
          2',/,' L L BENNETT ''RECOMMENDED FISSION PRODUCT CHAINS FOR USE IN  00021570
          3REACTOR EVALUATION STUDIES'' ORNL-TM-1658 (SEPT 1966)')            00021580
 9014     FORMAT('   FISSION PRODUCT YIELDS',/,' M E MEEK AND B F RIDER, ''    00021590
          1SUMMARY OF FISSION PRODUCT YIELDS FOR U-235, U-238, PU-239, AND PU 00021600
          2-241 AT THERMAL, FISSION SPECTRUM AND'' 14 MEV NEUTRON ENERGI      00021610
          3ES'' APED-5398-A(REV.),(OCT. 1968)',/,' S KATCOFF '' FISSION PRODUCT 00021620
          4YIELDS FROM NEUTRON INDUCED FISSION'' NUCLEONICS, VOL 18, NO 11,   00021630
          5(NOV 1960)',/,' N D DUDEY '' REVIEW OF LOW-MASS ATOM PRODUCTION IN  00021640
          6AST REACTORS'' ANL-7434,(APRIL 1968)')                            00021650
 9015     FORMAT(1H0,20X,'LIGHT ELEMENTS, MATERIALS OF CONSTRUCTION, AND ACT  00021660
          1IVATION PRODUCTS ',/,'O NUCL    DLAM      FB1      FP     FP1    FT     F 00021670
          2A   SIGTH  FNG1    FNA     FNP    RITH    FINA   FINP  SIGMEV  FN2N1  00021680
          3  FFNA   FFNP    Q     FG')                                        00021690
 9016     FORMAT(1H0,20X,'LIGHT ELEMENTS, MATERIALS OF CONSTRUCTION, AND ACT  00021700
          1IVATION PRODUCTS ',/,'O NUCL    DLAM      FB1      FP     FP1    FT     F 00021710
          2A   SIGNG  FNG1  SIGN2N  FN2N1.  SIGNP   SIGNP    Q    FG   ABU    00021720
          3NDANCE')                                                          00021730
 9017     FORMAT(1H ,A2,I3,A1,1PE9.2,0P5F6.3,1PE9.2,0P3F6.3,1PE9.2,0P2F6.3,  00021740
          11PE9.2,0P4F6.3,0P5F.2)                                            00021750
 9018     FORMAT(1H0,10X,'THERM= '1F10.5,5X,'RES= '1F10.5,5X,'FAST= '1F10.5,  00021760
          1//,1X,'NEUTRON SOURCE= '5I10.5X),5X,'NLIBE= 'I3)                   00021770
 9019     FORMAT(1H0,36X,'FISSION PRODUCTS',/,'O NUCL    DLAM      FB1      FP 00021780
          1   FP1    FT   SIGNG ',' FNG1    Y23    Y25     YO2    Y           00021790
          228    Y49     Q    FG')                                           00021800
 9020     FORMAT(1H0,36X,'FISSION PRODUCTS',/,'O NUCL    DLAM      FB1      FP 00021810
          1   FP1    FT   SIGNG   FNG1   Y25    Y28    Y49    Q    FG')       00021820
 9021     FORMAT(1H ,A2,I3,A1,1PE9.2,0P4F6.3,1PE9.2,0P4F6.3,1PE9.2,0P2F6.3,  00021830
          10P2F6.3)                                                          00021840
 9022     FORMAT(1H ,A2,I3,A1,1PE9.2,0P5F6.3,1P3E9.2,1P3E9.2,0P2F6.3)        00021850
 9023     FORMAT(1H0,32X,'ACTINIDES AND THEIR DAUGHTERS',//                  00021860
          1' NUCL    DLAM     FB1     FP     FP1    FT    FA    FSF  E+6  SIGNG  R 00021870
          2ING  FNG1  SIGF   RIF    SIGFF   SIGN2N  SIGN3N    Q    FG')      00021880
 9024     FORMAT(1H0,32X,'ACTINIDES AND THEIR DAUGHTERS',//                  00021890
```

1625.
1626.
1627.
1628.
1629.
1630.
1631.
1632.
1633.
1634.
1635.
1636.
1637.
1638.
1639.
1640.
1641.
1642.
1643.
1644.
1645.
1646.
1647.
1648.
1649.
1650.
1651.
1652.
1653.
1654.
1655.
1656.
1657.
1658.
1659.
1660.
1661.
1662.
1663.
1664.
1665.
1666.
1667.
1668.
1669.
1670.
1671.
1672.
1673.
1674.
1675.
1676.
1677.
1678.
1679.
1680.
1681.
1682.
1683.
1684.

```
1'  NUCL      DLAM      FB1      FP      FP1      FT      =A      FSF E+6  SIGNG              F00021900
2NG21  SIGF    SIGN2N    SIGN3N     Q       FG')                                               00021910
9025 FORMAT(1H ,A2,I3,A1,1PE9.2,0P5F6.3,6PF6.1,1P2E9.2,0PF6.3,1P5E9.2,                         00021920
   1   0PF6.3,F5.2)                                                                            00021930
9026 FORMAT(1H ,A2,I3,A1,1PE9.2,0P5F6.3,6PF9.1,1PE9.2,0PF6.3,1P3E9.2,                          00021940
   1   0PF7.3,F5.2)                                                                            00021950
9027 FORMAT('0SUM OF YIELDS OF ALL FISSION PRODUCTS =',15X,1P3E9.2)                            00021960
9028 FORMAT(I5,2X,1PE10.3,3X,E10.3,5(2X,E10.3,3X,I5)/(30X,5(2X,E10.3,                          00021970
   1   3X,I5)))                                                                                00021980
9029 FORMAT('1NON-ZERO MATRIX ELEMENTS AND THEIR LOCATIONS'/                                   00021990
   1' I        DIS(I)       CAP(I)     A(I,J)     J      A(I,J)     J      A(I,J)     J    ')   00022000
   2J      A(I,J)     J      A(I,J)     J      A(I,J)     J     ')                             00022010
9030 FORMAT('64H0SUM OF YIELDS OF ALL FISSION PRODUCTS                                         00022020
   1   ,1P5F9.2)                                                                               00022030
9031 FORMAT(5I10)                                                                              00022040
9032 FORMAT(I6,F5.3,I1,5F3.3,E5.2,2F3.3,E5.2,2F3.3,E5.2,3F3.3,F4.3,F3.300022050
   1,F6.4)                                                                                     00022060
9033 FORMAT(1H ,A2,I3,A1,1PE9.2,0P5F6.3,1PE9.2,0PF6.3,1PE9.2,0PF6.3,                           00022070
   1   1P2E9.2,0P2F6.3,F7.3)                                                                   00022080
9034 FORMAT(I7,F9.3,I1,5F5.3,1PE9.2,0P2F5.3,F7.3,2E6.0)                                        00022090
9035 FORMAT(7X,F9.2,3F5.3,F9.2,2F5.3,F9.2,3F5.3, 5X,I1)                                        00022100
9036 FORMAT(20A4)                                                                              00022110
9037 FORMAT(7X,2F9.2,F5.3,4F9.2,F4.3,F9.2,I1)                                                  00022120
9038 FORMAT(7X,2F9.2,F5.3,5F9.2, 4X,I1)                                                        00022130
9039 FORMAT('0  WARNING, MOUT OF RANGE IN NUDATA, =',I5)                                       00022140
9040 FORMAT('      7X,F9.2,3F8.6,F4.2,2F3.1,F9.2,3F5.3,5X,I1)                                  00022150
9041 FORMAT('0 NUN HAS EXCEEDED 2500, EQUAL TO '2I6)                                           00022160
     END                                                                                       00022170
     SUBROUTINE COLLECT(TMB,CWASTE,ILITE,ITOT)                                                 00022180
     COMMON/EQ/XZERO(800), XZH(800),XTEMP(800),XNEW(10,800),                                   00022190
   1   B(800),D(800)                                                                           00022200
     DIMENSION CWASTE(800)                                                                     00022210
     IF(TMB.LT.1) RETURN                                                                       00022220
     DO 10 I=1,ITOT                                                                            00022230
     B(I)=CWASTE(I)                                                                            00022240
     XTEMP(I)=0.0                                                                              00022250
  10 CALL DECAY(1,TMB,ITOT)                                                                    00022260
     CALL TERM(TMB,1,J,ITOT)                                                                   00022270
     CALL EQUIL(1,ITOT)                                                                        00022280
     DO 20 I=1,ITOT                                                                            00022290
  20 CWASTE(I)=XNEW(1,I)/TMB                                                                   00022300
     RETURN                                                                                    00022310
     END                                                                                       00022320
     SUBROUTINE STORAG(TMB,CWASTE,ILITE,ITOT)                                                  00022330
     COMMON/EQ/XZERO(800), XZH(800),XTEMP(800),XNEW(10,800),                                   00022340
   1   B(800),D(800)                                                                           00022350
     DIMENSION CWASTE(ITOT)                                                                    00022360
     IF(TMB.LT.1) RETURN                                                                       00022370
     DELT=TMB                                                                                  00022380
     DO 10 I=1,ITOT                                                                            00022390
     B(I)=0.0                                                                                  00022400
  10 XTEMP(I)=CWASTE(I)                                                                        00022410
     CALL DECAY(1,DELT,ITOT)                                                                   00022420
     CALL TERM(TMB,1,ILITE,ITOT)                                                               00022430
     CALL EQUIL(1,ITOT)                                                                        00022440
     DO 20 I=1,ITOT                                                                            00022450
  20 CWASTE(I)=XNFW(1,I)                                                                       00022460
     RETURN                                                                                    00022470
     END                                                                                       00022480
   C PROGRAM BLOCK DATA                                                                        00022490
```

```
      BLOCK DATA                                                        00022500
      INTEGER*2 ELE(99),STA(2)                                          00022510
      COMMON/LABEL/ ELE,STA                                             00022520
      DATA ELE/' H','HE',' LI','BE',' B',' C',' N',' O',' F','NE','NA','M00022530
     1G','AL','SI',' P',' S','CL','AR',' K','CA','SC','TI',' V','CR','MN00022540
     2','FE','CO','NI','CU','ZN','GA','GE','AS','SE','BR','KR','RB','SR'00022550
     3,' Y','ZR','NB','KC','TC','RU','RH','PD','AG','CD','IN','SN','SB',00022560
     4'TE',' I',' XE','CS','BA','LA','CE','PR','ND','PM','SM','EU','GD',00022570
     5TB','DY','HO','ER','TM','YB','LU','HF','TA',' W','RE','OS','IR','P00022580
     6T','AU','HG','TL','PB','BI','PO','AT','RN','FR','RA','AC','TH','PA00022590
     7,' U','NP','PU','AM','CM','BK','CF','ES'/                         00022600
      DATA STA/' ','M '/                                                00022610
      END                                                               00022620
      SUBROUTINE HALF(A,I)                                              00022630
C     SUBROUTINE HALF CONVERTS HALF-LIFE TO DECAY CONSTANT (1/SEC)      00022640
      DIMENSION C(9)                                                    00022650
      DATA C/6.9315E-01,1.1552E-02,1.9254E-04,8.0226E-06,2.1965E-08,0.0,00022660
     1    2.1965E-11,2.1965E-14,2.1965E-17/                             00022670
      IF(A.GT.0.0) GO TO 10                                             00022680
      IF(I.EQ.6) GO TO 20                                               00022690
      A=9.99                                                            00022700
      RETURN                                                            00022710
   10 A=C(I)/A                                                          00022720
      RETURN                                                            00022730
   20 A=0.0                                                             00022740
      RETURN                                                            00022750
      END                                                               00022760
      SUBROUTINE NOAH(NUCLI,NAME)                                       00022770
C     SUBROUTINE NOAH CONVERTS SIX DIGIT IDENTIFIER TO ALPHAMERIC SYMBOL00022780
      INTEGER*2 NAME(3)                                                 00022790
      INTEGER*2 ELE(99),STA(2)                                          00022800
      COMMON/LABEL/ ELE,STA                                             00022810
      IS=MOD(NUCLI,10)+1                                                00022820
      NZ =NUCLI/1000                                                    00022830
      MW=NUCLI/10-NZ *1000                                              00022840
      NAME(1)=ELE(NZ)                                                   00022850
      NAME(2)=MW                                                        00022860
      NAME(3)=STA(IS)                                                   00022870
      RETURN                                                            00022880
      END                                                               00022890
```

1745.
1746.
1747.
1748.
1749.
1750.
1751.
1752.
1753.
1754.
1755.
1756.
1757.
1758.
1759.
1760.
1761.
1762.
1763.
1764.
1765.
1766.
1767.
1768.
1769.
1770.
1771.
1772.
1773.
1774.
1775.
1776.
1777.
1778.
1779.
1780.
1781.
1782.
1783.
1784.

APPENDIX D

COMPUTER PROGRAMS FOR DOSE PARAMETERS

The following computer programs provide the NRC staff method for calculating various parameters used in the Technical Specifications.

PARTS, a computer program to calculate technical specification dose parameters for the iodine and particulate portions of gaseous effluents; available from the Radiological Assessment Branch of the Nuclear Regulatory Commission, Washington, D.C. 20555.

RABFIN, a computer program to calculate technical specification dose parameters for the noble gas portion of gaseous effluents; available from the Radiological Assessment Branch of the Nuclear Regulatory Commission, Washington, D.C. 20555.

LADTAP, a computer program to calculate the doses from radioactive effluents released to the hydrosphere; the program and a modification to calculate the technical specification dose parameters for radionuclides in liquid effluents is available from the Radiological Assessment Branch of the Nuclear Regulatory Commission, Washington, D.C. 20555.

The remainder of this Appendix contains the PARTS program listing, and modifying the routines to the LADTAP Code.

LADTAP MODIFICATIONS

An option has been added to the staff's code LADTAP to tabulate the $A_{i\tau}$ factors of Section 4.3.1 of this manual. Listed below are the routines which have been modified, the changes are indicated by the 'CHANGE 1' notation in columns 73-80.

To execute this option the standard LADTAP input is prepared with the following departures:

1. The 50 mile population (card 3 of the LADTAP input deck) should be set negative.
2. The release of all nuclides should be set to one Ci/yr.

Only the input data defining the ALARA determination of LADTAP is necessary. Following the input data deck structure of Enclosure 1 to the LADTAP program, data beyond card number 7 need not be prepared for the option.

PARTS INPUT DECK TABLE

Card No.	Format	Variable	Columns	Description
1	20 A4	Name	1-80	Plant Title Card, Name, Docket No. and Plant Type
2	F 5.2	H	1-5	Humidity absolute (default value = 8.0 gr/m^3)
	F 5.2	YL	6-10	Yield of leafy vegetables for human consumption (default value = 2.0 Kg/m^2)
	F 5.2	YV	11-15	Yield of produce other than leafy vegetables (default value = 2.0 Kg/m^2)
	F 5.2	YP	16-20	Agricultural productivity of animal pasture feed (default value = 0.70 Kg/m^2 wet weight)
	F 5.2	YC	21-25	Agricultural crop productivity of animal feed other than pasture grass (default value = 2.0 Kg/m^2 wet weight)
	F 5.2	QC	26-30	Milk cow and beef cattle consumption rate for feed or forage (default value = 50 Kg/day wet weight)
	F 5.2	QG	31-35	Goat consumption rate for feed or forage (default value = 6 Kg/day wet weight)
	E 8.2	DOQ	41-48	Annual average relative deposition rate (D/Q), determined for a specific plant airborne release and site location (meters^{-2}) (Optional Use For Reference & Information Only)
3	I1	IAGE	1	Identification of Controlling Age Group (1 is Infant, 2 is Child, 3 is Teen and 4 is Adult)
	I1	IORG	2	Identification of Controlling Organ (1 is Thyroid, 2 is the critical organ)
	6A4	ZLOC	3-26	Receptor Location identification, Name, Compass Sector and Distance
	F 5.0	GF	27-31	Fraction of yr. humans are exposed to ground surface radiation (default value = 1.0)
	F 5.0	ZIN	32-36	Annual occupancy factor for the inhalation pathway (default value = 1.0)
	F 5.0	FV	37-41	Fraction of yr. leafy vegetables are grown (default value = 1.0)
	F 5.0	FP	42-46	Fraction of yr. cows are on pasture (default value = 1.0)
	F 5.0	FG	47-51	Fraction of produce from local garden (default value = 0.76)
	F 5.0	FPF	52-56	Fraction of daily intake of cows derived from pasture while on pasture (default value - 1.0)
	F 5.0	FGT	57-61	Fraction of yr. goats are on pasture (default value = 1.0)
	F 5.0	FPG	62-66	Fraction of daily intake of goat from pasture while on pasture (default value = 1.0)
	F 5.0	FB	67-71	Fraction of yr. beef cattle are on pasture (default value 1.0)
	F 5.0	FBF	72-76	Fraction of daily intake of beef cattle derived from pasture while on pasture (default value = 1.0)

```
      BLOCK DATA BLKDAT                                      BLKDAT    2
      COMMON/ELEMEN/IELEM(100)                               BLKDAT    3
      INTEGER IELEM                                          BLKDAT    4
      COMMON/POPUL/PERA,PERT,PERC,US                         BNL01     1
      DATA IELEM/                                            BLKDAT    5
     1'H ','HE','LI','BE','B ','C ','N ','O ','F ','NE','NA','MG','AL', BLKDAT    6
     2'SI','P ','S ','CL','AR','K ','CA','SC','TI','V ','CR','MN','FE', BLKDAT.   7
     3'CO','NI','CU','ZN','GA','GE','AS','SE','BR','KR','RB','SR','Y ', BLKDAT    8
     4'ZR','NB','MO','TC','RU','RH','PD','AG','CD','IN','SN','SB','TE', BLKDAT    9
     5'I ','XE','CS','BA','LA','CE','PR','ND','PM','SM','EU','GD','TB', BLKDAT   10
     6'DY','HO','ER','TM','YB','LU','HF','TA','W ','RE','OS','IR','PT', BLKDAT   11
     7'AU','HG','TL','PB','BI','PO','AT','RN','FR','RA','AC','TH','PA', BLKDAT   12
     8'U ','NP','PU','AM','CM','BK','CF','ES','FM'/          BLKDAT   13
      DATA PERA/0.66/                                        BLKDAT   15
      DATA PERT/0.14/                                        BLKDAT   16
      DATA PERC/0.20/                                        BLKDAT   17
      DATA US/2.6E+08/                                       BLKDAT   18
      END                                                    BLKDAT   19
```

```
      PROGRAM LADTAP(INPUT,OUTPUT,TAPE5=INPUT,TAPE6=OUTPUT,TAPE10)          BNL01      2
      COMMON Q(200),PL,CFS,NSUR,LT,HECO(200),LIST(200,4),LCT,LZ ,CON,KIT    LADTAP     3
     + ,POP                                                                 LADTAP     4
      COMMON/POPUL/PEKA,PERT,PERC,US                                        LADTAP     5
      DIMENSION FACCF(100),FACCI(100),FACCA(100),SACCI(100),SACCF(100),     LADTAP     6
     + SACCA(100)                                                           LADTAP     7
      DIMENSION ITITLE(20)                                                  BNL01      8
      DATA FACCF/                                                           LADTAP     9
     +9.0E-01,1.0E+00,5.0E-01,2.0E+00,2.2E-01,4.6E-05,1.5E+05,9.2E-01,      LADTAP    10
     +1.0E+01,1.0E+00,1.0E+02,5.0E-01,2.5E+01,2.5E+01,7.5E+02,              LADTAP    11
     +5.0E+01,1.0E+00,1.0E+03,4.0E+01,1.0E+03,1.0E+02,                      LADTAP    12
     +4.0E+02,1.0E+02,5.0E-01,1.0E+02,5.0E+01,2.0E+03,3.3E+03,              LADTAP    13
     +1.0E+02,1.7E+02,4.2E+01,1.5E+01,1.0E+01,1.3E+00,                      LADTAP    14
     +3.0E+04,1.0E+01,1.5E+01,1.0E+01,1.0E+01,2.3E+02,2.0E+02,              LADTAP    15
     +1.0E+05,3.0E+03,1.0E+00,0.0E+00,1.5E+01,1.0E+00,2.0E+00,              LADTAP    16
     +2.5E+01,1.2E+01,2.5E+01,2.5E+01,2.5E+01,2.5E+01,                      LADTAP    17
     +3.0E+04,1.2E+03,1.0E+01,1.0E+02,1.0E+02,1.0E+03,                      LADTAP    18
     +2.5E+01,3.0E+01,1.5E+01,1.2E+01,1.0E+01,5.0E+00,2.5E+01,              LADTAP    19
     +2.5E+01,2.5E+01,1.1E+01,1.0E+01,3.5E+00,1.0E+01,2.5E+01,              LADTAP    20
     +2.5E+01,2.5E+01,1.0E+01,1.0E+01,1.0E+01/                              LADTAP    21
      DATA FACCI/                                                           LADTAP    22
     +9.0E-01,1.0E+00,4.0E+01,1.0E+01,5.0E+01,1.5E+05,9.2E-01,              LADTAP    23
     +1.0E+02,1.0E+00,1.0E+02,1.0E+02,2.5E+01,2.5E+04,1.0E+02,              LADTAP    24
     +1.0E+02,1.0E+00,8.3E+02,1.0E+03,3.0E+03,1.0E+02,                      LADTAP    25
     +9.0E+04,3.7E+03,2.0E+02,1.0E+03,1.0E+04,4.7E+02,3.5E+01,              LADTAP    26
     +4.0E+01,1.7E+02,3.3E+02,1.0E+00,1.0E+01,1.0E+02,6.7E+00,              LADTAP    27
     +1.0E+02,1.0E+02,1.5E+05,1.0E+05,1.0E+01,7.7E+02,2.0E+02,              LADTAP    28
     +1.0E+05,1.0E+00,4.0E+00,3.0E+03,1.0E+05,1.0E+03,1.0E+02,              LADTAP    29
     +1.0E+03,1.0E+03,1.0E+03,1.0E+03,1.0E+03,1.0E+03,                      LADTAP    30
     +1.0E+03,1.0E+03,1.0E+03,1.0E+03,1.0E+01,1.0E+03,6.7E+00,              LADTAP    31
     +6.7E+02,1.0E+02,1.0E+01,6.0E+01,3.0E+02,5.0E+01,1.0E+05,              LADTAP    32
     +1.5E+04,1.0E+02,2.4E+01,2.0E+04,5.0E+01,1.0E+02,2.5E+02,              LADTAP    33
     +1.0E+03,5.0E+01,1.1E+02,6.0E+01,1.0E+01,1.0E+02/                      LADTAP    34
     +1.0E+03,1.0E+03,1.0E+02/                                              LADTAP    35
      DATA FACCA/                                                           LADTAP    36
     +9.0E-01,1.0E+00,3.0E+02,2.0E+00,2.2E-01,4.6E-05,1.3E+04,9.2E-01,      LADTAP    37
     +2.0E+00,1.0E+00,5.0E+02,1.0E+02,4.2E+02,1.3E+02,2.5E+05,1.0E+02,      LADTAP    38
     +5.0E+01,1.0E+00,6.7E+02,1.3E+02,1.0E+03,2.0E+02,                      LADTAP    39
     +9.0E+04,1.0E+03,2.0E+02,5.0E+01,1.0E+04,5.0E+02,3.5E+01,              LADTAP    40
     +8.0E+03,1.0E+02,1.0E+02,1.5E+01,1.0E+02,5.0E+02,2.0E+02,              LADTAP    41
     +1.0E+01,1.0E+02,1.5E+02,4.0E+00,1.0E+01,1.0E+02,5.0E+02,              LADTAP    42
     +5.0E+03,4.0E+03,5.0E+03,5.0E+03,5.0E+03,1.0E+03,                      LADTAP    43
     +8.0E+02,1.2E+03,2.4E+01,2.0E+03,1.0E+03,1.0E+03,                      LADTAP    44
     +5.0E+03,5.0E+03,2.4E+02,1.0E+02,2.0E+00,8.0E+01,1.5E+05,              LADTAP    45
     +5.0E+03,1.1E+03,5.0E-01,1.1E+02,5.0E+01,1.0E+02,2.5E+02,              LADTAP    46
     +5.0E+03,5.0E+03,1.0E+03/                                              LADTAP    47
      DATA SACCF/                                                           LADTAP    48
     +9.0E-01,1.0E+00,5.0E-01,2.2E-01,1.8E+03,4.0E+04,9.6E-01,              LADTAP    49
     +3.0E+00,1.0E+00,6.7E-02,7.7E-02,1.0E+01,2.9E+04,1.7E+00,              LADTAP    50
     +1.3E-02,1.0E+00,1.1E+01,1.0E-01,2.0E+03,1.0E+02,                      LADTAP    51
     +5.5E+02,3.0E+03,1.0E+02,6.7E+02,2.0E+03,3.3E+03,                      LADTAP    52
     +3.3E+02,4.0E+03,1.5E-02,1.0E+00,8.3E+01,1.0E+02,2.0E+02,              LADTAP    53
     +3.0E+02,1.0E+01,3.0E+00,1.0E+01,3.0E+03,3.0E+03,                      LADTAP    54
     +1.0E+05,3.0E+03,1.0E+01,1.0E+01,1.0E+00,4.0E+01,1.0E+01/              LADTAP    55
```

```
      +2.5E+01,1.0E+01,2.5E+01,2.5E+01,2.5E+01,2.5E+01,2.5E+01,          LADTAP   58
      +2.5E+01,2.5E+01,2.5E+01,2.5E+01,2.5E+01,2.5E+01,2.0E+02,          LADTAP   59
      +3.0E+04,3.0E+01,4.4E+00,1.0E+01,1.0E+02,3.3E+01,1.7E+03,          LADTAP   60
      +1.0E+04,3.0E+02,1.5E+01,3.0E+02,1.0E+01,1.0E+01,5.0E+01,          LADTAP   61
      +2.5E+01,1.0E+01,1.0E+01,1.0E+01,3.0E+02,2.5E+01,2.5E+01,          LADTAP   62
      +2.5E+01,2.5E+01,1.0E+01,1.0E+01/                                   LADTAP   63
      DATA SACC/                                                          LADTAP   64
      +9.3E-01,1.0E+00,5.0E-01,2.0E-01,4.4E-01,1.7E+04,9.0E-01,          LADTAP   65
      +3.6E+00,1.0E+00,1.9E-01,7.7E-01,6.0E+01,3.0E+01,3.0E+04,4.4E-01,  LADTAP   66
      +4.0E-02,1.0E+00,6.6E+00,1.3E+01,1.0E+04,1.0E+01,1.7E+04,          LADTAP   67
      +3.3E+02,2.0E+02,1.7E+03,5.0E+04,6.7E+02,1.7E+04,                  LADTAP   68
      +3.3E+02,1.0E+01,5.0E+01,1.0E+00,1.7E+01,2.0E+03,4.0E+01,          LADTAP   69
      +1.0E+02,1.0E+01,5.0E+03,1.0E+00,1.0E+01,2.5E+05,                  LADTAP   70
      +1.0E+05,1.0E+03,1.0E+01,1.0E+03,1.0E+01,2.5E+01,1.0E+02,          LADTAP   71
      +1.0E+03,4.0E+02,1.0E+03,1.0E+03,1.0E+03,2.0E+01,                  LADTAP   72
      +1.0E+03,1.0E+03,1.0E+01,2.0E+03,3.3E+01,3.5E+04,                  LADTAP   73
      +1.7E+04,3.0E+01,6.2E-01,5.0E+01,1.0E+01,2.0E+01,1.0E+03,          LADTAP   74
      +1.0E+05,1.0E+01,3.2E+04,1.0E+01,1.0E+01,1.0E+01,1.0E+03,          LADTAP   75
      +1.0E+03,1.0E+01,1.0E+01,2.0E+01,1.0E+01,2.0E+01,1.0E+03,          LADTAP   76
      +1.0E+03,1.0E+01,1.0E+01,1.0E+01/                                   LADTAP   77
      DATA SACCA/                                                         LADTAP   78
      +9.3E-01,1.0E+00,3.0E+00,1.0E+03,2.2E+00,1.4E+03,1.4E+03,9.6E-01,  LADTAP   79
      +1.4E+00,1.0E+00,9.5E-01,7.7E-01,5.0E+00,1.3E+01,3.4E-01,          LADTAP   80
      +7.6E-02,1.0E+00,2.6E+00,5.0E+00,2.0E+01,5.0E+02,2.2E+02,          LADTAP   81
      +5.5E+03,7.3E+02,1.0E+01,2.5E+02,1.7E+03,1.7E+02,                  LADTAP   82
      +1.7E+03,1.0E+01,1.5E+01,1.0E+00,1.7E+01,5.0E+03,1.0E+03,          LADTAP   83
      +5.0E+02,1.0E+01,4.0E+03,7.0E+03,2.0E+03,2.0E+01,                  LADTAP   84
      +1.0E+05,1.0E+02,5.0E+03,1.0E+01,5.0E+01,1.0E+02,                  LADTAP   85
      +5.0E+03,1.0E+03,6.0E+02,1.0E+03,5.0E+03,5.0E+03,2.0E+01,          LADTAP   86
      +5.0E+03,1.0E+03,5.0E+03,5.0E+03,3.3E+01,1.0E+03,                  LADTAP   87
      +1.0E+03,3.0E+01,1.0E+02,1.0E+02,2.0E+01,1.0E+02,1.0E+03,          LADTAP   88
      +1.0E+05,5.0E+03,3.6E+00,6.7E+01,6.0E+01/                           LADTAP   89
      +5.0E+03,5.0E+03,6.0E+01,6.0E+01/                                   LADTAP   90
   10 FORMAT(2X,19A4,A2)                                                  LADTAP   91
   20 FORMAT(8F10.0)                                                      BNLO1     4
   24 FORMAT(I10,2E10.2,I10)                                              LADTAP   95
   25 FORMAT(1H0,2X,'DISCHARGE=',1PE8.2,' CFS',10X,'SOURCE TERM MULTIPLI LADTAP   96
      +ER=',EH.2)                                                         LADTAP   97
   26 FORMAT(1H0,2X,'FRESHWATER SITE')                                    LADTAP   98
   27 FORMAT(1H0,2X,'SALTWATER SITE')                                     LADTAP   99
   30 FORMAT(1H0,' 50-MILE POPULATION=',1PE8.2,5X,'FRACTION --- ADULT=   LADTAP  100
      +',0PF4.2,/,49X,'TEENAGER=',F4.2,/,49X,'CHILD=',F4.2)              LADTAP  101
   28 FORMAT(1H1)                                                         LADTAP  102
      PL=15.0                                                             LADTAP  103
      IPRNT=1                                                             LADTAP  104
      JSB=1                                                               LADTAP  105
   22 READ(5,10)TITLE                                                     LADTAP  106
      IF(EOF(5).NE.0)GOTO500                                             LADTAP  107
      PRINT 28                                                            LADTAP  108
      READ 24,L1,CFS,UML,LCT                                              LADTAP  109
      IF(UML.EQ.0.) UML=1.                                                LADTAP  110
      READ 20,POP,TR                                                      LADTAP  111
      IF(TR.GT.0.) READ 20,PERA,PERT,PERC                                 LADTAP  112
      PRINT 10,ITITLE                                                     LADTAP  113
      PRINT 25,CFS,UML                                                    LADTAP  114
      IF(POP.GT.0) PRINT 30,POP,PERA,PERT,PERC                            LADTAP  115
                                                                          LADTAP  116
```

D-5

```
115        IF(LT.EQ.0) PRINT 26                          LADTAP  117
           IF(LT.GT.0) PRINT 27                          LADTAP  118
           IF(JSR.EQ.1) CALL REDDF(IPRNT)                LADTAP  119
           JSR=JSR+2                                     LADTAP  120
120        CALL PLOP(DOSE,4)                             LADTAP  121
           CALL SOURCE(UML)                              LADTAP  122
           IF(LT.EQ.0) CALL ALARA(FACCF,FACCI,FACCA)     LADTAP  123
           IF(LT.GT.0) CALL ALARA(SACCF,SACCI,SACCA)     LADTAP  124
           IF(LT.EQ.0) CALL WHY(FACCF,1,1)               LADTAP  125
           IF(LT.GT.0) CALL WHY(FACCF,1,2)               LADTAP  126
           IF(LT.EQ.0) CALL WHY(FACCI,2,1)               LADTAP  127
125        IF(LT.GT.0) CALL WHY(FACCI,2,2)               LADTAP  128
           IF(LT.EQ.0) CALL WHY(SACCF,1,1)               LADTAP  129
           IF(LT.GT.0) CALL WHY(SACCF,1,2)               LADTAP  130
           IF(LT.EQ.0) CALL WHY(SACCI,2,1)               LADTAP  131
           IF(LT.GT.0) CALL WHY(SACCI,2,2)               LADTAP  132
130        CALL WATER                                    LADTAP  133
           CALL ACTIVE                                   LADTAP  134
           CALL FLOOD                                    LADTAP  135
           IF(LT.EQ.0) CALL WHO(FACCF,FACCI,FACCA)       LADTAP  136
           IF(LT.GT.0) CALL WHO(SACCF,SACCI,SACCA)       LADTAP  137
135        CALL PLOP(DOSE,3)                             LADTAP  138
           GO TO 22                                      LADTAP  139
500        STOP                                          LADTAP  140
           END                                           LADTAP  141
```

```
                SUBROUTINE REDDF(IPRNT)                                          REDDF     4
                COMMON/SURCE/IZ(300),IMASS(300),META(300),NLIBA,NLIBT,NLIBC,NLIBI REDDF     5
                COMMON/ELEMN/IELEM(100)                                          REDDF     6
                COMMON Q(200),PL,CFS,NSUR,LT,RECD(200),LIST(200,4),LCT,LZ ,CON,KIT REDDF     7
               +,PDP                                                             REDDF     8
                COMMON/DFLIB/DFL(300,7),DFA(300,7),EXG(300,2),TAU(300),EXS(300,2), REDDF     9
               +EFF(300,8)                                                       RNLO1    10
                DIMENSION LS(20)                                                 REDDF    12
           10   FORMAT(1H1)                                                      REDDF    13
           11   FORMAT(/,/)                                                      RNLO1     6
           12   FORMAT(2X,19A4,A2)                                               REDDF    15
           13   FORMAT('  CHILD DOSE FACTORS')                                   REDDF    16
           14   FORMAT('  ADULT DOSE FACTORS')                                   REDDF    17
           15   FORMAT('  TEENAGER DOSE FACTORS')                                REDDF    18
           16   FORMAT(1X,2I3,A1,5E8.0)                                          REDDF    19
           17   FORMAT(10E8.0)                                                   REDDF    20
           18   FORMAT('  ADULT HEADING GOES HERE')                             REDDF    21
           19   FORMAT(I4,A2,I4,A1,1P12E9.2,//56X,/,10X,1P8E10.2)                REDDF    22
           20   FORMAT('  TEENAGER HEADING GOES HERE')                           REDDF    23
           21   FORMAT(I4,A2,I4,A1,1P7E9.2,//,11X,1P7E9.2)                       REDDF    24
           22   FORMAT('  INFANT DOSE FACTORS')                                  REDDF    25
           23   FORMAT('  DOSE FACTOR LIBRARY CONTAINS',I4,' ENTRIES')           REDDF    26
           24   FORMAT(1X,9E8.2)                                                 REDDF    27
     C** READ ADULT DOSE FACTOR LIBRARY                                          REDDF    28
                READ (10,12)LS                                                   REDDF    29
                K=0                                                              REDDF    30
           39   K=K+1                                                            REDDF    31
                READ(10,16)IZ(K),IMASS(K),META(K),TAU(K),EXG(K,2),EXS(K,2),EXG(K,1 REDDF    32
               +),FXS(K,1)                                                       REDDF    33
                TAU(K)=TAU(K)*3600.                                              REDDF    34
                IF(IZ(K))45,45,40                                                REDDF    35
           40   READ(10,17)(DFL(K,J),J=1,7)                                      REDDF    36
                READ(10,17)(DFA(K,J),J=1,7)                                      REDDF    37
                READ(10,24)(EFF(K,J),J=1,8)                                      REDDF    38
                GOTO 39                                                          REDDF    39
           45   NLIBA=K-1                                                        REDDF    40
                K=K-1                                                            REDDF    41
     C** READ TEENAGER DOSEFACTOR LIBRARY                                        REDDF    42
                READ(10,12)LS                                                    REDDF    43
           49   K=K+1                                                            REDDF    44
                READ(10,16)IZ(K),IMASS(K),META(K)                                REDDF    45
                IF(IZ(K))55,55,50                                                REDDF    46
           50   READ(10,17)(DFL(K,J),J=1,7)                                      REDDF    47
                READ(10,17)(DFA(K,J),J=1,7)                                      REDDF    48
                GOTO 49                                                          REDDF    49
           55   NLIBT=K-1                                                        REDDF    50
                K=K-1                                                            REDDF    51
     C** READ CHILD DOSE FACTOR LIBRARY                                          REDDF    52
                READ(10,12)LS                                                    REDDF    53
           59   K=K+1                                                            REDDF    54
                READ(10,16)IZ(K),IMASS(K),META(K)                                REDDF    55
                IF(IZ(K))65,65,60                                                REDDF    56
           60   READ(10,17)(DFL(K,J),J=1,7)                                      REDDF    57
                READ(10,17)(DFA(K,J),J=1,7)                                      REDDF    58
                GOTO 59                                                          REDDF    59
           65   NLIBC=K-1                                                        REDDF    60
                K=K-1                                                            REDDF
```

```
         READ(10,12)L5
   66    K=K+1
         READ(10,16)IZ(K),IMASS(K),META(K)
         IF(IZ(K))66,68,67
   67    READ(10,17)(DFL(K,J),J=1,7)
         READ(10,17)(DFA(K,J),J=1,7)
         GO TO 66
   68    NLIBI=K-1
         IF(IPRNT.GT.0)GOTO 1000
C** PRINT OUT ADULT DOSE FACTORS
         PRINT 10
         PRINT 11
         PRINT 14
         PRINT 18
         DO 70 K=1,NLIBA
         KK=IZ(K)
   70    PRINT 19, IZ(K),IELEM(KK),IMASS(K),META(K),TAU(K),(EXG(K,J),J=1,2)
        1,(EXS(K,J),J=1,2),(DFL(K,J),J=1,7),(DFA(K,J),J=1,7),(EFF(K,J),J=1,
        2R)
         K1=NLIBA+1
C** PRINT OUT TEENAGER DOSE FACTORS
         PRINT 10
         PRINT 11
         PRINT 15
         PRINT 20
         DO 80 K=K1,NLIBT
         KK=IZ(K)
   80    PRINT 21,IZ(K),IELEM(KK),IMASS(K),META(K),(DFL(K,J),J=1,7),(DFA(K,
        1J),J=1,7)
         K1=NLIBT+1
C** PRINT OUT CHILD DOSE FACTORS
         PRINT 10
         PRINT 11
         PRINT 13
         PRINT 20
         DO 90 K=K1,NLIBC
         KK=IZ(K)
   90    PRINT 21,IZ(K),IELEM(KK),IMASS(K),META(K),(DFL(K,J),J=1,7),(DFA(K,
        1J),J=1,7)
         K1=NLIBC+1
C** PRINT OUT INFANT DOSE FACTORS
         PRINT 10
         PRINT 11
         PRINT 22
         PRINT 20
         DO 100 K=K1,NLIBI
         KK=IZ(K)
  100    PRINT 21,IZ(K),IELEM(KK),IMASS(K),META(K),(DFL(K,J),J=1,7),(DFA(K,
        1J),J=1,7)
         PRINT 23,NLIBC
 1000    RETURN
         END
```

```
      SUBROUTINE SOURCE(UML)
      COMMON Q(200),PL,CFS,NSUP,LT,REC0(200),LIST(200,4),LCT,L2 ,CON,KIT
     +,POP
      COMMON/CFL16/DFL(300,7),DFA(300,7),EXG(300,2),TAU(300),EXS(300,2),
     +EFF(300,8)
      COMMON/SORCE/IZ(300),IMASS(300),META(300),NLIBA,NLIBT,NLIBC,NLIBI
      COMMON/ELEMEN/IELEM(100)
      DIMENSION IM(5),NUM(12),ISOR(20)
      DATA NUM/'1','10','11','2','3','4','5','6','7','8','9','M'/
   11 FORMAT(8E10.0)
   12 FORMAT(2X,19A4,A2)
   13 FORMAT(' GRIEF ',A2,5A1,1PE10.2)
   21 FORMAT(2X,A2,5A1,1X,E10.0)
   22 FORMAT(1H ,I4,A2,I4,A1,1X,1P12F9.2)
   23 FORMAT(1H0,'TOTAL NUMBER IN SOURCE TERM IS ',I4,5X,'TOTAL RELEASE
     +IS ',1PE10.4)
   30 FORMAT(1H ,'NUCLIDE  CURIE/YEAR   BONE      LIVER  TOTAL BODY  THYR
     +OID KIDNEY   LUNG  GI-LLI   SKIN  TOTAL BODY  REC(N)')
   31 FORMAT(1H0,21X,'           SHORELINE  ')
     +                            INGESTION DOSE FACTORS
   35 FORMAT(1H ,45X,'(MREM/PCI INTAKE)',22X,'(MREM/HR)/(PCI/M**2)')
   32 FORMAT(1H1,30X,'*    *     TEENAGER DOSE FACTORS     *    *  *')
   33 FORMAT(1H0,30X,'*    *      CHILD DOSE FACTORS       *    *  *')
   34 FORMAT(1H0,30X,'*    *      INFANT DOSE FACTORS      *    *  *')
   36 FORMAT(1H0,30X,'*    *      ADULT DOSE FACTORS       *    *  *')
      READ 12,ISOR
      PRINT 12,ISOR
      I=0
      QTE0.
   75 I=I+1
      READ 21,IA,IM,QQ
      IF(QQ)101,101,76
   76 K=-1
      MASS=0
      MET=NUM(1)
      JJ=-JJ
      DO 90 JJ=1,5
      IF(IM(J).EQ.NUM(1))GOTO 90
      IF(IM(J).NE.NUM(12))GOTO 78
      MET=NUM(12)
      GOTO 90
   78 K=K+1
      DO 80 L=2,11
   80 IF(NUM(L).EQ.IM(J))GOTO 85
      PRINT 13,IA,IM,QQ
      I=I-1
      GOTO 75
   85 MASS=MASS+(L-2)*10.**K
   90 CONTINUE
C** FIND Z OF NUCLIDE
      DO 91 IK=1,100
   91 IF(IELEM(IK).EQ.IA)GOTO 92
      PRINT 13,IA,IM,QQ
      I=I-1
      GOTO 75
C**.FINE NUCLIDE IN ADULT LIBRARY
   92 DO 95 LL=1,NLIBA
```

```
SOURCE    3
SOURCE    5
SOURCE    6
SOURCE    7
SOURCE    8
SOURCE    9
SOURCE   10
BMLO1     7
SOURCE   12
BMLO1    13
SOURCE   15
SOURCE   16
SOURCE   17
SOURCE   18
SOURCE   19
SOURCE   20
SOURCE   21
SOURCE   22
SOURCE   23
SOURCE   24
SOURCE   25
SOURCE   26
SOURCE   27
SOURCE   28
SOURCE   29
SOURCE   30
SOURCE   31
SOURCE   32
SOURCE   33
SOURCE   34
SOURCE   35
SOURCE   36
SOURCE   37
SOURCE   38
SOURCE   39
SOURCE   40
SOURCE   41
SOURCE   42
SOURCE   43
SOURCE   44
SOURCE   45
SOURCE   46
SOURCE   47
SOURCE   48
SOURCE   49
SOURCE   50
SOURCE   51
SOURCE   52
SOURCE   53
SOURCE   54
SOURCE   55
SOURCE   56
SOURCE   57
SOURCE   58
SOURCE   59
SOURCE   60
```

```
         IF(IZ(LL).NE.IK)GOTO 95                                    SOURCE   61
         IF(MASS(LL).NE.MASS)GOTO 95                                SOURCE   62
         IF(META(LL).NE.MET)GOTO 95                                 SOURCE   63
         GOTO 96                                                    SOURCE   64
  95     CONTINUE                                                   SOURCE   65
         I=I-1                                                      SOURCE   66
         PRINT 13,IA,IM,UQ                                          SOURCE   67
         GOTO 75                                                    SOURCE   68
  96     LIST(I,1)=LL                                               SOURCE   69
C** FIND NUCLIDE IN TEENAGER LIBRARY                                SOURCE   70
         K1=NLIBA+1                                                 SOURCE   71
         DO 97 LL=K1,NLIBT                                          SOURCE   72
         IF(IZ(LL).NE.IK)GOTO 97                                    SOURCE   73
         IF(MASS(LL).NE.MASS)GOTO 97                                SOURCE   74
         IF(META(LL).NE.MET)GOTO 97                                 SOURCE   75
         GOTO 98                                                    SOURCE   76
  97     CONTINUE                                                   SOURCE   77
         LIST(I,2)=LIST(I,1)                                        SOURCE   78
         GOTO 99                                                    SOURCE   79
  98     LIST(I,2)=LL                                               SOURCE   80
         DFL(LL,5)=DFL(LIST(I,1),5)                                 SOURCE   81
         DFA(LL,5)=DFA(LIST(I,1),5)                                 SOURCE   82
C** FIND NUCLIDE IN CHILD DOSE FACTOR LIBRARY                       SOURCE   83
  99     K1=NLIBT+1                                                 SOURCE   84
         DO 106 LL=K1,NLIBC                                         SOURCE   85
         IF(IZ(LL).NE.IK)GOTO 106                                   SOURCE   86
         IF(MASS(LL).NE.MASS)GOTO 106                               SOURCE   87
         IF(META(LL).NE.MET)GOTO 106                                SOURCE   88
         GOTO 107                                                   SOURCE   89
  106    CONTINUE                                                   SOURCE   90
         LIST(I,3)=LIST(I,2)                                        SOURCE   91
         GOTO 108                                                   SOURCE   92
  107    LIST(I,3)=LL                                               SOURCE   93
         DFL(LL,5)=DFL(LIST(I,1),5)                                 SOURCE   94
         DFA(LL,5)=DFA(LIST(I,1),5)                                 SOURCE   95
  108    CONTINUE                                                   SOURCE   96
C** FIND NUCLIDE IN INFANT DOSE FACTOR LIBRARY                      SOURCE   97
         K1=NLIBC+1                                                 SOURCE   98
         DO 110 LL=K1,NLIAI                                         SOURCE   99
         IF(IZ(LL).NE.IK)GO TO 110                                  SOURCE  100
         IF(MASS(LL).NE.MASS)GO TO 110                              SOURCE  101
         IF(META(LL).NE.MET)GO TO 110                               SOURCE  102
         GO TO 115                                                  SOURCE  103
  110    CONTINUE                                                   SOURCE  104
         LIST(I,4)=LIST(I,3)                                        SOURCE  105
         GO TO 120                                                  SOURCE  106
  115    LIST(I,4)=LL                                               SOURCE  107
         DFL(LL,5)=DFL(LIST(I,1),5)                                 SOURCE  108
         DFA(LL,5)=DFA(LIST(I,1),5)                                 SOURCE  109
  120    CONTINUE                                                   SOURCE  110
         QT=QT+QQ                                                   SOURCE  111
         Q(I)=QQ*UML                                                SOURCE  112
         GOTO 75                                                    SOURCE  113
  101    NSON=I-1                                                   SOURCE  114
C** PRINT OUT SOURCE TERM                                           SOURCE  115
C**CALCULATES ANY RECONCENTRATION OF RADIONUCLIDES                  SOURCE  116
         CALL RECON                                                 SOURCE  117
```

```
      PRINT 36                                                       SOURCE   118
      PRINT 31                                                       SOURCE   119
      PRINT 35                                                       SOURCE   120
      PRINT 30                                                       SOURCE   121
      DO 105 I=1,NSOR                                                SOURCE   122
      LL=LIST(I,1)                                                   SOURCE   123
      IK=IZ(LL)                                                      SOURCE   124
  105 PRINT 22,IK,IELEM(IK),IMASS(LL),META(LL),Q(I),(DFL(LL,J),J=1,7),SOURCE  125
     +EXG(LL,1),EXG(LL,2),RECU(I)                                    SOURCE   126
      DO 210 JT=2,4                                                  SOURCE   127
      IF(JT.EQ.4) PRINT 34                                           SOURCE   128
      IF(JT.EQ.3) PRINT 33                                           SOURCE   129
      IF(JT.EQ.2) PRINT 32                                           SOURCE   130
      PRINT 31                                                       SOURCE   131
      PRINT 35                                                       SOURCE   132
      PRINT 30                                                       SOURCE   133
      DO 200 I=1,NSOR                                                SOURCE   134
      LL=LIST(I,1)                                                   SOURCE   135
      IK=IZ(LL)                                                      SOURCE   136
      LA=LIST(I,JT)                                                  SOURCE   137
      IF(LA.EQ.LL) GO TO 200                                         SOURCE   138
      PRINT 22,IK,IELEM(IK),IMASS(LL),META(LL),Q(I),(DFL(LA,J),J=1,7),SOURCE  139
  200 CONTINUE                                                       SOURCE   140
  210 CONTINUE                                                       SOURCE   141
      QT=QT+UML                                                      SOURCE   142
      PRINT 23,NSOR,QT                                              SOURCE   143
      RETURN                                                         SOURCE   144
      END                                                            SOURCE   145
```

```
      SUBROUTINE RECON                                                    RECON     2
      COMMON Q(200),PL,CFS,NSUR,LT,RECO(200),LIST(200,4),LCT,LZ ,CON,KIT  RECON     3
     +,PUP                                                                RECON     4
      COMMON/DFLIB/DFL(300,7),DFA(300,7),EXG(300,2),TAU(300),EXS(300,2),  RECON     5
     +EFF(300,8)                                                          RECON     6
      COMMON/SINCE/IZ(300),IMASS(300),META(300),NLIBA,NLIBT,NLIBC,NLIBI   RECON     7
      REAL MAKF                                                           RECON     8
   10 FORMAT(I10,5F10.2)                                                  RECON    10
   15 FORMAT(1H0,'NU RECONCENTRATION OF NUCLIDES ')                       RECON    11
   16 FORMAT(1H0,'RECONCENTRATION-- MAKE-UP',1PE8.2,5X,'CYCLE TIME=',     RECON    12
     +E8.2,' HR',5X,'VOL OF POND=',E8.2,' FT**3',/,20X,'TURNOVER RATE=',  RECON    13
     +E8.2,'/HR',5X,'COOLANT FLOW=',E8.2,' CFS')                         RECON    14
   17 FORMAT(1H0,'RECONCENTRATION==  CYCLE TIME=',F10.2,' HR',5X,'RECYC   RECON    15
     +LE FRACTION=',F10.2)                                                RECON    16
      READ(5,10)M,MAKF,CT,VOL,TR,RF                                       RECON    17
      IF(M.EQ.0)WRITE(6,15)                                              RECON    18
      IF(M.EQ.1)WRITE(6,16)MAKE,CT,VOL,TR,CFS                            RECON    19
      IF(M.EQ.2)WRITE(6,17)CT,RF                                         RECON    20
      IF(M-1)20,20,30                                                    RECON    21
   20 DO 50 J=1,NSUR                                                     RECON    22
      M=LIST(J,1)                                                        RECON    23
      ARGU=TAU(M-1)*CT                                                   RECON    24
      IF(ARGU.GT.100.)ARGU=100.                                          RECON    25
   50 RECO(J)=1./(1.-((CFS-MAKE)*EXP(-ARGU))/(CFS+VOL*TR/3600.))         RECON    26
      RETURN                                                             RECON    27
   30 TUTC=PL*365.25*24./CT                                              RECON    28
      N=1+INT(TUTC)                                                      RECON    29
      DO 60 J=1,NSUR                                                     RECON    30
      M=LIST(J,1)                                                        RECON    31
      ARGU=TAU(M)*100.*CT                                                RECON    32
      IF(ARGU.GT.100.)ARGU=100.                                          RECON    33
      STEW=RF*EXP(-ARGU)                                                 RECON    34
      TEST=TUTC*ALOG(STEW)                                               RECON    35
      IF(TEST.LT.-11.51)GO TO 40                                         RECON    36
      STEW=STEW**N                                                       RECON    37
      GO TO 60                                                           RECON    38
   40 STEW=1.0E-05                                                       RECON    39
   60 RECO(J)=(1.-STEW)/(1.-(RF*EXP(-ARGU)))                             RECON    40
      RETURN                                                             RECON    41
  100 DO 70 J=1,NSOR                                                     RECON    42
   70 RECO(J)=1.                                                         RECON    43
      RETURN                                                             RECON    44
      END                                                               RECON    45
```

```
            SUBROUTINE ALARA (ACCF,ACCI,ACCA)                              ALARA    2
            COMMON Q(200),PL,CFS,NSUP,LT,RECD(200),LIST(200,4),LCT,LZ ,CON,KIT  ALARA    3
           +,POP                                                           ALARA    4
            DIMENSION ACCF(100),ACCI(100),ACCA(100)                        ALARA    5
            DIMENSION LOCA (3)                                             ALARA    6
      C                                                                    ALARA    7
      C     PRINTS HEADINGS FOR THE APPENDIX I INDIVIDUAL                  ALARA    8
      C     DOSE TABLES AND THE SELECTED LOCATION DOSE                     ALARA    9
      C     TABLES-ALSO CALLS SUBROUTINE OUT WITH                          ALARA   10
      C     THE CORRECT USAGE PARAMETERS FOR A                            ALARA   11
      C     PARTICULAR AGE GROUP                                          ALARA   12
      C                                                                    ALARA   13
                                                                           ALARA   14
                                                                           ALARA   15
         10 FORMAT(1H1,35X,'*    *    AS LOW AS REASONABLY ACHIEVABLE *    ALARA   16
           C *')                                                           ALARA   17
         20 FORMAT(1H ,55X,'MREM PER YEAR')                                ALARA   18
         25 FORMAT(1H1)                                                    ALARA   19
         40 FORMAT(1H0,'PATHWAY      THYROID    SKIN    KIDNEY    BONE    LUNG  LI  ALARA   20
           1VER    TOTAL BODY                                   DOSE       ALARA   21
         50 F(FRMAT(1H0,17X,'                                     ')       ALARA   22
           +,(MREM PER YEAR INTAKE)                                        ALARA   23
         60 FORMAT(1H0,20X,'A D U L T   D O S E S')                        ALARA   24
         70 FORMAT(1H0,20X,'C H I L D   D O S E S')                        ALARA   25
         80 FORMAT(1H0,20X,'T E E N A G E R   D O S E S 3')                ALARA   26
         90 FORMAT(1H0,20X,'I N F A N T   D O S E S')                      ALARA   27
        160 FORMAT(1H0,'LOCATION IS ',3A4)                                 ALARA   28
      C                                                                    ALARA   29
        100 FORMAT(110,7E10.0)                                             ALARA   30
        110 FORMAT(7E10.0)                                                 ALARA   31
        130 FORMAT(1H1,35X,'*    *    SELECTED LOCATION *    *    *')       ALARA   32
        140 FORMAT(110,3E10.0,3A4)                                         ALARA   33
            CON=1.0                                                        ALARA   34
            KK=0                                                           ALARA   35
        150 CONTINUE                                                       ALARA   36
            DATA TDF,TDC,TDA,TDW,TD8,TD8W,TD8R/0.,0.,0.,0.,510.,0.,0.,0.,0.0/  ALARA   37
            DATA CHF,CHC,CHA,CHW,CHS,CHSW,CHR/6.9,0.,0.,0.,510.,18.,0.,0.,0.0/ ALARA   38
            IF(LT.GT.0) CHC=1.7                                            ALARA   39
            DATA TAF,TAC,TAA,TAW,TAS,TASW,TA8/16.,0.,0.,0.,510.,67.,0.,0.,0.0/ ALARA   40
            IF(LT.GT.0) TAC=3.8                                            ALARA   41
            DATA FIUS,CHUS,ALUS,WUSE,SHU,SWU,BUSE/21.,0.,0.,0.,730.,12.,0.,0.,0./ ALARA 42
      C                                                                    ALARA   43
            IF(LT.GT.0)CRUS=5.0                                            ALARA   44
            IF(KK.EQ.0)READ 100,N,SWF,DILU,SHD,DWD,T,TU                    ALARA   45
            IF(KK.GT.0) READ 140,N,DILU,T,SWF,(LOCA(J),J=1,3)              ALARA   46
            IF (N.EQ.0)GO TO 120                                           ALARA   47
            READ 110,FIUS,CKUS,ALUS,WUSE,SHU,SWU,BUSE                      ALARA   48
            READ 110,TAF,TAC,TAA,TAW,TAS,TASW,TA8                          ALARA   49
            READ 110,CHF,CHC,CHA ,CHW,CHS,CHSW,CH8                         ALARA   50
            READ 110,TDF,TDC,TDA,TDW,TD8,TD8W,TD8                          ALARA   51
        120 CONTINUE                                                       ALARA   52
            IF(DILU.EQ.0.)GO TO 200                                        ALARA   53
            IF(KK.GT.0) PRINT 130                                          ALARA   54
            IF(KK.EQ.0)PRINT 10                                            ALARA   55
            IF(KK.GT.0)SHD=DILU                                            ALARA   56
            SWD=SHD                                                        ALARA   57
                                                                           ALARA   58
```

```
             HUIL=DILU
             IF(KK.GT.1)DWD=DILU
             IF(KK.GT.1) PRINT 160,LUCA
             IF(KK.GT.1) TD=T
      C
 60          PRINT 60
             PRINT 50
             PRINT 40
             CALL OUT(1,ACCF,ACCI,ACCA,T,FIUS,CRUS,ALUS,NUSE,SMU,SWU,BUSE,DILU,
            +DWD,SWD,SWD,BDIL,SWF,KK,N,TD)
             IF(KK.GT.0.AND.LCT.GT.0)PRINT 130
             IF(KK.GT.1) PRINT 160,LUCA
 70          IF(KK.EQ.0.AND.LCT.GT.0)PRINT 10
             PRINT 80
             PRINT 50
             PRINT 40
             CALL OUT(2,ACCF,ACCI,ACCA,T,TAF,TAC,TAA,TAN,TAS,TASW,TAB,DILU,DWD,
            +SWD,SWD,BDIL,SWF,KK,N,TD)
 75          IF(KK.GT.0.AND.LCT.GT.0)PRINT 130
             IF(KK.GT.1) PRINT 160,LOCA
             IF(KK.EQ.0.AND.LCT.GT.0)PRINT 10
             PRINT 70
             PRINT 50
 80          PRINT 40
             CALL OUT(3,ACCF,ACCI,ACCA,T,CHF,CHC,CHC,CHA,CHW,CHS,CHSW,CHB,DILU,DWD,
            +SWD,SWD,BDIL,SWF,KK,N,TD)
             IF(TDW.EQ.0..OR.LT.GT.0) GO TO 145
 85          IF(KK.GT.0.AND.LCT.GT.0)PRINT 130
             IF(KK.GT.1) PRINT 160,LUCA
             IF(KK.EQ.0.AND.LCT.GT.0)PRINT 10
             PRINT 90
 90          PRINT 50
             PRINT 40
             CALL OUT(4,ACCF,ACCI,ACCA,T,TDF,TDC,TDA,TDW,TDS,TDSW,TDB,DILU,DWD,
            +SWD,SWD,BDIL,SWF,KK,N,TD)
 145         KK=KK+2
 95          GO TO 150
 200         CONTINUE
             RETURN
             END
```

ALARA   59
ALARA   60
ALARA   61
ALARA   62
ALARA   63
ALARA   64
ALARA   65
ALARA   66
ALARA   67
ALARA   68
ALARA   69
ALARA   70
ALARA   71
ALARA   72
ALARA   73
ALARA   74
ALARA   75
ALARA   76
ALARA   77
ALARA   78
ALARA   79
ALARA   80
ALARA   81
ALARA   82
ALARA   83
ALARA   84
ALARA   85
ALARA   86
ALARA   87
ALARA   88
ALARA   89
ALARA   90
ALARA   91
ALARA   92
ALARA   93
ALARA   94
ALARA   95
ALARA   96

```
      SUBROUTINE OUT(KUP,ACCF,ACCI,ACCA,T,FIUS,CRUS,ALUS,MUSE,SHU,SWU,BU     OUT      2
     +St,DILU,DMD,SHD,SWD,BDIL,SWF,SK,N,IU)                                   OUT      3
      COMMON D(200),PL,CFS,NSUP,LT,MECU(200),LIST(200,4),LC1,LZ,CON,KIT       OUT      4
     + ,PUP                                                                   OUT      5
      DIMENSION W(3),X(3),Y(3),Z(3),H(3),FDUSE(8),CDUSE(8),ADUSE(8),SDUS      OUT      6
     1E(8),SWDU(8),BDUSE(8),TDUSE(8),A(3),H(3),C(3),WDUSE(8)                  OUT      7
      DIMENSION ACCI(100),ACCA(100),DUSE(200,8)                              OUT      8
                                                                             OUT      9
C     CONTROLS THE CALLING OF THE CALCULATIONAL SUBROUTINES WITH THE        OUT     10    BNL01
C     APPROPRIATE USAGE PARAMETERS FOR THE PARTICULAR AGE GROUP             OUT     11
C                                                                           OUT     12
C                                                                           OUT     13
      DATA Y/'TOTA','L   '/                                                 OUT     14
      DATA X/'INVE','RTEH','RATE'/                                          OUT     15
      DATA Z/'ALGA','E   '/                                                 OUT     16
      DATA C/'HUAT','ING '/                                                 OUT     17
      DATA H/'DRIN','KING'/                                                 OUT     18
      DATA W/'FISH','    '/                                                 OUT     19
      DATA A/'SHOR','ELIN','E   '/                                          OUT     20
      DATA B/'SWIM','MING'/                                                 OUT     21
   10 FORMAT(1H ,3A4,15X,1P7E15.2)                                          OUT     22    BNL01
   20 FORMAT(1H ,3A4,1P8E15.2)                                              OUT     24
      T2=T+24.                                                              OUT     25
      T3=TD+12.                                                             OUT     26
      LZ=0                                                                  OUT     27
      KIT=0                                                                 OUT     28
      CALL AQUA(W,DILU,FIUS,T2,FDUSE,KOP,ACCF)                              OUT     29
      PRINT 10,W,(FDUSE(J),J=2,8)                                           OUT     30
      CALL AQHA(X,DILU,CRUS,T2,CDUSE,KUP,ACCI)                              OUT     31
      IF(CRUS.GT.0.0) PRINT 10,X,(CDUSE(J),J=2,8)                           OUT     32
      CALL AQUA(Z,DILU,ALUS,T2,ADUSE,KUP,ACCA)                              OUT     33
      IF(ALUS.GT.0.0) PRINT 10,Z,(ADUSE(J),J=2,8)                          OUT     34
      CALL DRIFK(DMD,T3,MUSE,WDUSE,KOP)                                     OUT     35
      IF(LT.EQ.0) PRINT 10,H,(WDUSE(J),J=2,8)                              OUT     36
      CALL SHOPE(A,SWF,SHD,T,SHU,SDOSE)                                    OUT     37
      PRINT 20,A,SDUSE                                                      OUT     38
      GEOM=1.                                                              OUT     39
      CALL SWIM(H,SHD,T,SWU,GEOM,SHDU)                                     OUT     40
      IF(SWU.GT.0.0) PRINT 20,B,SHDU                                        OUT     41
      GEOM=2.                                                              OUT     42
      CALL SWIM(C,HDIL,T,BUSE,GEOM,BDUSE)                                  OUT     43
      IF(BUSE.GT.0.) PRINT 20,C,BDUSE                                      OUT     44
      DO 40 J=1,R                                                          OUT     45
   40 TDUSE(J)=FDUSE(J)+CDUSE(J)+ADUSE(J)+SDUSE(J)+WDUSE(J)+SWDO(J)+BDOS    OUT     46
     1E(J)                                                                 OUT     47
      PRINT 20,Y,TDUSE                                                     OUT     48
   60 FORMAT(1H0,12X,'USAGE  (KG/YR,HR/YR)         DILUTION        TIME(HR  OUT     49
     +)',10X,'SHOREWIDTH FACTURE',F3.1)                                    OUT     50
   70 FORMAT(1H ,3A4,7X,F8.1,10X,F10.1,3X,F10.2)                           OUT     51
      PRINT 60,SWF                                                         OUT     52
      PRINT 70,W,FIUS,DILU,T2                                              OUT     53
      IF(CRUS.GT.0.) PRINT 70,X,CRUS,DILU,T2                               OUT     54
      IF(ALUS.GT.0.) PRINT 70,Z,ALUS,DILU,T2                               OUT     55
      IF(MUSE.GT.0.AND.LT.EQ.0) PRINT 70,H,MUSE,DMD,T3                     OUT     56
      IF(SHU.GT.0.0) PRINT 70,A,SHU,SHD,T                                  OUT     57
      IF(SWU.GT.0.0) PRINT 70,B,SWU,SWD,T                                  OUT     58
```

```
60        IF(BUSE.GT.0.0) PRINT 70,C,BUSE,BDIL,T        OUT    59
          KIT=10                                        OUT    60
80        CONTINUE                                      OUT    61
          IF(LCT.GT.0)CALL PERDOS(W,TDOSE,DOSE)         OUT    62
          RETURN                                        OUT    63
          END                                           OUT    64
```

```
      SUBROUTINE WHO(ACCF,ACCI,ACCA)
      COMMON G(200),PL,CFS,NSUR,LT,RECI(200),LIST(200,4),LCT,LZ,CON,KIT
     +,POP
      DIMENSION EXT(8),EXI(8),TDOSE(8),TYPE(3),A(3),B(3),C(3),D(3),W(3),
     CX(3),Z(3),ACCF(100),ACCI(100),ACCA(100)
C
C     CONTROLS THE CALLING OF THE CALCULATIONAL SUBROUTINES FOR THE
C     PRIMARY AND SECONDARY BIOTA DOSES
C
      DATA CSWF/2.0/
      DATA RAT,RAC,HERON,DUCK/6.,14.,11.,5./
      DATA RATMAS,RACMAS,HEMMAS,DUCMAS/1000.,12000.,4600.,1000./
      DATA RATUSE,RACUSE,MERUSE,DUCUSE/100.,200.,600.,100./
C     BIOTA TYPES
      DATA A/'MUSK','RAT ',' '/
      DATA B/'RACC','OON ',' '/
      DATA C/'HERO','N   ',' '/
      DATA D/'DUCK',' ',' '/
      DATA W/'FISH',' ',' '/
      DATA X/'INVE','RTEB','RATE'/
      DATA Z/'ALGA','E ',' '/
   70 FORMAT(1H0,                                                 ')
   20 FORMAT(1H ,3A4,1P3E15.2)
   60 FORMAT('DILUTION=',1PE10.2,10X,'TRANSIT TIME=',E10.2,' HR')
   10 FORMAT(1H1,'    *    DOSE TO BIOTA   *    *')
   30 FORMAT(1H0,20X,'MRADS PER YEAR')
   40 FORMAT(1H0,19X,'INTERNAL        EXTERNAL          TOTAL')
   50 FORMAT(RE10.0)
      CON=1.
      PRINT 10
      PRINT 30
   80 READ 50,DILU,T
      IF(DILU.EQ.0.)GO TO 100
      KIT=0
      LZ=0
      PRINT 70
      PRINT 40
      CALL CRITR(W,DILU,T,TDOSE,ACCF)
      CALL SHORE(TYPE,CSWF,DILU,T,4380.,EXT)
      CALL SWIP(TYPE,DILU,T,8760.,1.,EXI)
      TEXT=EXT(2)+EXI(2)
      TOT=TEXT+TDOSE(1)
      PRINT 20,W,TDOSE(1),TEXT,TOT
      CALL CRITR(X,DILU,T,TDOSE,ACCI)
      CALL SHORE(TYPE,CSWF,DILU,T,8760.,EXT)
      CALL SWIM (TYPE,DILU,T,8760.,1.,EXI)
      TEXT=EXT(2)+EXI(2)
      TOT=TEXT+TDOSE(1)
      PRINT 20,X,TDOSE(1),TEXT,TOT
      CALL CRITR(Z,DILU,T,TDOSE,ACCA)
      CALL SWIM(TYPE,DILU,T,8760.,1.,EXI)
      TOT=EXI(2)+TDOSE(1)
      PRINT 20,Z,TDOSE(1),EXI(2),TOT
      CALL EAT(A,RAT,RATMAS,RATUSE,DILU,T,TDOSE,ACCA)
```

D-17

```
                CALL SHORE(TYPE,CSWF,DILU,T,2922.,EXT)                    WHU    59
60              CALL SWIM(TYPE,DILU,T,2922.,1.,EXI)                       WHU    60
                TEXT=EXT(2)+EXI(2)                                        WHU    61
                TOT=TEXT+TDOSE(1)                                        WHU    62
                PRINT 20,A,TDOSE(1),TEXT,TOT                              WHU    63
                CALL EAT(H,HAC,HACMAS,HACUSE,DILU,T,TDOSE,ACCI)           WHU    64
65              CALL SHORE(TYPE,CSWF,DILU,T,2191.,EXT)                    WHU    65
                TOT=EXT(2)+TDOSE(1)                                       WHU    66
                PRINT 20,B,TDOSE(1),EXT(2),TOT                            WHU    67
                CALL EAT(C,HERIN,HERMAS,HERUSE,DILU,T,TDOSE,ACCF)         WHU    68
                CALL SHORE(TYPE,CSWF,DILU,T,2920.,EXT)                    WHU    69
70              CALL SWIM(TYPE,DILU,T,2920.,2.,EXI)                       WHU    70
                TEXT=EXT(2)+EXI(2)                                        WHU    71
                TOT=TEXT+TDOSE(1)                                        WHU    72
                PRINT 20,C,TDOSE(1),TEXT,TOT                              WHU    73
                CALL EAT(D,DUCK,DUCHAS,DUCUSE,DILU,T,TDOSE,ACCA)          WHU    74
75              CALL SHORE(TYPE,CSWF,DILU,T,4383.,EXT)                    WHU    75
                TEXT=EXT(2)+EXI(2)*3./2.                                  WHU    76
                TOT=TEXT+TDOSE(1)                                        WHU    77
                PRINT 20,D,TDOSE(1),TEXT,TOT                              WHU    78
                KIT=70                                                    WHU    79
80              IF(LCT.GT.0) CALL PERDUS(A,TDOSE,DOSE)                    WHU    80
                GO TO 80                                                  WHU    81
          100   CONTINUE                                                  WHU    82
                RETURN                                                    WHU    83
                END                                                       WHU    84
```

D-18

```
          SUBROUTINE WHY(ACC,I,N)                                        WHY    2
          COMMON/POPUL/PERA,PERT,PERC,US                                 WHY    3
          COMMON Q(200),PL,CFS,NSUR,LT,RECO(200),LIST(200,4),LCT,LZ ,CON,KIT  WHY  4
         +,PUP                                                           WHY    5
          DIMENSION ACC(100),X(3),W(3),CATH(20),DILU(20),T(20),TDUSE(8),DUSE  WHY  6
         +(200,8),A(3),W(3),C(3),TYPE(3),CONC(200)                       WHY    7
          DIMENSION D(3),PD(7)                                           WHY    8

    C                                                                    WHY    9
    C     CONTROLS THE CALCULATION OF THE SPORT                          WHY   10
    C     AND COMMERCIAL FISH AND INVERTEBRATE                           WHY   11
    C     POPULATION DOSES-ACTUAL CALCULATIONS                           WHY   12
    C     DONE BY SUBROUTINES PAFD AND CENT                              WHY   13
    C                                                                    WHY   14

          DATA X/'INVE','R   '/                                          WHY   15
          DATA W/'FISH','    '/                                          WHY   16
          DATA A/'ADUL','T   '/                                          WHY   17
          DATA B/'TEEN','AGER'/                                          WHY   18
          DATA C/'CHIL','D   '/                                          WHY   19
          DATA D/'TOTA','L   '/                                          WHY   20
     15   FORMAT(1H ,6A4,1P8E10.2)                                       WHY   21
     20   FORMAT(1H0,'PATHWAY       AGE GROUP   USAGE   BONE      LIVER   WHY   22
         + TOTAL BODY  THYROID  KIDNEY  LUNG  GI-LLI')                   WHY   23
     30   FORMAT(1H0,34X,'----------------------DOSE (MAN-REM)---------'  WHY   24
         +-----------------')                                            WHY   25
     60   FORMAT(1H0,' DILUTION  CATCH   TIME(HR) INCLUDES FOOD PROCESSING  WHY  26
         + TIME OF ',1PE4.2,' HR,5X,'POPULATION=',E8.2)                  WHY   27
     61   FORMAT(1H ,53X,'MAN-REM')                                      WHY   28
     64   FORMAT(1H1,35X,'*  * *  INVERTEBRATE CONSUMPTION POPULATION DOSES  WHY  29
         + *  * *')                                                      WHY   30
     65   FORMAT(1H1,35X,'*  * *  FISH CONSUMPTION POPULATION DOSES  *  *  WHY   31
         +*')                                                            WHY   32
     66   FORMAT(1H0,'                     SPORTFISH HARVEST_____')  WHY   33
     67   FORMAT(1H0,'                     COMMERCIAL HARVEST         ')  WHY   34
     68   FORMAT(1H0,'                     NEPA DOSES_____')          WHY   35
     69   FORMAT(1H0,'NOTE--TOTAL NEPA DOSE MUST INCLUDE SPORT CATCH, DOSES  WHY  36
         +BELOW ARE FOR COMMERCIAL CATCH ONLY')                         WHY   37
     70   FORMAT(8E10.2)                                                 WHY   38
     71   FORMAT(1H ,1P8E10.2)                                           WHY   39
     75   FORMAT(1H0,'AVERAGE INDIVIDUAL CONSUMPTION (KG/YR)    ADULT=',  WHY  40
         +1PE4.2,5X,'TEEN=',E8.2,5X,'CHILD=',E4.2)                       WHY   41
          P(AMT,AU,TU,CU)=AMT/(AU*PERA+TU*PERT+CU*PERC)                  WHY   42
          AUSE(PEO,AU)=PEO*PERA*AU                                       WHY   43
          TUSE(PEO,TU)=PEO*PERT*TU                                       WHY   44
          CUSE(PEO,CU)=PEO*PERC*CU                                       WHY   45
          CUP=1000.                                                      WHY   46
          LA=0                                                           WHY   47
          IF(N.EQ.1) NN=1                                                WHY   48
          IF(N.EQ.2) NN=2                                                WHY   49
          IF(I.EQ.1.AND.LT.EQ.0) HARV=4.0E+06                           WHY   50
          IF(I.EQ.2.AND.LT.EQ.0) HARV=2.30E+06                          WHY   51
          IF(I.EQ.1.AND.LT.GT.0) HARV=6.58E+08                          WHY   52
          IF(I.EQ.2.AND.LT.GT.0) HARV=4.10E+08                          WHY   53
          IF(N.EQ.1) FPT=168.                                            WHY   54
          IF(N.EQ.2) FPT=240.,                                          WHY   55
          J=1                                                            WHY   56
```

```
80  HEAD 70,CATH(J),DILU(J),T(J)                                    WHY    59
    T(J)=T(J)+FPT                                                   WHY    60
    J=J+1                                                           WHY    61
    M=M-1                                                           WHY    62
    IF(DILU(M).EQ.0.) GO TO 85                                      WHY    63
    GO TO 80                                                        WHY    64
85  M=M-1                                                           WHY    65
    IF(M.EQ.0) GO TO 100                                            WHY    66
    IF(I.EQ.1)PRINT 65                                              WHY    67
    IF(I.EQ.2)PRINT 64                                              WHY    68
    PRINT 61                                                        WHY    69
    IF(N.EQ.1)PRINT66                                               WHY    70
    IF(N.EQ.2)PRINT 67                                              WHY    71
    PRINT 30                                                        WHY    72
    PRINT 20                                                        WHY    73
    GO TO (21,22),I                                                 WHY    74
    GO TO 100                                                       WHY    75
21  AU=6.9                                                          WHY    76
    TU=5.2                                                          WHY    77
17  DO 17 J=1,3                                                     WHY    78
    TYPE(J)=W(J)                                                    WHY    79
    CU=2.2                                                          WHY    80
    GO TO 86                                                        WHY    81
22  AU=1.                                                           WHY    82
    TU=0.75                                                         WHY    83
    CU=0.33                                                         WHY    84
16  DO 16 J=1,3                                                     WHY    85
    TYPE(J)=X(J)                                                    WHY    86
    GO TO 86                                                        WHY    87
86  AMT=0.                                                          WHY    88
    IF(N.EQ.1) NL=1                                                 WHY    89
    IF(N.EQ.2) NL=2                                                 WHY    90
87  DO 87 IN=1,M                                                    WHY    91
    AMT=AMT+CATH(IN)                                                WHY    92
    IF(N.EQ.1)PEU=P(AMT,AU,TU,CU)                                   WHY    93
    IF(N.EQ.2)PEU=PUP                                               WHY    94
88  LZ=0                                                            WHY    95
    KIT=0                                                           WHY    96
    USE=AUSE(PEU,AU)                                                WHY    97
    CALL CENT(T,CATH,DILU,M,CONC,AMT,MARV,NL)                       WHY    98
    CALL PAFD(TYPE,ACC,CONC,1,USE,TDOSE,NN,LM)                      WHY    99
    PRINT 15,TYPE,A,USE,(TDOSE(JK),JK=1,7)                          WHY   100
89  DO 89 J=1,7                                                     WHY   101
    PD(J)=TDOSE(J)                                                  WHY   102
    SUM=USE                                                         WHY   103
    USE=TUSE(PEU,TU)                                                WHY   104
    CALL PAFD(TYPE,ACC,CONC,2,USE,TDOSE,NN,LM)                      WHY   105
    PRINT 15,TYPE,B,USE,(TDOSE(JK),JK=1,7)                          WHY   106
91  DO 91 J=1,7                                                     WHY   107
    PD(J)=PD(J)+TDOSE(J)                                            WHY   108
    SUM=SUM+USE                                                     WHY   109
    USE=CUSE(PEU,CU)                                                WHY   110
    CALL PAFD(TYPE,ACC,CONC,3,USE,TDOSE,NN,LM)                      WHY   111
    PRINT 15,TYPE,C,USE,(TDOSE(JK),JK=1,7)                          WHY   112
92  DO 92 J=1,7                                                     WHY   113
    PD(J)=PD(J)+TDOSE(J)                                            WHY   114
    SUM=SUM+USE                                                     WHY   115
```

```
115        PRINT 15,TYPE,D,SUM,(PD(J),J=1,7)        115
           IF(LM.GT.0)GO TO 100                     117
           PRINT 60,FPT,PFO                         118
           DO 90 J=1,M                              119
90         PRINT 71,OILU(J),CATH(J),T(J)            120
120        PRINT 75,AU,TU,CU                        121
           KIT=30                                   122
           IF(LCT.GT.0)CALL PERDOS(W,TDOSE,DOSE)    123
           IF(N.EQ.1)GO TO 100                      124
           LM=10                                    125
125        NL=1                                     126
           PRINT 68                                 127
           PRINT 69                                 128
           PRINT 30                                 129
           PRINT 20                                 130
130        PEO=P(AMT,AU,TU,CU)                      131
           GO TO 88                                 132
100        CONTINUE                                 133
           RETURN                                   134
           END                                      135
```

CARD NR. SEVERITY DETAILS   DIAGNOSIS OF PROBLEM

| 73 | I | AN IF STATEMENT MAY BE MORE EFFICIENT THAN A 2 OR 3 BRANCH COMPUTED GO TO STATEMENT. |
| 74 | I | THERE IS NO PATH TO THIS STATEMENT. |

```
                SUBROUTINE WATER                                                   WATER    2
                COMMON Q(200),PL,CFS,NSUR,LT,RECO(200),LIST(200,4),LCT,LZ ,CON,KIT  WATER    3
               +,PUP                                                               WATER    4
                COMMON/SORCE/IZ(300),IMASS(300),META(300),NLIBA,NLIBT,NLIBC,NLIBI   WATER    5
                DIMENSION TDOSE(8),A(3),B(3),C(3),D(3),TRI(3)                       WATER    6
                DIMENSION TYPE(3)                                                   WATER    7
                DIMENSION PD(8),CUM(8),E(3)                                         WATER    8
                DATA TRI/'WATE','R ',' '/                                           WATER    9
                DATA D/'TOTA','L ',' '/                                             WATER   10
                DATA E/'CUMU','L TO','TAL '/                                        WATER   11
                DATA A/'ADUL','T ',' '/                                            WATER   12
                DATA B/'TEEN','AGER',' '/                                          WATER   13
                DATA C/'CHIL','D ',' '/                                             WATER   14
                DATA TYPE/'DRIN','KING',' '/                                        WATER   15
             10 FORMAT(1H ,6A4,1P8E10.2)                                           WATER   16
             20 FORMAT(1H0,'PATHWAY        AGE GROUP    USAGE      BONE      LIVER  WATER   17
               + TOTAL BODY  THYROID   KIDNEY    LUNG    GI-LLI')                   WATER   18
             30 FORMAT(1H1,35X,' *  * POPULATION WATER CONSUMPTION DOSES  *  *     WATER   19
               +*)                                                                 WATER   20
             35 FORMAT(1H0,34X,'------------------------------------DOSE (MAN-REM)--------  WATER   21
               +------------------')                                              WATER   22
             50 FORMAT(1H0,'                                                    ') WATER   23
               +                                                                   WATER   24
             55 FORMAT(1H0,'POPULATION=',1PE8.2,5X,'D-LUTION=',1PE8.2,5X,'TRANSIT TI  WATER   25
               +ME=',E8.2,' HR (INCLUDING 24 HR FOR TREATMENT FACILITY)')          WATER   26
             60 FORMAT(8E10.0)                                                     WATER   27
             65 FORMAT(1H0,'---------HYDROSPHERE TRITIUM DOSE-------')             WATER   28
             66 FORMAT(1H0,'------CUMULATIVE TOTAL----')                           WATER   29
             80 FORMAT(1H0,'AVERAGE INDIVIDUAL CONSUMPTION (L/YR)    ADULT=',      WATER   30
               +1PE8.2,5X,'TEEN=',E8.2,5X,'CHILD=',E8.2)                           WATER   31
                DATA AU/370./                                                      WATER   32
                DATA TU/260./                                                      WATER   33
                DATA CU/260./                                                      WATER   34
                AUSE(P,AU)=P*PERA*AU                                               WATER   35
                TUSE(P,TU)=P*PERT*TU                                               WATER   36
                CUSE(P,CU)=P*PERC*CU                                               WATER   37
                CON=1000.                                                          WATER   38
                DO 56 J=1,8                                                        WATER   39
             56 CUM(JM)=0.0                                                        WATER   40
                EUS=0.0                                                            WATER   41
                PRINT 30                                                           WATER   42
             40 READ 60,P,DILU,T,GAL,GUS                                           WATER   43
                PRINT 50                                                           WATER   44
                IF(P.EQ.0..AND.GUS.GT.0.) P=GAL/GUS                                WATER   45
                IF(DILU.EQ.0.)GO TO 100                                            WATER   46
                PRINT 35                                                           WATER   47
                PRINT 20                                                           WATER   48
                DO 41 JM=2,8                                                       WATER   49
             41 PD(JM)=0.0                                                         WATER   50
                T=T+24.                                                            WATER   51
                USE=AUSE(P,AU)                                                     WATER   52
                KIT=0                                                              WATER   53
                LZ=0                                                               WATER   54
                CALL DRINK(DILU,T,USE,TDOSE,1)                                     WATER   55
                PRINT 10,TYPE,A,USE,(TDOSE(JK),JK=2,8)                             WATER   56
                DO 42 JM=2,8                                                       WATER   57
```

```
        SUBROUTINE ACTIVE                                                       ACTIVE        2
        COMMON Q(200),PL,CFS,NSUR,LT,RECO(200),LIST(20D,4),LCT,LZ ,CON,KIT      ACTIVE        3
       +,PUP                                                                    ACTIVE        4
        DIMENSION S(3),SW(3),D(3),A(3),B(3),C(3),TDUSE(8)                       ACTIVE        5
        DIMENSION LJCA(3)                                                       ACTIVE        6
        DATA S/'SHOK','ELIN','E  '/                                            ACTIVE        7
        DATA SW/'SWIM','MING',' '/                                             ACTIVE        8
        DATA D/'THIAT','INL,' '/                                               ACTIVE        9
        DATA A/'TOTA','L PUP','PUL '/                                          ACTIVE       10
     80 FORMAT(1H0,'LOCATION=',3A4)                                            ACTIVE       11
     15 FORMAT(1H0,'DILUTION=',E8.2,10X,'TRANSIT TIME=',E4.2,' HR',10X,'SW     ACTIVE       12
       +F=',F3.1)                                                              BNL01        13
     10 FORMAT(1H ,6A4,1P7E15.2)                                              BNL01        14
     16 FORMAT(1H1,35X,'*  *   RECREATION POPULATION DOSES   *  *             ACTIVE       15
       +*')                                                                    ACTIVE       16
     20 FORMAT(1H0,'PATHWAY           AGE GROUP       USAGE         SKIN       ACTIVE       17
       +         TOTAL BODY       THYROID')                                    ACTIVE       18
     30 FORMAT(1H1,'*      *     POPULATION DOSES  *      *')                  ACTIVE       19
     40 FORMAT(1H ,48X,'                 DOSE(MAN-REM)               ')        ACTIVE       20
     50 FORMAT(1H0,'                                                   ')      ACTIVE       21
       +                                                                       ACTIVE       22
     60 FORMAT(1H0,'DILUTION=',E8.2,10X,'TRANSIT TIME=',E8.2,' HR')            ACTIVE       23
     70 FORMAT(4E10.0,3A4)                                                     ACTIVE       24
     75 FORMAT(3E10.0,3A4)                                                     ACTIVE       25
        PRINT 16                                                               ACTIVE       26
        CON=1000.                                                              ACTIVE       27
        JL=10                                                                  ACTIVE       28
    100 READ 70,SWU,DILU,T,SWF,(LUCA(J),J=1,3)                                 ACTIVE       29
        PRINT 50                                                               ACTIVE       30
        IF(DILU.EQ.0.)GO TO 110                                                ACTIVE       31
        LZ=0                                                                   ACTIVE       32
        PRINT 40                                                               ACTIVE       33
        KIT=0.                                                                 ACTIVE       34
        PRINT 20                                                               ACTIVE       35
        CALL SHORE(S,SWF,DILU,T,SWU,TDOSE)                                     ACTIVE       36
        PRINT 10,S,A,SWU,(TDOSE(J),J=1,3)                                      ACTIVE       37
        PRINT 80,LOCA                                                          ACTIVE       38
        PRINT 15,DILU,T,SWF                                                    ACTIVE       39
        KIT=40                                                                 ACTIVE       40
        IF(JL.LT.0)GO TO 100                                                   ACTIVE       41
        IF(LCT.GT.0)CALL PERDOS(W,TDOSE,DUSE)                                  ACTIVE       42
        JL=-10                                                                 ACTIVE       43
        GO TO 100                                                              ACTIVE       44
    110 READ 75,SWU,DILU,T,(LOCA(J),J=1,3)                                     ACTIVE       45
        PRINT 50                                                               ACTIVE       46
        IF(DILU.EQ.0.)GO TO 120                                                ACTIVE       47
        LZ=0                                                                   ACTIVE       48
        KIT=0.                                                                 ACTIVE       49
        PRINT 40                                                               ACTIVE       50
        PRINT 20                                                               ACTIVE       51
        GEOM=1.                                                                ACTIVE       52
        CALL SWIM(SW,DILU,T,SWU,GEOM,TOUSE)                                    ACTIVE       53
        PRINT 10,SW,A,SWU,(TDOSE(J),J=1,3)                                     ACTIVE       54
        PRINT 80,LOCA                                                          ACTIVE       55
        PRINT 60,DILU,T                                                        ACTIVE       56
        KIT=40                                                                 ACTIVE       57
        IF(JL.GT.0)GO TO 110                                                   ACTIVE       58
```

```
      42  PD(JM)=PD(JM)+TDOSE(JM)                                                WATER  59
          DO 57 JM=2,8                                                          WATER  60
      57  CUM(JM)=CUM(JM)+TDOSE(JM)                                             WATER  61
          TUS=USE                                                               WATER  62
          USE=TUSE(P,TU)                                                        WATER  63
          CALL DRINK(DILU,T,USE,TDOSE,2)                                       WATER  64
          PRINT 10,TYPE,R,USE,(TDOSE(JK),JK=2,8)                               WATER  65
          DO 43 JM=2,8                                                          WATER  66
      43  PD(JM)=PD(JM)+TDOSE(JM)                                               WATER  67
          DO 58 JM=2,8                                                          WATER  68
      58  CUM(JM)=CUM(JM)+TDOSE(JM)                                             WATER  69
          TUS=TUS+USE                                                           WATER  70
          USE=CUSE(P,CU)                                                        WATER  71
          CALL DRINK(DILU,T,USE,TDOSE,3)                                       WATER  72
          PRINT 10,TYPE,C,USE,(TDOSE(JK),JK=2,8)                               WATER  73
          DO 44 JM=2,8                                                          WATER  74
      44  PD(JM)=PD(JM)+TDOSE(JM)                                               WATER  75
          DO 59 JM=2,8                                                          WATER  76
      59  CUM(JM)=CUM(JM)+TDOSE(JM)                                             WATER  77
          TUS=TUS+USE                                                           WATER  78
          EUS=FUS+TUS                                                           WATER  79
          PRINT 10,TYPE,D,TUS,(PD(JM),JM=2,8)                                  WATER  80
          KIT=20                                                                WATER  81
          PRINT 55,P,DILU,T                                                     WATER  82
          PRINT RO,AU,TU,CU                                                     WATER  83
          IF(LCT.GT.0) CALL PERDUS(TYPE,TDOSE,DOSE)                            WATER  84
          GO TO 40                                                              WATER  85
     100  CONTINUE                                                              WATER  86
          IF(PD(2).GT.0.0) PRINT 66                                            WATER  87
          IF(PD(2).GT.0.0) PRINT 20                                            WATER  88
          IF(PD(2).GT.0.0) PRINT 10,TYPE,E,EUS,(CUM(JM),JM=2,8)               WATER  89
          PRINT 65                                                              WATER  90
          PRINT 20                                                              WATER  91
          USE=2.2                                                               WATER  92
          DO 70 I=1,NSOR                                                        WATER  93
          M=LIST(I,1)                                                           WATER  94
          IF(M.EQ.1) CALL TRTIUM(Q(M),POP,H3B,H3T)                            WATER  95
          IF(M.EQ.1)PRINT 10,TRI,D,USE,H3B,H3T,H3B,H3B,H3B,H3B                 WATER  96
      70  CONTINUE                                                              WATER  97
          RETURN                                                                WATER  98
          END                                                                  WATER  99
```

D-24

```
          IF(LCT.GT.0)CALL PERDOS(W,TDOSE,DOSE)
          JL=10
          GO TO 110
60    120  READ 75,HUSE,DILU,T,(LOCA(J),J=1,3)
          PRINT 50
          IF(DILU.EQ.0.)GO TO 130
          LZ=0
65        KIT=0.
          GEOM=2.0
          PRINT 40
          PRINT 20
          CALL SWIM(O,DILU,T,HUSE,GEOM,TDOSE)
70        PRINT 10,O,A,HUSE,(TDOSE(J),J=1,3)
          PRINT 80,LOCA
          PRINT 60,DILU,T
      C
      C
75    130  GO TO 120
          CONTINUE
          RETURN
          END
```

ACTIVE   59
ACTIVE   60
ACTIVE   61
ACTIVE   62
ACTIVE   63
ACTIVE   64
ACTIVE   65
ACTIVE   66
ACTIVE   67
ACTIVE   68
ACTIVE   69
ACTIVE   70
ACTIVE   71
ACTIVE   72
ACTIVE   73
ACTIVE   74
ACTIVE   75
ACTIVE   76
ACTIVE   77
ACTIVE   78
ACTIVE   79

D-25

```
            SUBROUTINE AQUA (CRITR,DILU,USF,T,TDOSE,JJ,ACC)                    AQUA    2
            COMMON/DFLIB/DFL(300,7),DFA(300,7),EXG(300,2),TAU(300),EXS(300,2), AQUA    3
           +EFF(300,8)                                                         AQUA    4
            COMMON Q(200),PL,CFS,NSUR,LT,RECU(200),LIST(200,8),LCT,LZ ,CON,KIT AQUA    5
           + ,POP                                                             AQUA    6
            COMMON/SORCE/IZ(300),IMASS(300),META(300),NLIBA,NLIBT,NLIBC,NLIBI  AQUA    7
            DIMENSION ACC(100),TDOSE(8),DOSE(200,8),CRITR(3)                   AQUA    8
            DO 8 J=1,8                                                         AQUA    9
          8 TDOSE(J)=0.0                                                       AQUA   10
            IF(USF.EQ.0.)GO TO 50                                             AQUA   11
            DO 10 I=1,NSUR                                                     CHANGE1  1
            DOSE(I,1)=0.                                                       AQUA   13
            LL=LIST(I,JJ)                                                      AQUA   14
            LM=LIST(I,1)                                                       AQUA   15
            MU=IZ(LM)                                                          AQUA   16
            ARGU=TAU(LM)*T                                                     AQUA   17
            IF(ARGU.GT.20.)GO TO 20                                           AQUA   18
            FACT=119.*Q(I)*RECU(I)/CFS/DILU*EXP(-ARGU)*USF*ACC(MO)/CON         AQUA   19
            GO TO 30                                                           AQUA   20
         20 FACT=0.0                                                           AQUA   21
         30 DO 40 J=2,8                                                        AQUA   22
            L=J-1                                                              AQUA   23
            DOSE(I,J)=DFL(LL,L)*FACT                                           AQUA   24
            TDOSE(J)=TDOSE(J)+DOSE(I,J)                                        AQUA   25
         40 CONTINUE                                                           AQUA   26
         10 CONTINUE                                                           AQUA   27
            IF(LCT.GT.0) CALL PERDOS(CRITR,TDOSE,DOSE)                         AQUA   28
         50 CONTINUE                                                           AQUA   29
            RETURN                                                            
            END                                                               
```

D-26

```
      SUBROUTINE DRINK(DWD,T,USE,TDUSE,JJ)                               DRINK     2
      COMMON Q(200),PL,CFS,NSUR,LT,REC0(200),LIST(200,4),LCT,LZ ,CON,KIT DRINK     3
     +  ,PDP                                                             DRINK     4
      COMMON/SORCE/IZ(300),IMASS(300),META(300),NLIBA,NLIBT,NLIBC,NLIBI  DRINK     5
      COMMON/DFLIB/DFL(300,7),DFA(300,7),EXG(300,2),TAU(300),EXS(300,2), DRINK     6
     +EFF(300,8)                                                         DRINK     7
      COMMON/TRANS/DILM                                                  CHANGE1   2
      DIMENSION TDUSE(8),DUSE(200,8),TYPE(3)                             DRINK     8
      DATA TYPE/'DRIN','KING',' '/                                       DRINK     9
      DILM = DWD                                                         CHANGE1   3
      DO 8 J=1,8                                                         DRINK    10
    8 TDUSE(J)=0.0                                                       DRINK    11
      IF(USE.EQ.0.)GO TO 50                                             DRINK    12
      IF(LT.GT.0) GO TO 50                                              DPINK    13
      DO 10 I=1,NSUR                                                     DRINK    14
      DUSE(I,1)=0.                                                       CHANGE1   4
      LL=LIST(I,JJ)                                                      DRINK    15
      LM=LIST(I,1)                                                       DRINK    16
      MU=IZ(LM)                                                          DRINK    17
      ARGU=TAU(LM)*T                                                     DRINK    18
      IF(ARGU.GT.20.) GO TO 20                                          DRINK    19
      FACT=119.*MU(I)*REC0(I)/CF8/DWD*EXP(-ARGU)*USE/CON                 DRINK    20
      GO TO 30                                                           DRINK    21
   20 FACT=0.0                                                           DRINK    22
   30 DO 40 J=2,8                                                        DRINK    23
      L=J-1                                                              DRINK    24
      DUSE(I,J)=DFL(LL,L)*FACT                                           DRINK    25
   40 TDUSE(J)=TDUSE(J)+DUSE(I,J)                                        DRINK    26
   10 CONTINUE                                                           DRINK    27
      IF (LCT.GT.0) CALL PERDUS(TYPE,TDUSE,DUSE)                         DRINK    28
      IF(CON.GT.10.)CALL PLOP(DUSE,7)                                    DRINK    29
   50 CONTINUE                                                           DRINK    30
      RETURN                                                             DRINK    31
      END                                                               DRINK    32
```

```
         SUBROUTINE SHURE(TYPE,SWF,DILU,T,USE,TDOSE)                    SHURE      2
         COMMON W(200),PL,CFS,NSUR,LT,RECO(200),LIST(200,4),LCT,LZ ,CON,KIT  SHURE 3
        +,PUP                                                           SHURE      4
         COMMON/DFL(IH/DFL(300,7),DFA(300,7),EXG(300,7),EXS(300,2),TAU(300),EXS(300,2),  SHURE  5
        +EFF(300,8)                                                     SHURE      6
         COMMON/SORCE/IZ(300),IMASS(300),META(300),NLIBA,NLIBT,NLIBC,NLIBI  SHURE  7
         DIMENSION TYPE(3),TDOSE(8),DOSE(200,8)                         SHURE      8
         DO 8 J=1,8                                                     SHURE      9
       8 TDOSE(J)=0.0                                                   SHURE     10
         IF(USE.EQ.0.)GO TO 50                                          SHURE     11
         DO 10 I=1,NSUR                                                 SHURE     12
         LM=LIST(I,1)                                                   SHURE     13
         MU=IZ(LM)                                                      SHURE     14
         ARGU=TAU(LM)*PL*8760.                                          SHURE     15
         IF(ARGU.GT.100.)ARGU=100                                       SHURE     16
         TP=TAU(LM)*T                                                   SHURE     17
         IF(TP.GT.100)TP=100                                            SHURE     18
         FACT=10000.*(.693/TAU(LM)/24.)*Q(I)*RECU(I)/CFS/DILU*EXP(-TP)*SWF  SHURE  19
        C*(1.-EXP(-ARGU))*USE/CON                                       SHURE     20
         DO 20 J=1,8                                                    CHANGE1    5
         IF(J.GT.2)GOTO 15                                              CHANGE1    6
         DOSE(I,J)=FACT*EXG(LM,J)                                       SHURE     22
         TDOSE(J)=TDOSE(J)+DOSE(I,J)                                    CHANGE1    7
         GOTO 20                                                        CHANGE1    8
      15 DOSE(I,J)=DOSE(I,2)                                            CHANGE1    9
      20 CONTINUE                                                       CHANGE1   10
      10 CONTINUE                                                       SHURE     24
         IF(USE.GT.1000..AND.CON.LT.10.) GO TO 50                       SHURE     25
         IF(LCT.GT.0)CALL PERDOS(TYPE,TDOSE,DOSE)                       SHURE     26
      50 CONTINUE                                                       SHURE     27
         DO 40 J=3,8,1                                                  SHURE     28
      40 TDOSE(J)=TDOSE(2)                                              SHURE     29
         IF(CON.GT.10..AND.USE.GT.0.)CALL PLOP(DOSE,5)                  SHURE     30
         RETURN                                                         SHURE     31
         END                                                           SHURE     32
```

```
      SUBROUTINE SWIM(TYPE,DILU,T,USE,GEOM,TDOSE)                    SWIM   2
      COMMON Q(200),PL,CFS,NSUR,LT,RECO(200),LIST(200,4),LCT,LZ ,CON,KIT  SWIM   3
     +,FUP                                                          SWIM   4
      COMMON/DFLIB/DFL(300,7),DFA(300,7),EXG(300,2),TAU(300),EXS(300,2),   SWIM   5
     +EFF(300,8)                                                    SWIM   6
      COMMON/SINCE/IZ(300),IMASS(300),META(300),NLIBA,NLIBT,NLIBC,NLIBI   SWIM   7
      DIMENSION TDOSE(8),DOSE(200,8)                                SWIM   8
      DO 8 J=1,8                                                    SWIM  10
    8 TDOSE(J)=0.0                                                  SWIM  11
      IF(USE.EN.0.)GO TO 50                                         SWIM  12
      IF(DILU.EQ.0.)GO TO 50                                        SWIM  13
      DO 10 I=1,NSUR                                                SWIM  14
      LM=LIST(I,1)                                                  SWIM  15
      MU=IZ(LM)                                                     SWIM  16
      ARGU=TAU(LM)*T                                                SWIM  17
      IF(ARGU.GT.20.)GO TO 20                                       SWIM  18
      FACT=119.*U(I)*RECO(I)/CFS/DILU*EXP(-ARGU)/GEOM*USE/CON        SWIM  19
      GO TO 30                                                      SWIM  20
   20 FACT=0.0                                                      SAIM  21
   30 DOSE(I,1)=EXS(LM,1)*FACT                                      SWIM  22
      DOSE(I,2)=EXS(LM,2)*FACT                                      CHANGE1 11
      DO 15 J=3,8                                                   CHANGE1 12
   15 DOSE(I,J)=DOSE(I,2)                                           SWIM  23
      TDOSE(1)=TDOSE(1)+DOSE(I,1)                                   SWIM  24
   10 TDOSE(2)=TDOSE(2)+DOSE(I,2)                                   SWIM  25
      IF(INT(GEOM).EQ.2) GO TO 50                                   SWIM  26
      IF(USE.GT.1000.AND.CON.LT.10.) GO TO 50                       SWIM  27
      IF(LCT.GT.0) CALL PERDOS(TYPE,TDOSE,DOSE)                     SWIM  28
      IF(CON.GT.10.)CALL PLOP(DOSE,5)                               SWIM  29
   50 CONTINUE                                                      SWIM  30
      DO 40 J=3,8,1                                                 SWIM  31
   40 TDOSE(J)=TDOSE(2)                                             SWIM  32
      RETURN                                                        SWIM  33
      END
```

```
 1        SUBROUTINE CRITR(CRITR,DILU,T,TDOSE,ACC)              CRITR    2
          COMMON G(200),PL,CFS,NSUR,LT,RECO(200),LIST(200,4),LCT,LZ ,CON,KIT    CRITR    3
         + ,POP                                                 CRITR    4
 5        COMMON/SURCE/IZ(300),IMASS(300),META(300),NLIBA,NLIBT,NLIHC,NLIBI    CRITR    5
          COMMON/DFLIB/DFL(300,7),DFA(300,7),EXG(300,2),TAU(300),EXS(300,2),    CRITR    6
         +EFF(300,8)                                            CRITR    7
          DIMENSION TDOSE(8),ACC(100),CRITR(3),DOSE(290,8)      CRITR    8
          DO 8 J=1,M                                            CRITR    9
 8        TDOSE(J)=0.0                                          CRITR   10
10        DO 10 I=1,NSUR                                        CRITR   11
          LM=LIST(I,1)                                          CRITR   12
          MU=IZ(LM)                                             CRITR   13
          ARGU=TAU(LM)*T                                        CRITR   14
15        IF(ARGU.GT.40.)GO TO 9                                CRITR   15
          FACT=21.*G(I)*RECO(I)/CFS/DILU*EXP(-ARGU)*EFF(LM,2)   CRITR   16
          GO TO 11                                              CRITR   17
 9        FACT=0.0                                              CRITR   18
11        DOSE(I,1)=FACT*ACC(MO)                                CRITR   19
20 10     TDOSE(1)=TDOSE(1)+DOSE(I,1)                           CRITR   20
          IF(LCT.GT.0) CALL PERDOS(CRITR,TDOSE,DUSE)            CRITR   21
          RETURN                                                CRITR   22
          END                                                   CRITR   23
```

D-30

```
                 SUBROUTINE EAT(BIOT,RAD,MASS,CONS,DILU,T,TDOSE,ACC)              EAT    2
                 COMMON D(200),PL,CFS,NSUR,LT,RECO(200),LIST(200,4),LCT,LZ ,CON,KIT  EAT    3
                +,PUP                                                             EAT    4
                 COMMON/DFLIB/DFL(300,7),DFA(300,7),EXG(300,2),TAU(300),EXS(300,2), EAT    5
                +EFF(300,8)                                                       EAT    6
                 COMMON/SOURCE/IZ(300),IMASS(300),META(300),NLIBA,NLIBT,NLIBC,NLIBI EAT    7
                 REAL MASS                                                        EAT    8
                 DIMENSION HIOT(4),STAN(9),ACC(100),TDOSE(8),DOSE(200,8)          EAT    9
                 DATA STAN/0.,1.,2.,3.,5.,7.,10.,20.,30./                         EAT   10
                 TDOSE(1)=0.0                                                     EAT   11
                 TDOSE(2)=0.0                                                     EAT   12
                 DO 10 J=2,8                                                      EAT   13
                 IF(RAD.LE.1.4)GO TO 50                                           EAT   14
                 JJ=J-J                                                           EAT   15
                 PT=(STAN(JJ)+STAN(J))/2.                                         EAT   16
                 JE=J+1                                                           EAT   17
                 TP=(STAN(J)+STAN(JEB))/2.                                        EAT   18
                 IF(RAD.GE.PT.AND.RAD.LT.TP)GO TO 50                              EAT   19
              10 CONTINUE                                                         EAT   20
              50 L=J-1                                                            EAT   21
                 DO 20 I=1,NSOR                                                   EAT   22
                 MO=LIST(I,1)                                                     EAT   23
                 MT=IZ(MO)                                                        EAT   24
                 ARGU=TAU(MO)*T                                                   EAT   25
                 IF(ARGU.GT.40.)GO TO 9                                           EAT   26
                 IF(EFF(MO,8).EQ.0.) GO TO 9                                      EAT   27
                 FACT=2.AAE+07*Q(I)*RECO(I)*REGO(I)*CFS/DILU*EXP(-ARGU)*CONS/MASS/EFF(MO,8) EAT   28
                +*(DFL(MO,5)*EFF(MO,L)                                            EAT   29
                 GO TO 8                                                          EAT   30
               9 FACT=0.0                                                         EAT   31
               8 CONTINUE                                                         EAT   32
                 DOSE(I,1)=FACT*ACC(MT)                                           EAT   33
              20 TDOSE(1)=TDOSE(1)+DOSE(I,1)                                      EAT   34
                 IF(LCT.GT.0)CALL PERDOS(BIOT,TDOSE,DOSE)                         EAT   35
             100 CONTINUE                                                         EAT   36
                 RETURN                                                           EAT   37
                 END                                                             EAT   38
```

```
        SUBROUTINE PAFD(TYPE,ACC,CINC,JJ,USE,TDUSE,NN,LM)                      PAFD      2
        COMMON/SINCE/IZ(300),IMASS(300),META(300),NLIBA,NLIBT,NLINC,NLINT      PAFD      3
        COMMON Q(200),PL,CFS,NSUR,LT,RECO(200),LIST(200,4),LCT,LZ ,CON,KIT     PAFD      4
       + ,POP                                                                  PAFD      5
        COMMON/DFLIB/DFL(300,7),DFA(300,7),EXG(300,2),TAU(300),EXS(300,2),     PAFD      6
       +EFF(300,8)                                                             PAFD      7
        DIMENSION TYPE(3),ACC(100),CUNC(200)                                   PAFD      8
        DIMENSION DUSE(200,8),TDUSE(A)                                         PAFD      9
        DO 50 KJ=1,NSUR                                                        PAFD     10
        ML=LIST(KJ,1)                                                          PAFD     11
        LL=LIST(KJ,JJ)                                                         PAFD     12
        MU=IZ(ML)                                                              PAFD     13
        FACT=CUNC(KJ)*ACC(MU)/CUM*1100.                                        PAFD     14
        DU 60 J=1,7                                                            PAFD     15
        IF(KJ.EW.1)TDUSE(J)=0.                                                 PAFD     16
        DUSE(KJ,J)=FACT*DFL(LL,J)*USE                                          PAFD     17
     60 TDUSE(J)=TDUSE(J)+DUSE(KJ,J)                                           PAFD     18
     50 CONTINUE                                                               PAFD     19
        IF(LM.EQ.0.AND.NN.EQ.1)CALL PLOP(DOSE,6)                               PAFD     20
        IF(LM.EQ.0.AND.NN.EQ.2)CALL PLOP(DOSE,6)                               PAFD     21
        IF(LCT.GT.0)CALL PERDUS(TYPE,TDUSE,DOSE)                               PAFD     22
        RETURN                                                                 PAFD     23
        END                                                                    PAFD     24
```

```
         SUBROUTINE CENT(T,CATH,DILU,J,CONC,AMT,HARV,N)       CENT     2
         COMMON Q(200),PL,CFS,NSUR,LT,NEC(200),LIST(200,4),LCT,LZ ,CON,KJT   CENT     3
        + ,PUP                                                 CENT     4
         COMMON/SURCE/IZ(300),IMASS(300),META(300),NLIBA,NLIBT,NLIBC,NLIBI   CENT     5
         COMMON/UFLIN/UFL(300,7),DFA(300,7),EXG(300,2),TAU(300),EXS(300,2),   CFNT     6
        +EFF(300,8)                                            CENT     7
         DIMENSION  CATH(20),DILU(20),T(20),CONC(200)          CENT     8
         DO 20 K=1,J                                           CENT    10
         DO 40 KK=1,NSUR                                       CENT    11
         IF(K.EQ.1)CONC(KK)=0.0                                CFNT    12
         LM=LIST(KK,1)                                         CENT    13
         MU=IZ(LM)                                             CENT    14
         ARGU=TAU(LM)*T(K)                                     CENT    15
         IF(ARGU.GT.20.)GO TU 40                               CFNT    16
         IF(N.EQ.2) CONC(KK)=CONC(KK)+CATH(K)*Q(KK)*RECO(KK)*CFS/DILU(K)*    CENT    17
        +EXP(-ARGU)/HARV                                       CENT    18
         IF(N.EQ.1)CONC(KK)=CONC(KK)+CATH(K)*Q(KK)*RECO(KK)/CFS/DILU(K)*EXP   CENT    19
        +(-ARGU)/AMT                                           CENT    20
      40 CONTINUE                                              CENT    21
      20 CONTINUE                                              CENT    22
         RETURN                                                CENT    23
         END
```

D-33

```
      SUBROUTINE TRTIUM(CIYR,P,H3R,H3T)                              TRTIUM    2
      COMMON Q(200),PL,CFS,NSUR,LT,RFCD(200),LIST(200,4),LCT,LZ ,CON,KIT TRTIUM    3
     + ,PDP                                                          TRTIUM    4
      COMMON/POPUL/PERA,PERT,PERC,US                                 TRTIUM    5
      COMMON/DFLIB/DFL(300,7),DFA(300,7),EXG(300,2),TAU(300),EXS(300,2), TRTIUM    6
     +FFF(300,8)                                                     TRTIUM    7
      DATA HYDRU/2.7E+19/                                            TRTIUM    8
      DATA CONSUM/800./                                              TRTIUM    9
      ARGUSTAU(1)*PL*8760.                                           TRTIUM   10
      IF(ARGU.GT.40.)ARGU=40.                                       TRTIUM   11
      H3CON=CIYR*1.0E+12*(1.-EXP(-ARGU))/(TAU(1)*8760.*HYDRO)        TRTIUM   12
      H3R=H3CON*CONSUM*DFL(1,3)/CON*US                               TRTIUM   13
      H3T=H3CON*CONSUM*DFL(1,4)/CON*US                               TRTIUM   14
      RETURN                                                         TRTIUM   15
      END                                                            TRTIUM   16
```

```
      SUBROUTINE FLOOD                                                  FLOOD     2
      COMMON D(200),PL,CF9,NSUR,L1,RECO(200),LIST(200,4),LCT,LZ ,CON,KIT FLOOD    3
     +,PUP                                                              FLOOD     4
      COMMON/PUPIL/PERA,PERT,PERC,US                                    FLOOD     5
      REAL IRRIG                                                        FLOOD     6
      DIMENSION TYPE(3),A(3),B(3),C(3),TDOSE(8)                         FLOOD     7
      DIMENSION D(3),VEG(3),LV(3),MLK(3),MET(3),AALD(7),TALD(7),        FLOOD     8
     +TAND(7),CALD(7),CAND(7)                                          FLOOD     9
      DIMENSION DILU(20),T(20),PROD(20),CONC(200)                       FLOOD    10
      DIMENSION GUID(7),BAD(7)                                          FLOOD    11
      DATA D/'TOTA','L  ',' '/                                          FLOOD    12
      DATA TYPE/'IRRI','FOO',' D '/                                     FLOOD    13
      DATA VFG/'VEGE','TATI','ON '/                                     FLOOD    14
      DATA LV/'LEAF','Y VE','GE '/                                      FLOOD    15
      DATA MLK/'MILK',' ',' '/                                          FLOOD    16
      DATA MET/'MEAT',' ',' '/                                          FLOOD    17
      DATA A/'ADUL','T   ',' '/                                         FLOOD    18
      DATA B/'TEEN','AGER',' '/                                         FLOOD    19
      DATA C/'CHIL','D   ',' '/                                         FLOOD    20
   10 FORMAT(1H1,35X,'*                      IRRIGATED FOOD PATHWAY     *     *') FLOOD    21
   40 FORMAT(1H0,22X,'BONE          LIVER       TOTAL BODY            THYROID  FLOOD    22
     *  KIDNEY          LUNG          GI-LLI')                          FLOOD    23
    C                                                        INDIVIDUAL FLOOD    24
   41 FORMAT(1H0,19X,'                                                        FLOOD    25
     + DOSES(MREM PER YEAR INTAKE)                      ')              FLOOD    26
   42 FORMAT(1H0,16X,'                                  POPULATION DOSES(MAN-REM) FLOOD    27
     + ')                                                              FLOOD    28
   43 FORMAT(1H0,15X,'NOTE- INDIVIDUAL DOSES CALCULATED WITH DILUTION=', FLOOD    29
     +1PE8.2,' AND TRANSIT TIME=',E8.2,' HRS.')                        FLOOD    30
   50 FORMAT(2I10,6E10.0)                                               FLOOD    31
   60 FORMAT(8E10.2)                                                    FLOOD    32
   84 FORMAT(17X,1P5E10.2)                                              FLOOD    33
   85 FORMAT(1H0,'INDEX FOR FOOD PATHWAY DOES NOT EXIST')               FLOOD    34
   90 FORMAT(1H0,'$  $  $  ALARA DOSES  $  $  $')                       FLOOD    35
   91 FORMAT(1H0,'$  $  $  NEPA DOSES  *  *  *')                        FLOOD    36
   96 FORMAT(1H0,3A4,5X,'IRRIGATION RATE=',1PE8.2,' L/M**2/MIN',5X,'YIEL FLOOD    37
     +D=',1PE8.2,' KG/M**2',5X,'GROWING PERIOD=',E8.2,' DAYS',/,17X,    FLOOD    38
     +'TOTAL 50 MILE GROW=',E8.2,' KG/YR',5X,'TOTAL CROP IRRIGATION=',ER FLOOD    39
     +.2,/,17X,' DILUTION HARVEST TRANSIT TIME')                       FLOOD    40
   97 FORMAT(1H0,'INDIVIDUAL CONSUMPTION RATES    ADULT=',1PE8.2,' KG',  FLOOD    41
     +5X,'TEEN=',E8.2,5X,'CHILD=',E8.2,5X,'FOOD PROCESS TIME=',E8.2,' HR FLOOD    42
     +')                                                               FLOOD    43
   98 FORMAT(1H ,'POPULATION CONSUMPTION RATES    ADULT=',1PE8.2,' KG',  FLOOD    44
     +5X,'TEEN=',E8.2,5X,'CHILD=',E8.2,5X,'FOOD PROCESS TIME=',E8.2,' HR FLOOD    45
     +')                                                               FLOOD    46
  100 READ 50,N,KZ,IRRIG,YIELD,GROW,TFMG                                FLOOD    47
      TTIG=0.0                                                         FLOOD    48
      IF(N.EQ.0) GO TO 200                                             FLOOD    49
      IF(KZ.GT.0)READ 80,ACON,TCON,CCON,AC,TC,CC,HOLD,HLD1             FLOOD    50
      J=1                                                             FLOOD    51
  104 READ 80,DILU(J),PROD(J),T(J)                                     FLOOD    52
      M=J-1                                                           FLOOD    53
      IF(DILU(J).EQ.0.) GO TO 105                                     FLOOD    54
      J=J+1                                                           FLOOD    55
      GO TO 104                                                       FLOOD    56
  105 CONTINUE                                                         FLOOD    57
      TMT(1)                                                          FLOOD    58
```

D-35

```
            DL=DILU(1)
            DO 107 J=1,M
    107     IF(DILU(J).LT.DL) DL=DILU(J)
            IF(DILU(J).LT.DL) TMAT(J)
            PRINT 10
            DO 106 J=1,M
    106     TTIG=TTIG+PKOD(J)
            IF(K/.GT.0)GO TO 160
            GO TO (120,130,140,150),N
            PRINT 85
            RETURN
    120     AC=190.
            TC=240.
            CC=200.
            ACON=520.
            TCON=630.
            CCON=520.
            HLD1=1440.
            HOLD=340.
            GO TO 160
    130     AC=30.
            TC=20.
            CC=10.
            ACON=64.
            TCON=42.
            CCON=26.
            HOLD=50.
            HLD1=24.
            GO TO 160
    140     AC=110.
            TC=200.
            CC=170.
            ACON=310.
            TCON=400.
            CCON=330.
            HOLD=96.
            HLD1=48.
            GO TO 160
    150     AC=95.
            TC=59.
            CC=37.
            ACON=110.
            TCON=65.
            HOLD=440.
            HLD1=440.
    160     CONTINUE
            IF(N.EQ.1) PRINT 60,VEG
            IF(N.EQ.2) PRINT 60,LV
            IF(N.EQ.3) PRINT 60,MLK
            IF(N.EQ.4) PRINT 60,MET
            IF(N.GT.4) PRINT 85
            P=TFMG/(AC*PEHA+TC*PERT+CC*PERC)
            TP=TTIG/(AC*PERA+TC*PERT+CC*PERC)
            IF(P.GT.PUP)P=PUP
            KIT=0
            LZ=0
```

```
115        CALL CENT(T,PROD,DILU,M,CONC,AMT,TFMG,2)                                          FLUDD    116
           CALL FRUD(TYPE,CONC,HOLD,MLD1,ACUN,IRRIG,YIELD,GRUW,TFMG,TTIG,TP                  FLUDD    117
          +,AC,TDOSE,AALD,AAND,N,1,P,TM,DL)                                                  FLUDD    118
           PRINT 41                                                                          FLUDD    119
           PRINT40                                                                           FLUDD    120
120        PRINT 60,A,(TDOSE(J),J=1,7)                                                       FLUDD    121
           CALL FRUD(TYPE,CONC,HOLD,MLD1,TCON,IRRIG,YIELD,GRUW,TFMG,TTIG,TP                  FLUDD    122
          +,TC,TDOSE,TALD,TAND,N,2,P,TM,DL)                                                  FLUDD    123
           PRINT 60,H,(TDOSE(J),J=1,7)                                                       FLUDD    124
           CALL FRUD(TYPE,CONC,HOLD,MLD1,CCON,IRRIG,YIELD,GRUW,TFMG,TTIG,TP                  FLUDD    125
125       +,CC,TDOSE,CALD,CAND,N,3,P,TM,DL)                                                  FLUDD    126
           PRINT 40,C,(TDOSE(J),J=1,7)                                                       FLUDD    127
           PRINT 43,OL,TM                                                                    FLUDD    128
           PRINT 42                                                                          FLUDD    129
           PRINT 91                                                                          FLUDD    130
130        PRINT 40                                                                          FLUDD    131
           PRINT 60,A,(AAND(JM),JM=1,7)                                                      FLUDD    132
           PRINT 60,H,(TAND(JM),JM=1,7)                                                      FLUDD    133
           PRINT 60,C,(CAND(JM),JM=1,7)                                                      FLUDD    134
           DU 165 JM=1,7                                                                     FLUDD    135
135    165 GUDD(JM)=AAND(JM)+TAND(JM)+CAND(JM)                                               FLUDD    136
           PRINT 60,U,(GUDD(JM),JM=1,7)                                                      FLUDD    137
           PRINT 90                                                                          FLUDD    138
           PRINT 40                                                                          FLUDD    139
           PRINT 60,A,(AALD(JM),JM=1,7)                                                      FLUDD    140
140        PRINT 60,H,(TALD(JM),JM=1,7)                                                      FLUDD    141
           PRINT 60,C,(CALD(JM),JM=1,7)                                                      FLUDD    142
           DU 166 JM=1,7                                                                     FLUDD    143
       166 HAD(JM)=AALO(JM)+TALD(JM)+CALD(JM)                                                FLUDD    144
           PRINT 60,U,(HAD(JM),JM=1,7)                                                       FLUDD    145
145        PRINT 96,TYPE,IRRIG,YIELD,GRUW,TFMG,TTIG                                          FLUDD    146
           DU 170 J=1,M                                                                      FLUDD    147
170        PRINT 40,DILU(J),PRUD(J),T(J)                                                     FLUDD    148
           PRINT 97,ACUN,TCUN,CCUN,MLD1                                                      FLUDD    149
150        PRINT 98,AC,TC,CC,HULD                                                            FLUDD    150
           KIT=30                                                                            FLUDD    151
           IF(LCT.GT.0) CALL PERDOS(TYPE,TDOSE,DUSE)                                         FLUDD    152
           GO TO 100                                                                         FLUDD    153
       200 CONTINUE                                                                          FLUDD    154
           RETURN                                                                            FLUDD    155
155        END                                                                              FLUDD    156
```

CARD NR. SEVERITY DETAILS   DIAGNOSIS OF PROBLEM

67   I   THERE IS NO PATH TO THIS STATEMENT.

```
            SUBROUTINE FOOD(TYPE,CONC,HOLD,HLD1,CUNSUM,IRRIG,YIELD,GROW,          FOOD     2
           +TMG,TTIC,TP,C,IDUSE,ALD,AND,N,JJ,P,TM,DL)                            FOOD     3
            COMMON Q(200),PL,CFS,NSUR,LT,RFCI1(200),LIST(200,4),LCT,LZ ,CUN,KIT   FOOD     4
           +,PUP                                                                 FOOD     5
            COMMON/POPUL/PERA,PERT,PERC,US                                       FOOD     6
            COMMON/DFLIH/DFL(300,7),DFA(300,7),EXG(300,2),TAU(300),EXS(300,2),    FOOD     7
           +EFF(300,8)                                                           FOOD     8
            COMMON/SURCE/IZ(300),IMASS(300),META(300),NLIBA,NLIBT,NLIBC,NLIBI     FOOD     9
            REAL IPRIG                                                           FOOD    10
            DIMENSION ALD(7),AND(7),TYPE(3),IDUSE(8),DUSE(200,8),POOL(200,8)      FOOD    11
            DIMENSION CINC(200)                                                  FOOD    12
            DIMENSION SUTL(100),ZMET(100),ZMLK(100)                              FOOD    13
            DATA Q1,Q2,Q3,Q4/50.,60.,50.,50./                                    FOOD    14
            DATA FRAC/0.25/                                                      FOOD    15
            DATA ZMET/                                                           FOOD    16
           +2.1E-02,2.0E-02,1.0E-03,8.0E-04,5.1E-02,7.7E-02,1.6E-02,             FOOD    17
           +1.5E-01,2.0E-02,3.0E-05,4.0E-05,2.4E-01,2.3E-03,7.4E-03,             FOOD    18
           +4.0E-02,2.0E-02,1.2E-02,4.0E-03,1.6E-02,2.3E-03,7.4E-03,             FOOD    19
           +8.0E-04,4.0E-02,1.3E-02,5.3E-03,8.0E-02,1.3E-02,00,2.0E-01,          FOOD    20
           +2.8E-01,8.0E-01,1.5E-02,2.6E-02,3.1E-02,6E-03,3.4E-02,               FOOD    21
           +8.0E-03,4.0E-02,4.0E-01,4.0E-01,7.7E-02,2.9E-02,5.3E-03,             FOOD    22
           +2.0E-04,1.2E-03,4.7E-03,3.3E-03,2.2E-03,4.0E-03,3.2E-03,             FOOD    23
           +1.6E-00,5.3E-03,4.4E-05,0E-03,4.0E-03,4.4E-03,4.0E-01,               FOOD    24
           +4.0E-02,2.2E-04,1.3E-02,1.2E-02,8.0E-02,2.0E-02,3.4E-01,             FOOD    25
           +6.0E-02,2.0E-04,8.0E-03,3.4E-02,2.0E-04,1.0E-05,2.0E-04,             FOOD    26
           +6.0E-04,2.2E-04,2.0E-04,2.0E-04/                                     FOOD    27
            DATA SOIL/                                                           FOOD    28
           +4.8  ,5.0E-02,4.3E-04,2E-04,1.2E-01,5.5   ,7.5   ,1.6,               FOOD    29
           +26.5E-00,1.4E-01,5.2E-01,1.4E-04,1.5E-04,1.1E+00,5.9E-01,            FOOD    30
           +35.0E+00,6.0E-01,3.7E-01,3.6E-02,1.1E-03,5.4E-05,1.3E-04,            FOOD    31
           +42.9E-02,6.6E-04,9.4E-03,1.9E-01,1.2E-01,4.0E-01,2.5E-04,            FOOD    32
           +51.1E-02,1.3E-00,7.6E-01,5.0E-00,1.3E-01,1.7E-02,2.6E-03,            FOOD    33
           +69.4E-03,1.8E-04,3.0E-02,1.5E-05,0E-02,1.3E+01,5.0E-01,              FOOD    34
           +72.5E-01,2.5E-01,1.1E-02,1.3E-00,2.2E-02,9E-02,2.5E-05,              FOOD    35
           +82.5E-03,2.5E-02,2.6E-03,2.4E-03,2.5E-02,2.5E-03,2.4E-03,            FOOD    36
           +42.6E-03,2.5E-03,2.6E-02,5.2E-03,2.5E-03,2.4E-03,1.7E-04,            FOOD    37
           +A6.5E-03,1.8E-02,2.5E-01,1.5E-01,2.5E-00,1.0E-01,5.1E-01,            FOOD    38
           +42.5E-01,1.8E-04,2.1E-01,1.5E-01,2.5E-03,2.5E-03,3.4E-01,            FOOD    39
           +C2.5E-03,2.5E-03,2.5E-01,1.5E-01,2.5E-03,2.5E-04,2.7E-05,            FOOD    40
           +D2.5E-03,2.5E-03,2.5E-03/                                            FOOD    41
            DATA ZMLK/                                                           FOOD    42
           +1.3E-02,2.0E-02,5.0E-02,1.0E-04,2.7E-02,2.2E-02,2.0E-02,             FOOD    43
           +1.4E-02,2.0E-02,2.0E-02,4.0E-04,1.0E-04,2.5E-02,1.4E-02,             FOOD    44
           +5.0E-02,2.0E-02,8.0E-02,3.5E-06,2.0E-03,1.0E-03,2.7E-03,             FOOD    45
           +2.5E-04,1.2E-02,3.5E-02,7.6E-03,2.0E-02,2.5E-05,5.0E-04,             FOOD    46
           +2.5E-03,7.5E-03,2.5E-02,5.0E-04,2.0E-04,1.0E-05,1.2E-04,             FOOD    47
           +1.0E-04,2.5E-03,1.5E-03,1.0E-06,2.0E-03,6.0E-06,2.1E-02,             FOOD    48
           +5.0E-06,6.0E-05,5.0E-05,5.0E-06,5.0E-06,6.5E-06,5.0E-06,             FOOD    49
           +5.0E-05,2.5E-02,5.0E-02,2.5E-03,5.0E-03,5.0E-03,3.8E-02,             FOOD    50
           +2.2E-02,6.2E-04,3.0E-04,3.0E-05,0E-02,2.0E-02,8.0E-03,               FOOD    51
           +5.0E-05,6.0E-06,5.0E-06,5.0E-04,5.0E-06,2.0E-06,5.0E-06,             FOOD    52
           +5.0E-06,6.0E-06,5.0E-06,5.0E-06/                                     FOOD    53
            IF(JJ.EQ.1) TERM=PERA                                                FOOD   158
```

```
60        IF(JJ.EQ.3)TERM=PERC
          IF(JJ.EQ.2)TERM=PERT
          DO 8 J=1,8
        8 TDOSE(J)=0.0
          IF(N.EQ.0)GO TO 50
          TRANS=1.
65        DO 10 I=1,NSOR
          MO=LIST(I,1)
          MT=1/(MO)
          LL=LIST(I,JJ)
          CNC1=0.0
70        ARGU=TAU(MO)*TM
          IF(ARGU.GT.20.) GO TO 25
          CNC1=Q(I)*PECU(I)/CFS/DL*EXP(-ARGU)*1100.
25        CONTINUE
          IF(JJ.EQ.1) CUNC(I)=CONC(I)*1100.
          DECAY=0.693/14.*24.*TAU(MO)
75        ARGU=DECAY*GROW
          IF(ARGU.GT.20.) ARGU=20.
          LEAF=FRAC*TRANS/YIELD*(1.-EXP(-ARGU))/(DECAY*30.)
          ARG1=TAU(MO)*PL*8766.
          IF(ARG1.GT.20.) ARG1=20.
80        ROOT=SOIL(MT)*(1.-EXP(-ARG1))/(TAU(MO)*240.*730.)
          PCON=CONC(I)*IRRIG*(LEAF+ROOT)
          PCN1=CNC1*IRRIG*(LEAF+ROOT)
          IF(MO.EQ.1) PCON=CONC(I)
          IF(MO.EQ.1) PCN1=CNC1
85        ARGU=TAU(MO)*HOLD
          ARG1=TAU(MO)*HOLD
          IF(ARGU.GT.60.) ARGU=60.
          IF(ARG1.GT.60.) ARG1=60.
          IF(N.GT.2)GO TO 30
90        FCN2=PCN1*EXP(-ARG1)
          FCON=PCON*EXP(-ARGU)
          GO TO 40
30        IF(N.EQ.3)FCON=Q1*PCON+Q2*CONC(I)*ZMLK(MT)*EXP(-ARGU)
          IF(N.EQ.3) FCN1=Q1*PCN1+Q2*CNC(I)*ZMLK(MT)*EXP(-ARG1)
95        IF(N.EQ.4)FCON=Q3*PCON+Q4*CONC(I)*ZMET(MT)*EXP(-ARGU)
          IF(N.EQ.4) FCN1=Q3*PCN1+Q4*CNC1*ZMET(MT)*EXP(-ARG1)
          IF(N.EQ.3.AND.MO.EQ.1) FCON=(0.0028*CONC(I)/0.28)*(38.+60.)
          IF(N.EQ.3.AND.MO.EQ.1) FCN1=(0.0028*CNC1/0.28)*(38.+60.)
          IF(N.EQ.4.AND.MO.EQ.1) FCON=(0.0041*CONC(I)/0.32)*(28.+50.)
100       IF(N.EQ.4.AND.MO.EQ.1) FCN1=(0.0041*CNC1/0.32)*(28.+50.)
          GO TO 40
     C
40        DO 60 J=1,7
          IF(I.EQ.1) ALD(J)=0.
105       IF(I.EQ.1) AND(J)=0.
          DOSE(I,J)=DFL(LL,J)*FCN1*CONSUM
          FACT=TERM*P*C
          FCT1=TERM*TP*C
          POOL(I,J)=DFL(LL,J)*FCON*FACT/1000.
110       POL1=DFL(LL,J)*FCON*FCT1*TFMG/TTIG/1000.
          ALD(J)=ALD(J)+POOL(I,J)
          AND(J)=AND(J)+POL1
60        TDOSE(J)=TDOSE(J)+DOSE(I,J)
10        CONTINUE
```

```
115        CALL PL(IP(PUDL,6)
           IF(LCT.GT.0)CALL PERDUS(TYPE,TDUSE,DUSE)
      50   CONTINUE
           RETURN
           END
```

FOUD   116
FOUD   117
FOUD   118
FOUD   119
FOUD   120

```
  1        SUBROUTINE PERDOS(SPECIE,IDOSE,DOSE)                                    PERDOS    2
           COMMON D(200),PL,CF5,NSUR,LT,MECU(200),LIST(200,4),LCT,LZ,CIN,KIT      PERDOS    3
          +,POP                                                                   PERDOS    4
  5        COMMON/ELEMEN/IELEM(100)                                               PERDOS    8
           COMMON/SURCE/IZ(300),IMASS(300),META(300),NLIBA,NLIAT,NLIBC,NLIBI      PERDOS    9
           DIMENSION SPECIE(3),TDOSE(8),DOSE(200,8),PATH(8,3),SET(12),A1(7,8,     PERDOS   10
          +20),A2(7,8,20),A3(7,8,20),ISOT(7,8,20),IMET(7,8,20),NADS(7,8)          PERDOS   11
 10        DIMENSION B1(7,8,20),B2(7,8,20),B3(7,8,20)                             PERDOS   12
           COMMON/TRANS/OIL*                                                      CHANGE1   13
     C     DIMENSION DOS(8,100,8)                                                 CHANGE1   14
           DATA SET/1H1,1H2,1H3,1H4,1H5,1H6,1H7,1H8,1H9,1H0,1H ,1H*/              PERDOS   13
 10        FORMAT(1H0,'PATHWAY       SKIN     KIDNEY     BONE          LI         BNL01    11
          +VER     TOTAL BODY     THYROID                      LUNG              PERDOS   15
          *        GI-LLI')                                                       PERDOS   16
 15        FORMAT(1H0,'PATHWAY                            BODY')                  PERDOS   17
           DATA BLAK/'  '/                                                        PERDOS   18
110        FORMAT(1H0,'AGE GROUP           TOTAL BODY        THYROID')            PERDOS   14
115        FORMAT(1H0,'AGE GROUP           SKIN          TOTAL BODY')             PERDOS   20
120        FORMAT(1H0,*         * ISOTOPE CONTRIBUTION  *   *')       TOTAL       PERDOS   21
130        FORMAT(1H0,'AGE GROUP            LUNG      LIVER              GI-LLI') PERDOS   22
          +BODY        THYROID      KIDNEY        LUNG                            PERDOS   23
           IF(LZ.GT.0) GO TO 50                                                   PERDOS   24
           DO 65 J=1,7                                                            PERDOS   25
 25        DO 66 K=1,8                                                            PERDOS   26
 66        NADS(J,K)=1                                                            PERDOS   27
 65        CONTINUE                                                               PERDOS   28
           DO 70 J=1,7                                                            PERDOS   29
 30        DO 80 K=1,8                                                            PERDOS   30
           DO 90 I=1,20                                                           PERDOS   31
           A1(J,K,I)=BLAK                                                         PERDOS   32
           A2(J,K,I)=BLAK                                                         PERDOS   33
           A3(J,K,I)=BLAK                                                         PERDOS   34
 35        ISOT(J,K,I)=BLAK                                                       PERDOS   35
           M1(J,K,I)=BLAK                                                         PERDOS   36
           M2(J,K,I)=BLAK                                                         PERDOS   37
           M3(J,K,I)=BLAK                                                         PERDOS   38
           IMET(J,K,I)=BLAK                                                       PERDOS   39
 90        CONTINUE                                                               PERDOS   40
 40     80 CONTINUE                                                               PERDOS   41
        70 CONTINUE                                                               PERDOS   42
        50 IF(KIT.EQ.40) GO TO 300                                               PERDOS   43
           IF(KIT.EQ.30)GO TO 300                                                PERDOS   44
 45        IF(KIT.EQ.10)GO TO 200                                                PERDOS   45
           IF(KIT.EQ.50)GO TO 300                                                PERDOS   46
           IF(KIT.EQ.20) GO TO 300                                               PERDOS   47
           IF(KIT.EQ.70) GO TO 200                                               PERDOS   48
           LZ=L/4                                                                 PERDOS   49
 50        PATH(LZ,1)=SPECIE(1)                                                   PERDOS   50
           PATH(LZ,2)=SPECIE(2)                                                   PERDOS   51
           PATH(LZ,3)=SPECIE(3)                                                   PERDOS   52
           DO 20 J=1,NSUR                                                         PERDOS-  53
           N1=LIST(J,1)                                                           PERDOS-  54
           N2=IZ(N1)                                                              PERDOS   55
 55        IMUR = IMASS(N1)/100                                                   CHANGE1  15
           ITFN =(IMASS(N1)-IMUR*100)/10                                          CHANGE1  16
           IMIT= IMASS(N1)-IMUR*100-ITFN*10                                      CHANGE1  17
```

```
        IF(IHUN.GT.0.AND.ITEN.EQ.0) ITEN = 10          CHANGE1   18
        IF(IHUN.EQ.0.AND.ITEN.EQ.0) ITEN = 11          CHANGE1   19
        IF(IHUN.EQ.0) IHUN = 11                         CHANGE1   20
        IF(IUNIT.EQ.0) IUNIT = 10                       CHANGE1   21
        C1=SET(IHUN)                                    CHANGE1   22
        C2=SET(ITEN)                                    CHANGE1   23
        C3=SET(IUNIT)                                   CHANGE1   24
        DO 30 JJ=1,8                                    PERDOS    57
        DOS(LZ,J,JJ)=101.94*CFS*DOSE(J,JJ)             CHANGE1   25
        LENADS(LZ,JJ)                                   CHANGE1   26
        IF(L.GT.20)GOTO 30                              CHANGE1   27
        IF(TDOSE(JJ).LT.1.E-10)GOTO 30                 CHANGE1   28
        PERDOSE(J,JJ)/TDOSE(JJ)*100.                    PERDOS    60
        ITEN=INT(PER/10.)                               CHANGE1   24
        IUNIT=INT(PER)-ITEN*10                          PERDOS    62
        IF(ITEN.EQ.0)ITEN=11                            PERDOS    63
        IF(IUNIT.EQ.0)IUNIT=10                          PERDOS    64
        A1(LZ,JJ,L)=SET(ITEN)                           PERDOS    65
        A2(LZ,JJ,L)=SET(IUNIT)                          PERDOS    66
        A3(LZ,JJ,L)=SET(I2)                             PERDOS    67
        ISOT(LZ,JJ,L)=IELEM(MT)                         PERDOS    68
        MT(LZ,JJ,L)=C1                                  PERDOS    64
        H2(LZ,JJ,L)=C2                                  CHANGE1   30
        H3(LZ,JJ,L)=C3                                  CHANGE1   31
        IMET(LZ,JJ,L)=META(MI)                          CHANGE1   32
        NADS(LZ,JJ)=NADS(LZ,JJ)+1                       CHANGE1   33
   30   CONTINUE                                        CHANGE1   34
   20   CONTINUE                                        PERDOS    81
        RETURN                                          PERDOS    83
C                                                       PERDOS    84
C   *   INDIVIDUAL PERCENTAGE                           PERDOS    85
  200   CONTINUE                                        PERDOS    86
  210   FORMAT(1H0,3A4,8(4X,A2,1X,4A1,1X,3A1))         PERDOS    87
  220   FORMAT(1H ,12X,8(4X,A2,1X,4A1,1X,3A1))         PERDOS    88
        PRINT 120                                       PERDOS    89
        IF(KIT.EQ.10) PRINT 10                          PERDOS    90
        IF(KIT.EQ.70) PRINT 15                          PERDOS    91
        DO 240 K=1,LZ                                   PERDOS    92
        LIM=NADS(K,1)                                   PERDOS    93
        DO 250 JS=1,8                                   PERDOS    94
        IF(NADS(K,JS).GT.LIM)LIM=NADS(K,JS)            PERDOS    95
  250   CONTINUE                                        PERDOS    96
        IF(LIM.GT.20)LIM=20                             PERDOS    97
        PRINT 210,(PATH(K,KL),KL=1,3),(ISOT(K,J,1),B1(K,J,1),B2(K,J,1),B3(    CHANGE1   35
       *K,J),IMET(K,J,1),A1(K,J,1),A2(K,J,1),A3(K,J,1),J=1,8)                 PERDOS    98
        DO 260 KJ=2,LIM                                 PERDOS    94
        PRINT 220,(ISOT(K,J,KJ),B1(K,J,KJ),B2(K,J,KJ),B3(K,J,KJ),IMET(K,J,    PERDOS   100
       *KJ),A1(K,J,KJ),A2(K,J,KJ),A3(K,J,KJ),J=1,8)                           PERDOS   101
  260   CONTINUE                                        PERDOS   102
  240   CONTINUE                                        PERDOS   103
        IF(POP.GE.0.)RETURN                             PERDOS   104
  599   PRINT 599                                       CHANGE1   36
        FORMAT(1H1,32X,'TABLE 4.11-2'/24X,'LIQUID EFFLUENT DOSE PARAMETERS    CHANGE1   37
       *'//37X,'A(I)',MREM/HR PER UCI/ML'/16X,'RADIONUCLIDE',6X,'TOTAL BODY   CHANGE1   38
       *',5X,'CRITICAL ORGAN'/)                         CHANGE1   39
        DO 503 J=1,630W                                 CHANGE1   40
                                                        CHANGE1   41
```

```
115         MI=LIST(J,1)
            MI=IZ(MI)                                                        CHANGE1    42
            DOS1 = DOS(1,J,4) + DOS(2,J,4)                                   CHANGE1    43
            CDOS = 0.                                                        CHANGE1    44
            DO 510 JJ=2,8                                                    CHANGE1    45
120         DOS2 = DOS(1,J,JJ) + DOS(2,J,JJ)                                 CHANGE1    46
            IF(DOS2.GT.CDOS) CDOS = DOS2                                     CHANGE1    47
        510 CONTINUE                                                         CHANGE1    48
        505 PRINT 505,IELEM(MI),INASS(MI),META(MI),DOS1,CDOS                 CHANGE1    49
                                                                            CHANGE1    50
        503 CONTINUE                                                         CHANGE1    51
125         PRINT 506                                                        CHANGE1    52
        506 FORMAT(////////////////)                                        CHANGE1    53
        507 PRINT 507,(PATH(2,KL), KL=1,3),DIL"                              CHANGE1    54
                                                                            CHANGE1    55
130     507 FORMAT(2X,3A4,' DILUTION IN ADDITION TO THAT FOR FISH=',F5.1)   CHANGE1    56
            STOP                                                             CHANGE1    57
      C   *  IRRIGATED FOODS AND PND.                                        PERDUS    106
        520 FORMAT(1H ,12X,2(4X,A2,1X,4A1,1X,3A1))                          PERDUS    107
        300 CONTINUE                                                         PERDUS    108
135     510 FORMAT(1H ,12X,7(4X,A2,1X,4A1,1X,3A1))                          PERDUS    109
        380 FORMAT(1H0,'ADULT')                                             PERDUS    110
        390 FORMAT(1H0,'TEENAGER')                                          PERDUS    111
        595 FORMAT(1H0,'CHILD')                                             PERDUS    112
            PRINT 120                                                        PERDUS    113
140         IF(KIT.EQ.20) PRINT 380                                         PERDUS    114
            IF(KIT.EQ.50) PRINT 110                                         PERDUS    115
            IF(KIT.EQ.30)PRINT 130                                          PERDUS    116
            IF(KIT.EQ.40) PRINT 115                                         PERDUS    117
            DO 340 K=1,LZ                                                    PERDUS    118
145         IF(K.EQ.1)PRINT 380                                             PERDUS    119
            IF(K.EQ.2)PRINT 390                                             PERDUS    120
            IF(K.EQ.3) PRINT 395                                            PERDUS    121
            LOW=NADS(K,1)                                                    PERDUS    122
            DO 350 JS=1,7                                                    PERDUS    123
150         IF(NADS(K,JS).GT.LOW)LOW=NADS(K,JS)                             PERDUS    124
        350 CONTINUE                                                         PERDUS    125
            IF(LOW.GT.20)LOW=20                                             CHANGE1    56
            DO 360 KJ=1,LOW                                                  PERDUS    126
            IF(KJ.IMET(K,J,KJ).EQ.30) PRINT 310,(ISOT(K,J,KJ),B1(K,J,KJ),B2(K,J,KJ),B3(K,J,KJ),J=1,7)    PERDUS    127
155        +KJ),IMET(K,J,KJ),A1(K,J,KJ),A2(K,J,KJ),B1(K,J,KJ),J=1,7)       PERDUS    128
            IF(KJ.IMET(K,J,KJ).EQ.20) PRINT 310,(ISOT(K,J,KJ),B1(K,J,KJ),B2(K,J,KJ),B3(K,J,KJ),J=2,6)    PERDUS    129
           +KJ),IMET(K,J,KJ),A1(K,J,KJ),A2(K,J,KJ),A3(K,J,KJ),B1(K,J,KJ),B3(K,J,KJ),J=2,6)   PERDUS    130
            IF(KJ.IMET(K,J,KJ).EQ.50)PRINT 320,(ISOT(K,J,KJ),B1(K,J,KJ),B2(K,J,KJ),H2(K,J,KJ),B3(K,J,KJ),J=3,4)   PERDUS    131
           +KJ),IMET(K,J,KJ),A1(K,J,KJ),A2(K,J,KJ),A3(K,J,KJ),J=3,4)       PERDUS    132
            IF(KIT.EQ.40) PRINT 320,(ISOT(K,J,KJ),B1(K,J,KJ),B2(K,J,KJ),M3(K,J,KJ),J=1,2)    PERDUS    133
160        +KJ),IMET(K,J,KJ),A1(K,J,KJ),A2(K,J,KJ),A3(K,J,KJ),J=1,2)       PERDUS    134
        360 CONTINUE                                                         PERDUS    135
        340 CONTINUE                                                         PERDUS    136
            RETURN                                                           PERDUS    137
            END                                                             PERDUS    138
```

```
          SUBROUTINE PLUP(DOSE,N)                                                  PLUP      2
          INTEGER*ELEM                                                             PLUP      3
          LOGICALMETA                                                              PLUP      4
          COMMON/SORCE/IZ(300),IMASS(300),META(300),NETHA,NLIHT,NLIHC,NLIHI        PLUP      5
          COMMON/ELEMEN/IELEM(100)                                                 PLUP      6
          COMMON Q(200),PL,CFS,NSUR,LT,RECU(200),LIST(200,4),LCT,LZ ,CON,KIT       PLUP      7
         +,POP                                                                     PLUP      8
          DIMENSION DOSE(200,8),CUHEAD(200,8)                                      PLUP      9
       10 FORMAT(1H1,20X,'* * COST-BENEFIT ANALYSIS * * *')                        PLUP     10
       11 FORMAT(1H0,' NUCLIDE    RELEASE ------MAN-REM DOSE------                  PLUP     11
         +----MAN-REM PER CURIE----')                                             PLUP     12
       12 FORMAT(1H ,13X,'    CI/YR      | TOTAL BODY |   THYROID  | TOTAL BOD      BNL01    13
         +Y |  THYROID |')                                                         BNL01    14
       13 FORMAT(1H ,I4,A2,I4,A1,'    ',1PE8.2,'  |  ',E8.2,' |  ',E8.2,            BNL01    15
         +'  |  ',E8.2,'  |')                                                      HNL01    16
       14 FORMAT(1H0,'    TOTAL',20X,1PE8.2,5X,E8.2)                               PLUP     17
          IF(N.EQ.6,OR.N.EQ.7)GO TO 15                                            PLUP     18
          IF(N.EQ.5)GO TO 20                                                       PLUP     19
          IF(N.EQ.3) GO TO 100                                                     PLUP     20
          IF(N.EQ.4) GO TO 50                                                      PLUP     21
       15 DO 30 J=1,NSUR                                                           PLUP     22
          CUHEAD(J,1)=CUHEAD(J,1)+DOSE(J,N-3)                                      PLUP     23
          CUHEAD(J,2)=CUHEAD(J,2)+DOSE(J,N-2)                                      PLUP     24
       30 CONTINUE                                                                 PLUP     25
          RETURN                                                                   PLUP     26
       20 DO 40 J=1,NSUR                                                           PLUP     27
          CUHEAD(J,1)=CUHEAD(J,1)+DOSE(J,2)                                        PLUP     28
          CUHEAD(J,2)=CUHEAD(J,2)+DOSE(J,2)                                        PLUP     29
       40 CONTINUE                                                                 PLUP     30
          RETURN                                                                   PLUP     31
       50 DO 60 J=1,200                                                            PLUP     32
          CUHEAD(J,1)=0.                                                           PLUP     33
          CUHEAD(J,2)=0.                                                           PLUP     34
       60 CONTINUE                                                                 PLUP     35
          TOB=0.0                                                                  PLUP     36
          TOT=0.0                                                                  PLUP     37
          RETURN                                                                   PLUP     38
      100 PRINT 10                                                                 PLUP     39
          PRINT 11                                                                 PLUP     40
          PRINT 12                                                                 PLUP     41
          DO 110 J=1,NSUR                                                          PLUP     42
          LL=LIST(J,1)                                                             PLUP     43
          IK=IZ(LL)                                                                PLUP     44
          CIH=CUHEAD(J,1)/Q(J)                                                     PLUP     45
          CIT=CUHEAD(J,2)/Q(J)                                                     PLUP     46
          PRINT 13,IK,IELEM(IK),IMASS(LL),META(LL),Q(J),CUHEAD(J,1),CUHEAD(J       PLUP     47
         +,2),CIH,CIT                                                              PLUP     48
          TOB=TOB+CUHEAD(J,1)                                                      PLUP     49
          TOT=TOT+CUHEAD(J,2)                                                      PLUP     50
      110 CONTINUE                                                                 PLUP     51
          PRINT 14,TOB,TOT                                                         PLUP     52
          RETURN                                                                   PLUP     53
          END                                                                      PLUP     54
```

S C O P E   2   L O A D   M A P

PROGRAM WILL BE ENTERED AT LADTAP   (340)

BLOCK	ADDRESS	LENGTH
/ELEMEN/	100	144
/POPUL/	244	4
HLMDAT	250	0
LADTAP	250	1623
/SURCE/	2073	1610
/INFLTR/	3703	17644
RENUF	23547	1306
SOURCE	25055	724
PECON	26001	244
ALRA	26245	1000
PUT	27245	3714
WHO	33161	626
WHY	34007	4516
WATER	40525	637
ACTIVE	41364	513
AQUA	42077	3242
/TRANS/	45341	1
DRINK	45342	3252
SHORE	50614	3311
SWIM	54125	3266
CRITTR	57413	3213
EAT	62626	3264
PAFO	66112	3240
CENT	71352	121
TRTIUM	71473	40
FLUID	71533	1743
FUID	73476	7410
PEROUS	103106	40467
PLUP	143575	3333
/FCL.C./	147130	23
/48.10./	147153	134
IBNTRYE	147307	1
COMID=	147310	44
BIF	147354	20
FECMSK=	147374	41
FLTIN=	147435	154
FLTOUT=	147611	314
FMTAP=	150125	372
FORSYS=	150517	556
FORUTL=	151275	16
GETFIT=	151313	43
INCOM=	151356	257
INPC=	151635	173
KIDER=	152030	447
KHAKER=	152517	454
IHUTC=	153173	171
IHUTCOM=	153364	203
GUTUER=	153567	14
ALIR=	153603	77
EXP.	153702	100
SYSAID=	154002	1
SYS=1ST	154003	62

SCOPE 2 LOAD MAP

XTUI=   154065   10
//   154075   2271

LADTAP TEST DECK FOR LIQUID EFFLUENT T/S IN FRESH WATER

DISCHARGE=2.00E+01 CFS   SOURCE TERM MULTIPLIER=1.00E+00

FRESHWATER SITE
TECH SPEC NUCLIDES

NO RECONCENTRATION OF NUCLIDES

* * * ADULT DOSE FACTORS * * *

INGESTION DOSE FACTORS
(MREM/PCI INTAKE)

SHORELINE
(MREM/HR)/(PCI/M**2)

NUCLIDE	CURIE/YEAR	BONE	LIVER	TOTAL BODY	THYROID	KIDNEY	LUNG	GI-LLI	SKIN	TOTAL BODY	MPC(N)
1H 3	1.00E+00	0.	1.34E-07	1.34E-07	1.34E-07	1.34E-07	1.34E-07	1.34E-07	0.	0.	1.00E+00
15P 32	1.00E+00	1.93E-04	1.21E-05	7.47E-06	0.	0.	0.	2.17E-05	0.	0.	1.00E+00
24CR 51	1.00E+00	0.	0.	2.66E-09	1.59E-09	5.87E-10	3.53E-09	6.69E-07	2.60E-10	2.20E-10	1.00E+00
25MN 54	1.00E+00	0.	4.57E-06	8.73E-07	0.	1.36E-06	0.	1.40E-05	6.70E-09	5.40E-09	1.00E+00
26FE 55	1.00E+00	6.20E-06	2.79E-05	7.33E-06	0.	0.	3.23E-05	1.03E-05	0.	0.	1.00E+00
26FE 59	1.00E+00	4.34E-06	1.03E-05	3.92E-06	0.	0.	2.86E-06	9.40E-09	8.00E-09	7.00E-09	1.00E+00
27CO 58	1.00E+00	0.	7.46E-07	1.67E-06	0.	0.	0.	1.51E-05	8.20E-09	7.00E-09	1.00E+00
27CO 60	1.00E+00	0.	2.15E-06	4.72E-06	0.	1.03E-05	0.	4.02E-05	2.00E-08	1.70E-08	1.00E+00
30ZN 65	1.00E+00	4.85E-06	1.54E-05	6.97E-06	0.	2.48E-07	0.	9.70E-06	4.00E-09	2.90E-09	1.00E+00
30ZN 69M	1.00E+00	1.70E-07	3.73E-04	0.	0.	0.	2.49E-05	3.40E-09	3.40E-09		1.00E+00
37RB 86	1.00E+00	0.	2.11E-05	9.84E-06	0.	0.	0.	4.16E-06	7.20E-10	6.30E-10	1.00E+00
38SR 89	1.00E+00	3.09E-04	0.	8.45E-06	0.	0.	0.	4.04E-05	4.50E-13	5.40E-13	1.00E+00
38SR 90	1.00E+00	7.61E-03	0.	1.46E-03	0.	0.	0.	1.02E-04	0.	0.	1.00E+00
39Y 90	1.00E+00	9.63E-09	0.	2.58E-10	0.	0.	0.	1.02E-02	2.60E-12	2.20E-12	1.00E+00
39Y 91	1.00E+00	1.41E-07	0.	3.7E-09	0.	0.	0.	7.76E-03	2.70E-11	2.40E-11	1.00E+00
40ZR 95	1.00E+00	3.04E-08	9.76E-09	6.61E-09	0.	1.54E-08	0.	3.03E-05	5.40E-09	5.00E-09	1.00E+00
40ZR 97	1.00E+00	1.64E-09	3.39E-10	1.56E-10	0.	5.12E-10	0.	1.05E-04	4.40E-09	5.50E-09	1.00E+00
41NB 95	1.00E+00	6.23E-09	3.40E-09	1.56E-09	0.	3.43E-09	0.	2.10E-05	5.10E-09	5.10E-09	1.00E+00
42MO 99	1.00E+00	0.	4.31E-06	8.20E-07	0.	9.77E-06	0.	9.99E-06	2.20E-09	1.90E-09	1.00E+00
44RU 103	1.00E+00	1.85E-07	0.	7.98E-08	0.	7.07E-07	0.	2.16E-05	4.20E-09	3.60E-09	1.00E+00
44RU 106	1.00E+00	2.75E-06	0.	3.44E-07	0.	5.32E-06	0.	1.78E-04	1.80E-09	1.50E-09	1.00E+00
47AG 110M	1.00E+00	1.62E-07	1.04E-07	8.80E-08	0.	2.91E-07	0.	6.04E-05	2.10E-08	1.80E-08	1.00E+00
48CD 113M	1.00E+00	3.11E-05	1.02E-07	0.	0.	3.50E-06	0.	2.56E-05	2.60E-12	2.30E-12	1.00E+00
50SN 123	1.00E+00	5.16E-07	1.60E-07	4.38E-07	0.	0.	6.33E-05	6.46E-08			1.00E+00
50SN 126	1.00E+00	2.46E-05	1.64E-06	2.41E-06	0.	2.43E-05	9.00E-09				1.00E+00
51SB 124	1.00E+00	2.41E-06	5.30E-08	1.11E-06	0.	7.95E-05	1.50E-08	1.30E-08		2.18E-06	1.00E+00
51SB 125	1.00E+00	2.23E-06	2.40E-08	4.44E-07	0.	1.97E-05	3.50E-08	3.10E-09		2.33E-04	1.00E+00
52TE 125M	1.00E+00	2.64E-06	9.73E-07	3.59E-07	1.00E-05	1.07E-05	4.80E-11	3.50E-11			1.00E+00
52TE 127M	1.00E+00	6.74E-06	2.37E-06	8.26E-07	1.73E-06	2.27E-05	1.10E-12	1.10E-12			1.00E+00
52TE 129M	1.00E+00	1.15E-05	4.30E-06	1.62E-06	4.80E-05	5.79E-05	9.00E-10	7.70E-10			1.00E+00
52TE 131M	1.00E+00	1.74E-06	4.47E-07	7.64E-07	1.34E-06	8.40E-05	9.90E-09	8.40E-09			1.00E+00
52TE 132	1.00E+00	2.53E-05	1.64E-06	1.53E-06	1.80E-06	7.71E-05	1.70E-09	1.70E-09			1.00E+00
53I 131	1.00E+00	1.14E-06	5.96E-06	3.41E-06	1.95E-03	1.02E-05	3.40E-09	3.40E-09			1.00E+00
53I 133	1.00E+00	1.36E-06	2.48E-06	7.57E-07	4.77E-04	2.18E-06	4.50E-09	4.40E-09			1.00E+00
55CS 134	1.00E+00	6.22E-05	1.48E-04	1.21E-04	0.	4.40E-05	1.59E-05	2.59E-06	1.40E-08	1.20E-08	1.00E+00
55CS 136	1.00E+00	6.51E-06	2.57E-05	1.85E-05	0.	1.43E-05	1.96E-06	2.92E-06	1.70E-08	1.50E-08	1.00E+00
55CS 137	1.00E+00	7.94E-05	1.09E-04	7.15E-05	0.	3.71E-05	1.23E-05	2.10E-06	4.90E-09	4.20E-09	1.00E+00
56BA 140	1.00E+00	2.03E-05	2.55E-08	3.34E-06	0.	8.64E-09	1.46E-08	4.18E-06	2.10E-08	2.10E-08	1.00E+00
57LA 140	1.00E+00	2.50E-09	1.26E-09	3.34E-10	0.	0.	9.25E-05	1.70E-08	1.50E-08		1.00E+00
58CE 141	1.00E+00	9.37E-09	6.34E-09	7.18E-10	0.	2.94E-09	2.42E-05	6.20E-10	5.50E-10		1.00E+00
58CE 143	1.00E+00	1.65E-09	1.22E-09	1.35E-10	0.	5.38E-10	4.50E-05	2.50E-09	2.20E-09		1.00E+00
58CE 144	1.00E+00	4.89E-07	2.04E-07	1.17E-07	0.	2.13E-07	1.65E-04	3.70E-10	3.20E-10		1.00E+00
59PR 143	1.00E+00	9.21E-09	3.70E-09	4.57E-10	0.	2.13E-09	4.03E-05	0.	0.		1.00E+00
93NP 239	1.00E+00	1.20E-09	1.18E-10	6.46E-11	0.	3.65E-10	2.40E-05	1.10E-09	9.50E-10		1.00E+00

D-47

* * * TEENAGER DOSE FACTORS * * *

INGESTION DOSE FACTORS (MREM/PCI INTAKE) — SHORELINE (MREM/HR)/(PCI/M**2)

NUCLIDE		CURIE/YEAR	BONE	LIVER	TOTAL BODY	THYROID	KIDNEY	LUNG	GI-LLI	SKIN	TOTAL BODY	RECON
1H	3	1.00E+00	0.	1.0E-07	1.0E-07	1.0E-07	1.34E-07	1.0E-07	1.0E-07			
27CO	58	1.00E+00	0.	9.92E-07	2.20E-07	0.	0.	0.	1.34E-05			
27CO	60	1.00E+00	0.	2.7E-06	6.30E-06	0.	0.	0.	3.31E-05			
38SR	89	1.00E+00	4.60E-04	0.	1.32E-05	0.	0.	0.	4.99E-05			
38SR	90	1.00E+00	1.04E-02	2.57E-03	0.	0.	3.75E-05	2.20E-04				
39Y	90	1.00E+00	3.3E-04	8.87E-10	0.	0.	0.	1.09E-04				
39Y	91	1.00E+00	1.96E-07	5.23E-09	0.	0.	0.	7.53E-05				
40ZR	95	1.00E+00	3.72E-08	1.24E-08	1.54E-08	0.	0.	2.68E-05				
41NB	95	1.00E+00	7.24E-09	4.36E-09	3.43E-09	0.	0.	1.78E-05				
44RU	103	1.00E+00	2.57E-07	0.	7.07E-07	0.	0.	1.85E-05				
44RU	106	1.00E+00	4.06E-06	0.	5.32E-06	0.	0.	1.81E-04				
50SN	123	1.00E+00	3.8E-05	7.22E-07	5.78E-07	1.08E-06	0.	6.31E-05				
52TE	125M	1.00E+00	3.83E-06	1.37E-06	1.08E-07	5.08E-07	0.	1.07E-05				
52TE	129M	1.00E+00	1.66E-05	6.15E-06	5.30E-06	4.80E-06	0.	5.80E-05				
52TE	132	1.00E+00	3.55E-06	2.22E-06	2.10E-06	1.54E-05	0.	8.00E-05				
53I	131	1.00E+00	5.57E-06	7.87E-06	4.69E-06	2.27E-03	0.	1.49E-06				
53I	133	1.00E+00	2.03E-06	3.44E-06	1.06E-06	6.25E-04	0.	2.50E-06				
55CS	134	1.00E+00	8.05E-05	9.06E-04	4.80E-05	2.35E-05	2.24E-06					
55CS	137	1.00E+00	1.07E-04	1.44E-04	5.05E-05	3.71E-05	1.91E-05	1.92E-06				
56BA	140	1.00E+00	2.83E-05	3.48E-08	1.82E-06	8.68E-09	2.33E-08	4.14E-06				
57LA	140	1.00E+00	1.26E-08	1.72E-09	4.55E-10	0.	0.	4.48E-05				
58CE	141	1.00E+00	1.26E-08	4.46E-09	9.70E-10	2.94E-09	0.	2.29E-09				
58CE	144	1.00E+00	7.22E-07	2.96E-07	3.83E-08	1.21E-07	0.	1.70E-04				

* * * CHILD DOSE FACTORS * * *

INGESTION DOSE FACTORS (MREM/PCI INTAKE) — SHORELINE (MREM/HR)/(PCI/M**2)

NUCLIDE		CURIE/YEAR	BONE	LIVER	TOTAL BODY	THYROID	KIDNEY	LUNG	GI-LLI	SKIN	TOTAL BODY	RECON
1H	3	1.00E+00	0.	2.03E-07	2.03E-07	2.03E-07	1.34E-07	2.03E-07	2.03E-07			
27CO	58	1.00E+00	0.	1.85E-06	5.58E-06	0.	0.	0.	1.10E-05			
27CO	60	1.00E+00	0.	5.17E-06	1.55E-05	0.	0.	0.	2.86E-05			
38SR	89	1.00E+00	1.34E-03	0.	3.45E-05	0.	0.	0.	5.15E-05			
38SR	90	1.00E+00	1.72E-02	4.30E-03	0.	0.	0.	2.29E-04				
39Y	90	1.00E+00	4.21E-06	1.13E-09	0.	0.	0.	2.20E-04				
39Y	91	1.00E+00	5.85E-07	1.56E-08	0.	0.	0.	7.77E-05				
40ZR	95	1.00E+00	1.04E-07	2.02E-08	1.54E-08	0.	0.	2.50E-05				
41NB	95	1.00E+00	1.95E-08	8.32E-09	3.43E-09	0.	0.	1.44E-05				
44RU	103	1.00E+00	6.78E-07	0.	7.07E-07	0.	0.	1.78E-05				
44RU	106	1.00E+00	1.19E-05	0.	1.46E-06	5.32E-06	0.	1.85E-04				
50SN	123	1.00E+00	1.31E-05	1.64E-06	1.73E-06	3.22E-06	0.	5.50E-05				
52TE	125M	1.00E+00	1.14E-05	3.04E-06	3.20E-06	1.52E-06	0.	1.10E-05				
52TE	129M	1.00E+00	4.95E-05	1.38E-05	1.58E-05	7.65E-06	0.	5.96E-05				
52TE	132	1.00E+00	1.02E-05	6.50E-06	6.62E-06	5.42E-06	0.	7.89E-05				
53I	131	1.00E+00	1.63E-05	1.67E-05	5.43E-03	1.26E-05	0.	1.43E-06				
53I	133	1.00E+00	5.98E-06	7.38E-06	1.78E-03	2.90E-06	0.	2.99E-06				
55CS	134	1.00E+00	2.24E-04	3.77E-04	8.02E-05	4.80E-05	4.19E-05	2.04E-06				
55CS	137	1.00E+00	3.12E-04	3.02E-04	4.50E-05	3.71E-05	3.54E-05	1.44E-06				
56BA	140	1.00E+00	8.26E-05	7.25E-08	4.85E-06	8.68E-09	4.32E-08	4.21E-06				
57LA	140	1.00E+00	1.01E-07	3.52E-09	1.19E-08	0.	0.	1.30E-04				
58CE	141	1.00E+00	3.76E-08	1.88E-08	2.80E-09	2.94E-09	0.	2.36E-05				
58CE	144	1.00E+00	2.14E-06	6.70E-07	1.14E-07	1.21E-07	0.	1.74E-04				

* * * INFANT DOSE FACTORS * * *

INGESTION DOSE FACTORS
(MREM/PCI INTAKE)

SHORELINE
(MREM/HR)/(PCI/M**2)   RECON

NUCLIDE		CURIE/YEAR	BONE	LIVER	TOTAL BODY	THYROID	KIDNEY	LUNG	GI-LLI	SKIN	TOTAL BODY
1H	3	1.00E+00	0.	3.07E-07	3.07E-07	3.07E-07	1.34E-07	3.07E-07	3.07E-07		
27CO	58	1.00E+00	0.	3.7E-06	4.26E-06	0.	0.	0.	9.79E-06		
27CO	60	1.00E+00	0.	1.07E-05	2.56E-05	0.	0.	0.	2.64E-05		
38SR	89	1.00E+00	2.93E-03	0.	8.42E-05	0.	0.	0.	5.9E-05		
38SR	90	1.00E+00	2.51E-02	0.	6.40E-03	0.	0.	0.	2.43E-04		
39Y	90	1.00E+00	8.97E-08	0.	2.41E-09	0.	0.	0.	1.29E-04		
39Y	91	1.00E+00	1.25E-06	0.	3.33E-08	0.	0.	0.	8.27E-05		
40ZR	95	1.00E+00	2.11E-07	5.32E-08	3.78E-08	0.	1.54E-08	0.	2.34E-05		
41NB	95	1.00E+00	3.99E-08	1.75E-08	1.03E-08	0.	3.43E-09	0.	1.40E-05		
44RU	103	1.00E+00	1.41E-06	0.	4.85E-07	0.	7.07E-07	0.	1.74E-05		
44RU	106	1.00E+00	2.54E-05	0.	3.12E-06	0.	5.32E-06	0.	1.97E-05		
50SN	123	1.00E+00	2.79E-04	4.33E-06	6.86E-06	4.33E-06	0.	0.	6.91E-05		
52TE	125M	1.00E+00	2.43E-05	4.19E-06	3.24E-06	8.00E-06	1.00E-05	0.	1.17E-05		
52TE	129M	1.00E+00	1.05E-04	3.61E-05	1.60E-05	3.95E-05	4.40E-05	0.	6.33E-05		
52TE	132	1.00E+00	2.13E-05	1.05E-05	9.76E-06	1.55E-05	1.54E-05	0.	8.08E-05		
53I	131	1.00E+00	3.42E-05	4.07E-05	2.34E-05	1.31E-02	1.02E-05	0.	1.53E-06		
53I	133	1.00E+00	1.26E-05	1.44E-05	5.58E-06	4.35E-03	4.33E-06	0.	3.27E-06		
55CS	134	1.00E+00	4.54E-04	4.24E-04	6.97E-05	0.	4.80E-05	9.42E-05	1.96E-06		
55CS	137	1.00E+00	6.53E-04	7.31E-04	4.20E-05	0.	3.71E-05	9.81E-05	1.89E-06		
56BA	140	1.00E+00	1.74E-04	1.75E-04	7.99E-06	0.	8.68E-09	1.07E-07	1.04E-04		
57LA	140	1.00E+00	2.12E-08	8.37E-09	2.16E-09	0.	-0.	0.	1.04E-04		
58CE	141	1.00E+00	8.00E-08	4.91E-08	5.75E-09	0.	2.94E-09	0.	2.38E-05		
58CE	144	1.00E+00	4.49E-06	1.77E-06	2.42E-07	0.	1.21E-07	0.	1.85E-04		

TOTAL NUMBER IN SOURCE TERM IS   44   TOTAL RELEASE IS 4.4000E+01

D-49

ADULT DOSES

DOSE (MREM PER YEAR INTAKE)

PATHWAY	SKIN	HONE	LIVER	TOTAL BODY	THYROID	KIDNEY	LUNG	GI-LLI
FISH		2.27E+04	2.12E+03	1.45E+03	4.26E+01	3.06E+02	7.50E+01	3.66E+03
DRINKING		3.46E+02	1.65E+01	8.73E+01	8.98E+01	1.02E+01	1.23E+01	6.99E+03
SHORELINE	8.01E+00	6.49E+00	6.49E+00	6.49E+00	6.49E+00	6.49E+00	6.49E+00	6.49E+00
TOTAL	8.01E+00	2.30E+04	2.14E+03	1.54E+03	1.59E+02	3.23E+02	9.38E+01	3.74E+03

USAGE (KG/YR,HR/YR)

	USAGE	DILUTION	TIME (HR)
FISH	21.0	1.0	24.00
DRINKING	730.0	1.0	12.00
SHORELINE	12.0	1.0	-0.00

SHOREWIDTH FACTOR=1.0

* * * ISOTOPE CONTRIBUTION * * *

PATHWAY columns: SKIN | BONE | LIVER | TOTAL BODY | THYROID | KIDNEY | LUNG | GI-LLI

FISH

BONE	LIVER	TOTAL BODY	THYROID	KIDNEY	LUNG	GI-LLI
P 32 95%	P 32 63%	P 32 57%	SN 123 5%	ZN 65 7%	FE 55 5%	P 32 66%
SR 90 1%	ZN 65 1%	ZN 65 1%	SN 126 4%	TE 125M 1%	CS 134 49%	NB 95 19%
SN 126 1%	RB 86 2%	RB 86 1%	TE 127M 1%	TE 127M 4%	CS 136 5%	SN 123 6%
	CS 134 16%	SR 90 4%	TE 129M 4%	TE 129M 7%	CS 137 38%	SN 126 2%
	CS 137 12%	CS 134 19%	I 132 1%	I 132 1%		
		CS 136 2%	I 131 73%	CS 134 36%		
		CS 137 11%	I 133 .8%	CS 136 10%		
				CS 137 28%		

DRINKING

BONE	LIVER	TOTAL BODY	THYROID	KIDNEY	LUNG	GI-LLI
P 32 2%	P 32 2%	SR 90 87%	I 131 84%	ZN 65 4%	FE 55 10%	P 32 1%
SR 89 3%	MN 54 1%	CS 134 5%	I 133 14%	MN 99 3%	SB 125 77%	FE 59 1%
SR 90 89%	FE 55 6%	CS 137 3%		RU 106 2%	CS 134 5%	CU 60 2%
	FE 59 2%			CD 113M 1%	CS 137 4%	SR 89 2%
	ZN 65 3%			TE 125M 4%		SR 90 5%
	RB 86 5%			TE 127M 11%		Y 90 5%
	TE 129M 1%			TE 129M 19%		Y 91 4%
	I 131 1%			TE 131M 2%		ZR 95 1%
	CS 134 36%			TE 132 5%		ZR 97 3%
	CS 136 6%			I 131 3%		NB 95 1%
	CS 137 27%			I 133 1%		RU 103 1%
				CS 134 19%		RU 106 10%
				CS 136 5%		AG 110M 3%
				CS 137 14%		CD 113M 1%
						SN 123 3%
						SN 126 1%
						SB 124 4%
						SB 125 1%
						TE 127M 1%
						TE 129M 3%

SHORELINE

SKIN	GI-LLI
MN 54 1%	MN 54 1%
CO 60 27%	CO 60 28%
AG 110M 4%	AG 110M 4%
SN 123 6%	SN 126 34%
SN 126 31%	SB 125 3%
SB 125 2%	CS 134 9%
CS 134 8%	CS 137 13%
CS 137 12%	

TABLE 4.11-2

LIQUID EFFLUENT DOSE PARAMETERS

RADIONUCLIDE	A(I),MREM/HR PER UCI/ML	
	TOTAL BODY	CRITICAL ORGAN
H 3	1.14E+01	1.14E+01
P 32	1.71E+06	4.41E+07
CR 51	1.46E+00	3.66E+02
MN 54	9.07E+02	1.45E+04
FE 55	2.36E+03	1.04E+04
FE 59	1.25E+03	1.08E+04
CO 58	3.36E+02	3.04E+03
CO 60	9.54E+02	8.16E+03
ZN 65	3.39E+04	7.49E+04
ZN 69M	5.55E+01	3.70E+04
RB 86	4.62E+04	9.91E+04
SR 89	1.36E+03	4.75E+04
SR 90	2.49E+05	1.18E+06
Y 90	5.37E-02	1.22E+04
Y 91	5.99E-01	1.10E+04
ZR 95	8.40E-03	2.75E+03
ZR 97	9.59E+01	5.65E+03
NB 95	7.55E+01	1.48E+06
MO 99	8.47E+00	9.19E+02
RU 103	3.73E+01	2.29E+03
RU 106	7.80E+00	1.91E+04
AG 110M	5.74E+01	5.35E+03
CD 113M	5.50E+03	1.44E+04
SN 123	1.75E+04	4.58E+05
SN 126	9.45E+01	6.15E+05
SB 124	3.84E+01	6.77E+03
SB 125	3.70E+02	2.00E+04
TE 125M	8.55E+02	2.12E+04
TE 127M	1.86E+03	2.85E+04
TE 129M	4.53E+02	5.91E+04
TE 131M	1.30E+03	5.15E+04
TE 132	3.84E+02	6.55E+04
I 131	5.45E+01	2.20E+05
I 133	5.49E+05	3.43E+04
CS 134	8.55E+04	7.21E+05
CS 136	3.46E+05	1.19E+05
CS 137	1.21E+02	5.31E+05
BA 140	3.59E-02	3.77E+03
LA 140	6.08E-02	9.93E+03
CE 141	8.93E-03	2.05E+03
CE 143	2.24E+00	3.02E+03
CE 144	6.31E-02	1.41E+04
PR 143	5.79E-03	5.56E+03
NP 239		2.15E+03

DRINKING   DILUTION IN ADDITION TO THAT FOR FISH= 1.0

ADDENDUM

Setpoint Calculations

The radiological effluent Technical Specifications require alarm/trip setpoints for radiation monitors and flow measurement devices for each effluent line. Setpoint values are to be calculated to assure that alarm and trip actions occur prior to exceeding the limits of 10 CFR 20 at the release point to the unrestricted area. The calculated alarm and trip action setpoints to be specified in the ODCM for each radioactive liquid effluent line monitor and flow measurement device must satisfy the following equation:

$$\frac{cf}{F+f} \leq C$$

where:

C = the effluent concentration limit (Specification 3.11.1) implementing 10 CFR 20 for the site, in $\mu Ci/ml$

c = the setpoint, in $\mu Ci/ml$, of the radioactivity monitor measuring the radioactivity concentration in the effluent line prior to dilution and subsequent release; the setpoint, which is proportional to the volumetric flow of the effluent line and inversely proportional to the volumetric flow of the dilution stream plus the effluent stream, represents a value which, if exceeded, would result in concentrations exceeding the limits of 10 CFR 20 in the unrestricted area

f = the flow setpoint as measured at the radiation monitor location, in volume per unit time, but in the same units as F, below

F = the dilution water flow setpoint as measured prior to the release point, in volume per unit time.

[Note that if no dilution is provided, $c \leq C$. Also, note that when (F) is large compared to (f), then $F+f \approx F$.]

The equation is satisfied when the following alarm/trip setpoints are provided for each effluent line in the ODCM:

$$f \leq \frac{CF}{c} \quad \text{(in ml/sec; for example).}$$

$$F \leq \frac{cf}{C} \quad \text{(in ml/sec; for example).}$$

$$c \leq \frac{CF}{f} \quad \text{(in } \mu Ci/ml; \text{ for example).}$$

Some plants may be operated using a fixed value for one or more of these three variables, c, f or F.

Example 1

By using a constant capacity radwaste system discharge pump (on the undiluted stream) the value of (f) is fixed; therefore, the setpoints to be given in the ODCM are:

$$f = \underline{\hspace{5cm}} \text{ ml/sec (fixed)}$$

$$F > \underline{\hspace{5cm}} \text{ ml/sec} = cf/C$$

$$c = \underline{\hspace{5cm}} xF \ \mu Ci/ml \leq CF/f$$

If $C = 3 \times 10^{-8} \ \mu Ci/ml$, $f = 4000$ ml/sec and $F > 4 \times 10^6$ ml/sec, the radiation monitor setpoint is calculated as follows:

$$c \leq CF/f$$

$$= \frac{(3 \times 10^{-8})F}{4000} = 7.5 \times 10^{-12}F \ \mu Ci/ml.$$

If F is measured at some value in excess of the limiting value (the limiting value is 4×10^6 ml/sec in this example), then c may be established proportionately. If $F = 8 \times 10^6$ ml/sec, the alarm setpoint is:

$$c = 7.5 \times 10^{-12}F \ (\mu Ci/ml \text{ per ml/sec})(ml/sec)$$

$$= 7.5 \times 10^{-12}(8 \times 106) = 6 \times 10^{-5} \ \mu Ci/ml.$$

In this case, the alarm setpoint for the radioactive liquid effluent line monitor can be established at $6 \times 10^{-5} \ \mu Ci/ml$, _provided_ that an automatic isolation/control trip action occurs to satisfy the condition:

$$c/F < 7 x 5 \times 10^{-12} \ \mu Ci/ml \text{ per ml/sec.}$$

Example 2

By using a constant capacity dilution pump (on the dilution stream prior to a mixing box), the value of (F) is fixed; therefore, the setpoints to be given in the ODCM are:

$$f < \underline{\hspace{5cm}} \text{ ml/sec} = CF/c$$

$$F = \underline{\hspace{5cm}} \text{ ml/sec (fixed)}$$

$$c = \underline{\hspace{5cm}} x(1/f)\mu Ci/ml \leq CF/f$$

If $C = 3 \times 10^{-8} \ \mu Ci/ml$, $F = 4 \times 10^6$ ml/sec and $f < 4000$ ml/sec, the radiation monitor setpoint is calculated as follows:

$$c \leq CF/f$$

$$= \frac{(3 \times 10^{-8} \ X \ 4 \times 10^6)}{f} = 0.12(1/f) \ \mu Ci/ml.$$

If f is measured at some value less than the limiting value (the limiting value is 4000 ml/sec in this example), then c may be established proportionately. If $f = 1000$ ml/sec, the alarm setpoint is:

$$c = 0.12(1/f)(\mu Ci/sec)(sec/ml)$$

$$= \frac{0.12}{1000} = 1.2 \times 10^{-4} \ \mu Ci/ml.$$

In this case, the alarm setpoint for the radioactive liquid effluent line monitor can be established at 1.2×10^{-4} µCi/ml, <u>provided</u> that an automatic isolation/control trip action occurs to satisfy the condition:

$$cf > 0.12 \text{ µCi/sec.}$$

Value of c

A detailed description of the method to be used to obtain the value of (c) should be provided in the ODCM. Since (c) is dependent on the radionuclide distribution, yields, calibration and the monitor's parameters, each of these variables should be considered and the fixed or adjustable setpoint method of determination described in the ODCM for each effluent monitor. This may be accomplished by tabulation. Changes to the ODCM shall be provided in the SEMIANNUAL RADIOACTIVE EFFLUENT RELEASE REPORT.

NRC FORM 335
(7-77)

U.S. NUCLEAR REGULATORY COMMISSION

BIBLIOGRAPHIC DATA SHEET

		1. REPORT NUMBER (Assigned by DDC)
		NUREG-0133

4 TITLE AND SUBTITLE (Add Volume No., if appropriate)	2. (Leave blank)
"Preparation of Radiological Effluent Technical Specifications for Nuclear Power Plants" A Guidance Manual for Users of Standard Technical Specifications	3 RECIPIENT'S ACCESSION NO. N/A

7. AUTHOR(S)	5. DATE REPORT COMPLETED	
J. S. Boegli, R. R. Bellamy, W. L. Britz, R. L. Waterfield	MONTH October	YEAR 1978

9 PERFORMING ORGANIZATION NAME AND MAILING ADDRESS (Include Zip Code)	DATE REPORT ISSUED	
Division of Site Safety and Environmental Analysis U.S. Nuclear Regulatory Commission Office of Nuclear Reactor Regulation Washington, D.C. 20555	MONTH October	YEAR 1978
	6 (Leave blank)	
	8 (Leave blank)	

12. SPONSORING ORGANIZATION NAME AND MAILING ADDRESS (Include Zip Code)	10 PROJECT/TASK/WORK UNIT NO. N/A
N/A	11. CONTRACT NO. N/A

13 TYPE OF REPORT	PERIOD COVERED (Inclusive dates)
N/A	N/A

15 SUPPLEMENTARY NOTES	14. (Leave blank)

16. ABSTRACT (200 words or less)

This guidance manual provides the NRC staff methodology for calculating parameters for limiting conditions of operation required in the radiological effluent Technical Specifications for light-water-cooled nuclear power plants. It provides guidance in using the model specifications reported in NUREG-0472 (Rev. 1)* and NUREG-0473 (Rev. 1),* applicable to operating PWR and BWR licensees, and users of the Standard Technical Specifications packages available for various vendor designs. The manual addresses the implementation of the Regulations and current NRC staff positions as related to the radioactive waste management systems, effluent control and radiological monitoring programs and provides equations, references, computer codes, and guidelines pertinent to these limiting conditions for operation.

*October 1978

17. KEY WORDS AND DOCUMENT ANALYSIS	17a DESCRIPTORS
N/A	

17b. IDENTIFIERS/OPEN-ENDED TERMS

18 AVAILABILITY STATEMENT	19. SECURITY CLASS (This report)	21 NO. OF PAGES
Unlimited	20 SECURITY CLASS (This page)	22 PRICE $

NRC FORM 335 (7-77)

*U.S.GOVERNMENT PRINTING OFFICE:1987-202-292:60279

www.ingramcontent.com/pod-product-compliance
Lightning Source LLC
Chambersburg PA
CBHW080251290526
45790CB00005B/1774